The next step in learning the Korean language

GO! Billy Korean

Korean Made Simple 2: The next step in learning the Korean language
Volume 2, Edition 1

Written by: Billy Go
Edited by: Sohyun Sohn and Patricia Brooks
Published by: GO! Billy Korean

Audio files for this book are available for free download from gobillykorean.com.

Cover and inside illustrations by: HeeJin Park (heejindraws.tumblr.com)

Copyright © 2014 GO! Billy Korean
http://www.gobillykorean.com
All rights reserved

Printed by CreateSpace
Available from Amazon.com and other retail outlets
ISBN: 1502722216
ISBN-13: 978-1502722218

TABLE OF CONTENTS

	Preface	v
Chapter 1	Progressive Tense	11
Chapter 2	If and When	23
Chapter 3	Future Tense	37
Chapter 4	Complex Sentences	51
Chapter 5	More Complex Sentences	65
Chapter 6	Adverbs	77
Chapter 7	Comparisons	93
Chapter 8	Honorifics	109
Chapter 9	Verb Endings	127
Chapter 10	Introduction to Casual Korean	139
Chapter 11	Shall We?	161
Chapter 12	Let's	171
Chapter 13	Doing and Asking Favors	181
Chapter 14	Don't	197
Chapter 15	More Negative Sentences	211
Chapter 16	Have to Do	225
Chapter 17	Try to Do	235
Chapter 18	Have Ever	245
Chapter 19	Verbs to Nouns	253
Chapter 20	While	269
	Answer Keys	281
	Appendix A. Introduction to Idioms	293
	Appendix B. Major Korean Holidays	301
	Appendix C. Reading Practice	307
	Special Thanks	319
	Glossary	320

Preface

Welcome back! Or for those of you who are new to this series, welcome! If this is your first time seeing "Korean Made Simple," I'd highly recommend scanning through the first book and making sure that you have a strong understanding of each concept before continuing. This book will follow in the footsteps of "Korean Made Simple," and will strive to explain Korean concepts as simply as possible. Opening up this book means that you've decided to continue your journey toward mastering the Korean language. Congratulations, and good luck!

About this Sequel

Nobody likes a sequel that doesn't add something new. The major difference between this book and the previous one is that while the previous book focused on building a foundation for studying the Korean language, this book is geared toward increasing your communication skills. Also, while the previous book focused more on themes and common, day-to-day situations – including introducing yourself, shopping, and telling the time – this book will focus more on grammatical concepts.

There is also no need for additional introductory lessons in this book, as the basic introductory concepts were covered in the previous book, so we'll have more space to learn the essential grammar that you'll need to progress toward the next level. I'll be teaching everything just as simply as in the first book, so you should have no trouble keeping up.

Preface

We will be covering more serious, key topics through this book. Expect to learn a lot, and to be able to express yourself better and in more detail than you could before. After all, the previous book ended right after teaching past tense! Surely, we will need to learn more if we want to progress toward more natural Korean. What about future tense? Yes, we'll be learning this, and a whole lot more.

Just as with the previous book, do not expect to be speaking fluent Korean by the end, as there is simply too much that needs to be covered before you will be able to converse in Korean without any difficulties. However, I promise that you will gain an even more extensive introductory knowledge of the Korean language through this book, building on the foundation laid by the first "Korean Made Simple."

Buckle up. Turn on your headlights. Check your airbag. Wait – bad analogies. We're not going to crash. We're going to cruise. We're going to expand our Korean knowledge and learn how to read, write, speak and understand *real* Korean.

And like before, I'll be there every step of the way guiding you along.

Before Reading This Book

You should be able to read and write the Korean alphabet (한글) before beginning this book. The previous book completely covers how to learn it. Using this book without having read the previous one can be acceptable as a review, but know that you might have missed important vocabulary and grammar that were covered in the first book. You also might have missed advanced language and cultural notes, depending on how in-depth you studied. I recommend keeping a dictionary handy if you choose to read this book without having read the first one, and consulting additional sources to make sure that you understand everything along the way.

If you have already read the previous book, I would also strongly recommend reading all of the "Advanced Notes" before beginning this book (if you haven't done so already).

How to Use This Book

Just like "Korean Made Simple," this book builds upon itself with each chapter. I recommend that you take your time going through each lesson in order and avoid skipping any sections. If you're in a rush – "I'm leaving to Korea tomorrow to give a speech in Korean to the President of Korea!" – then complete all of the lessons but skip the Practice sections. Know that you'll only be able to improve when you combine studying with practice, so the best way to use this book is by completing every section, including the Practice sections.

Preface

If you notice a grammar form that you are not yet familiar with, you may have skipped it in a previous chapter. There's no need to rush through the basics of Korean; If you find something that you missed, I recommend that you read through the book more slowly. Later on you will be able to learn new concepts more quickly, but it's important to take things slowly and carefully in the beginning.

The first time you go through this book, read each "Culture Notes" section along the way, but skip the "Advanced Notes" sections. Save the "Advanced Notes" for your second or third reading of this book, as they were designed to provide additional information that can be confusing if you don't yet understand the overall concepts first.

Take notes along the way as you complete each chapter. Write down your own example sentences using the concepts that you're learning. You know best which concepts are the most difficult to *you*, and taking notes will help you to remember and master those concepts more efficiently.

Practice reading, writing, and speaking the language as much as possible. It will also be extremely beneficial if you have a friend with whom you can practice speaking and listening Korean. If you live in an area where it is difficult to meet native Koreans – such as most areas outside of Korea – try to find an online penpal. There are numerous simple websites where you can do this, so I won't name any specifically here.

Also make sure to download the free audio files for this book at gobillykorean.com.

About the Answer Keys

The more Korean you know, the more "right answers" there will be when speaking the language. While completing each Practice section, don't be surprised if your answers are different from what the Answer Keys section shows. You'll learn many new forms of speech in this book, including *honorific speech* and *casual speech*, as well as new vocabulary words and grammar forms. Compare your answers with the ones in this book and learn from them, but know that they might not match what you've written – and know that this is perfectly fine.

For your first time, I would recommend focusing on using the 요 form when completing the Practice sections, unless it's specified that you should use another form. The 요 form is the most commonly used form in Korea, and it will greatly benefit you to have a strong understanding of how to use it.

Preface

About the Vocabulary

I've taken special care when selecting each word that appears in these books, choosing the most important ones for you to know when beginning to learn Korean.

Every vocabulary word added to this book was picked for a good reason. I'd recommend learning as much of the vocabulary contained in this book and the previous book as possible.

As you complete this book, refer to the vocabulary list at the end of each chapter whenever you find words that you're not familiar with. Since this is the second book in the "Korean Made Simple" series, if you run into any vocabulary words that are not in the vocabulary lists or Glossary section, know that these words were covered in the first book. For this reason, if you have a copy of the first book, I'd recommend keeping it handy while studying. Or, you can also use a dictionary to look up words with which you are unfamiliar.

How to Memorize Vocabulary

There are many methods for memorizing vocabulary, and many of them will work fine. I recommend trying multiple ways to find out which method works best for you and then studying as often as you can using that method.

I'd also like to point out a few effective methods for memorizing vocabulary. Some of these were mentioned in the previous book, and others are new.

1. Quiz yourself frequently on words you are learning, or have somebody else quiz you.

2. Force yourself to create sentences using the words (and grammar forms) that you are learning.

Preface

3. Write vocabulary words that you're learning on sticky notes and place them over objects and places that they correspond to. For example, you can write the Korean word for "pencil" on your favorite pencil, or the word for "pretty" on your girlfriend's face (or boyfriend's face, if you have a pretty boyfriend. I'm not going to judge.).

4. Associate funny and odd ideas with Korean words; sometimes a nonsensical phrase can make memorizing a difficult word much simpler. For example, you can remember that the word 열쇠 means "key" by thinking of someone saying, "*You'll say* where the *key* is." At the risk of ruining this entire book I'm not going to list any other odd sentences, but feel free to use whatever random ideas you'd like.

5. Flash cards are still a popular yet traditional way of learning large amounts of words. If using flash cards, I recommend saying the word in Korean out loud while writing the English side, and saying the word out loud in English while writing the Korean side. This way you can become familiar with speaking the word, hearing yourself say it, and writing and reading it all at once.

No matter which method you use to study vocabulary, pick one that you can see yourself doing frequently. Keep a regular study schedule – studying 30 minutes a day for 5 days a week will be more effective than trying to cram for 150 minutes at once.

Regarding Numbers

While the previous book spelled all numbers *phonetically* (일, 이, 삼, ...), this book uses only *Arabic numerals* (1, 2, 3, ...) as this is how Koreans write numbers. Of course, when introducing new *counters*, I'll let you know whether to use Sino Korean or Pure Korean numbers with each one. As you go through the book, read each sentence out loud to yourself. This will help you to adjust to reading numbers in Korean while looking at the number in Arabic numerals.

A Few Speaking Tips

Here's a tip for sounding a bit more natural when speaking Korean. When you're just starting out, it'll be difficult to put together complete sentences quickly enough to hold a conversation. You might feel like you're stumbling to compose each sentence, and may become frustrated that what you're saying isn't anything like what you wanted to express. But don't worry at all. Unless you were born in South Korea, everyone is like this at first when learning Korean. I remember that I was like this too!

Preface

Keep your sentences short and to the point. I'm not saying "Don't try to express yourself fully because you're still a beginner" at all. Express yourself in the simplest, most compact form that you can, because it will help you to sound more natural while you're still learning the language. This is a real tip for sounding more natural when speaking. Koreans prefer sentences that get to the point much more than English speakers do. If your sentences are only a few words, you're doing fine. If some of your sentences are just one word, you're right on track as well. In fact, even as you improve, keep your sentences short and to the point. Long sentences are for later, when you want to have a discussion about a topic in much more detail.

As a beginner, it's much easier to create short, simple sentences than long, drawn-out ones that run on. Making short sentences is easier, and will also sound more natural to the average Korean. It's a win-win scenario. Keep your sentences simpler, and your Korean will sound better.

Good Luck

I'm not trying to scare you by making the title of this section "Good Luck." The Korean language, just like English or any other language can be easy at times and difficult at other times. It's just a language, and there will be times where you will feel frustrated learning a concept or feel like you might want to give up. While good quality books and teachers can help make the process much easier, even using the best teachers and books you are likely to still have times that frustrate you with learning Korean. I've been there before, and I want to let you know that it does get better.

The secret to becoming fluent in Korean is to keep studying and practicing Korean. Just like running a marathon, if your goal is to finish the marathon, you will never get to the end if you give up half way. You need to keep going until you've reached the mark that you're looking at.

I understand exactly how difficult learning Korean can be, especially when transitioning from basic phrases ("Hello! Goodbye!") to more complex grammar and concepts. I also know many people who've gone through this process too, and the only thing that they all have in common is that they never gave up learning the language. I also hope that whatever your goals for Korean are, whether they be fluency, basic conversation, or anything, that you will keep going until you've reached them, because I truly believe that anyone can learn Korean with study and practice. Good luck in your studies. I'll be here for you if you need me.

Progressive Tense

Chapter 1

Conversation

정윤원:	지금 뭐해요?
강신애:	숙제를 하고 있어요.
정윤원:	그래요? 무슨 숙제요?
강신애:	수학 숙제요. 너무 지루해요. 정말 하고 싶지 않아요.
정윤원:	하하. 저는 심심해요.
강신애:	윤원 씨는 공부하고 있지 않아요? 시험 준비를 안 하고 있어요?
정윤원:	시험이요?
강신애:	네, 내일 수학 시험이 있어요. 몰랐어요?
정윤원:	....

In the final chapter of the previous book, we learned how to use the *past tense* to express events that happened in, well... the past. But what if you want to express something that's happening *right now*? So far, we've been able to do this by simply conjugating the verb in the *present tense*. In fact, this is the most common way to express that something's happening now.

저는 지금 공부해요.
"I'm studying now."

11

Chapter 1: Progressive Tense

This *-ing* ending on verbs, which shows that something is currently happening, is what we call the *progressive tense* in English. In Korean, as we previously learned, we can simply use the *present tense* to express this *-ing* meaning most of the time. However, in some situations we will need to use the progressive tense, as we will soon see.

First, let's go over how to make the progressive tense in Korean. Then we'll learn how and when to use it.

Verb Stem + 고 있다

Take a verb stem (a verb minus the 다 at the end) and attach 고. Then add the verb 있다 and conjugate it. Here are a few examples:

하다 → 하 + 고
→ 하고 있다

이미 하고 있어요.
"I'm already doing it."

마시다 → 마시 + 고
→ 마시고 있다

김 씨는 술을 마시고 있어요.
"Mr. Kim is drinking alcohol."

공부하다 → 공부하 + 고
→ 공부하고 있다

저는 지금 공부하고 있어요.
"I'm studying now."

Although this might seem the same as using the regular present tense, we can use the progressive tense to emphasize that something is currently happening. Because of this, the progressive tense can be used to clarify *when* an action is happening – specifically, that it's currently happening. This difference might not always translate into English, so it's important to be aware of its meaning in Korean.

As we learned before, the present tense can be used for things that are currently happening, or for things that happen in general, without specifying the time:

Progressive Tense

저는 숙제를 해요.

This sentence can mean "I do homework." It can also mean "I am (currently) doing homework."

저는 숙제를 하고 있어요.

This sentence only means, "I am (currently) doing homework." Here are a few more examples of the same sentences written using the present tense and the progressive tense.

시간이 없어요. 공부해요.
"I don't have any time. I'm studying."

시간이 없어요. 공부하고 있어요.
"I don't have any time. I'm (currently) studying."

저는 집에 가요.
"I'm going home."

저는 집에 가고 있어요.
"I'm (currently) going home."

Since the progressive tense is used for actions that are currently happening, it can only be used with *action verbs*, and not with *descriptive verbs*. For example, using 춥다 ("to be cold") in this form as 춥고 있다 would be *incorrect*. Instead, it should be left as 추워요 ("It is cold.") or 추웠어요 ("It was cold."), among other possible conjugations.

알다 and 가지다

Some verbs are used more commonly with the progressive tense than with the present tense. One such verb is 알다 ("to know"). In the previous book, we learned that we can conjugate 알다 in the present tense like this:

저는 그분을 알아요.
"I know him."

While using 알다 in the present tense is fine, it's also common to use the progressive tense – 알고 있다.

저는 그분을 알고 있어요.
"I know him (currently)."

Chapter 1
Progressive Tense

Both of these are grammatically correct, and acceptable to use. Just know that you will see the progressive tense used more commonly.

Another verb that's commonly used with the progressive tense is 가지다 ("to have" or "to hold"). In the previous book, we learned that it's more natural to use 가지고 싶다 than 원하다 when expressing that you *want* something.

저는 펜을 가지고 싶어요.
"I want to have a pen."

가지다 is also commonly used in place of 있다 when you want to say that you *have* something. When it's used to mean "to have," such as when saying "I have something," it must be used in the progressive tense.

저는 펜을 가지고 있어요.
"I have a pen."

It's fine to use either 가지고 있다 or 있다 to mean "to have," so pick whichever one you'd like.

저는 연필이 있어요.
저는 연필을 가지고 있어요.
"I have a pencil."

Past Progressive Tense

The progressive tense can also be used for talking about things that happened in the past (as well as in the future, which we'll cover in Chapter 3). To say that something was happening, use this form with 고 있었다 instead, making sure to conjugate 있었다. This 있었다 is simply the verb 있다 conjugated in the past tense.

저는 공원에 가고 있어요.
"I am going to the park."

저는 공원에 가고 있었어요.
"I was going to the park."

먹고 있어요.
"I'm eating."

먹고 있었어요.
"I was eating."

Progressive Tense

지금 하고 있습니다.
"I am doing it now."

어제 하고 있었습니다.
"I was doing it yesterday."

Now that we've learned the basics of the progressive tense, let's go over the conversation.

> 정윤원: 지금 뭐해요?
> "What are you doing now?"

뭐 is a common shorter version of 무엇 ("what"). In fact, 뭐 is so common that 무엇 is rarely used outside of textbooks and formal speeches. Nevertheless, remember that 뭐 comes from 무엇, as their usage is the same. From now on, I'd recommend using 뭐 instead of 무엇.

뭐해요 is a common way to ask what someone is doing. Keep in mind that it is *informal*, and therefore shouldn't be used to strangers or in formal situations. We'll learn another version of this phrase that can be used to strangers or in formal situations in Chapter 8.

> **Adv** Note that 뭐해요 comes directly from the verb 뭐하다, which means "to do what." Of course, 뭐하다 is a shorter version of 무엇하다. Also note that both 뭐하다 and 무엇하다 are written as one word, without a space.

> 강신애: 숙제를 하고 있어요.
> "I'm doing homework."

Here, it would also be grammatically correct if 강신애 said 숙제를 해요. However, using the progressive tense emphasizes that she is *currently* studying. Perhaps 강신애 thinks that 정윤원 is going to ask her to play, so she wants to make sure that she tells him that she's currently busy studying... but I can't read minds.

> 정윤원: 그래요? 무슨 숙제요?
> "Really? What homework?"

그래요 is a common way to say that something is *really* a certain way, or to ask if it is. Its literal meaning is, "It is so." Or as a question, its literal meaning is, "Is it so?" 그래요 has the same use as 그렇습니다 (or 그렇습니까?) which we learned in the previous book.

> 그래요?
> "Really?"
> "Is that so?"

15

Chapter 1

Progressive Tense

그래요.
"Really."
"It is so."

강신애: 수학 숙제요. 너무 지루해요. 정말 하고 싶지 않아요.
"Math homework. It's too boring. I really don't want to do it."

Compound Nouns

We've already learned many compound nouns in the previous book, but I haven't yet given you a proper introduction to them.

In Korean, just like in English, two nouns can be combined together to form one new noun; this is called a compound noun because the nouns have been *compounded* together. In the conversation example, 수학 숙제 ("math homework") is a combination of 수학 ("math") and 숙제 ("homework"). Here are a few more examples:

과학 시험
"science test"

한국 음식
"Korean food"

고양이 카페
"cat café"

Culture Notes

In Korea, cat cafés and dog cafés are popular in some cities, but you don't go there to eat your pets. These are cafés where you can enjoy hot or cold drinks, just like a regular café, while interacting and playing with live animals. The animals are free to walk around the cafés, and you're free to pet them. Each café has its own theme, and each pet has its own personality. I'd highly recommend visiting one if you are in Korea. Sometimes drinking tea while sitting next to a cat that doesn't acknowledge your existence can be the perfect way to spend a few hours of your afternoon.

Progressive Tense

Chapter 1

Let's go back to the conversation.

너무, as we learned in the previous book, means "too (much)" or "overly," and is an *adverb*. It can be added before a verb. Here it's added before 지루하다 ("to be boring"), to mean "to be too boring" or "to be *overly* boring."

> 정윤원: 하하. 저는 심심해요.
> "Haha. I'm bored."

심심하다 and 지루하다

As we just learned, 지루하다 means "to be boring;" it's used to express that a *thing* or an *activity* is boring or uninteresting. 심심하다 means "to be bored," and is used to mean that a *person* is bored and has nothing interesting to do. Make sure to remember their difference. Saying that a person is 지루하다 can be taken as an insult, and saying that an activity is 심심하다 would sound awkward.

> 엄마의 잔소리가 **지루해요**.
> "Mom's nagging is boring."

> 요즘 매일 **심심해요**.
> "Lately I'm bored every day."

Remember that *things* or *activities* can be 지루하다, and a *person* can be 심심하다.

> 강신애: 윤원 씨는 공부하고 있지 않아요? 시험 준비를 안 하고 있어요?
> "You're not studying? You're not preparing for the test?"

The progressive tense can use either 지 않다 or 안 in a *negative sentence*. Notice how 지 않다 is only used after 있다, but not after the first verb (here, 하다). The above sentence is correct, but asking, "공부하지 않고 있어요?" would be *incorrect* (probably understandable to a Korean, but *incorrect*).

When using 안, however, put it before the *first* verb, and not before 있다. For example, using 안 하고 있다 would be *correct*, but using 하고 안 있다 would be *incorrect* (and probably not understandable to a Korean). In addition, changing 있다 to 없다 for a negative sentence (such as 하고 없다) would also be *incorrect*. When using the progressive tense, only the verb 있다 is used.

Chapter 1 — Progressive Tense

정윤원: 시험이요?
"Test?"

강신애: 네, 내일 수학 시험이 있어요. 몰랐어요?
"Yes, tomorrow there's a math test. You didn't know?"

정윤원: ....
"...."

A period, or a dot, is called a 점. If you wanted to say the above sentence, you would say "점 점 점."

Decimals

You can also use 점 to say numbers with decimals in them. When saying numbers in this way, use Sino Korean numbers (일, 이, 삼, etc.).

1.3 → 1 점 3
8.9 → 8 점 9
100.03 → 100 점 0, 3

There are two main ways to say the number zero. In the previous book we learned 영, but in daily usage 공 is equally as common.

0 → 영 or 공

However, when reading numbers with *decimals*, only 영 is used.

100.03 → 100 점 **영** 3
10.0 → 10 점 **영**

> **Adv**: In addition, you might find 제로 being used from time to time, which is the Konglish version of the word "zero."

Percentage

To say a percentage in Korean, you only need to learn one word – 퍼센트 ("percent").

50 퍼센트
"50 percent"

Progressive Tense

10 퍼센트
"10 percent"

You can also use 프로 instead, which is another version of 퍼센트.

33 프로
"33 percent"

| Adv | If you were curious, 프로 comes from the Dutch word "procent," which means the same thing as "percent." |

Fractions

Fractions in Korean (such as "one half," or "two thirds") are simple to make, but work in the opposite way from English. Let's take a look at a few fractions:

1/2
2/3
5/8

In English, we'd have to learn words like "half" (to say "one half"), "thirds" (to say "two thirds") and even "eighths" (to say "five eighths"), but in Korean it's much simpler. The same fractions in Korean would be "1 part of 2," "2 parts of 3," and "5 parts of 8." We can use the Sino Korean word 분 ("part," "portion") to say this.

1/2 → "2 분의 1"
2/3 → "3 분의 2"
5/8 → "8 분의 5"

| Advanced | **To Marry: 시집가다 and 장가가다**

While you can use 결혼(을) 하다 to mean "to marry," there are two more important verbs that also mean "to marry" – 시집(을) 가다 and 장가(를) 가다.

시집(을) 가다 is used for when a *woman* gets married.

언제 시집갈 거예요?
"When will you get married?" (asking a woman)

장가(를) 가다 is used for when a *man* gets married.

철수 씨가 어제 장가갔어요.
"Chul-soo got married yesterday." (Chul-soo is a man)

If you ever forget which one to use while speaking, know that 결혼(을) 하다 is still correct in both situations. |

Chapter 1

Progressive Tense

Practice

Translate to Korean:

1. "I'm busy now. I am eating a delicious steak."

    _____.

2. "I have three books."

    _____.

3. "Tomorrow I have a science test."

    _____.

4. "I'm bored, but I don't want to do that boring homework."

    _____.

5. "I understood only 80%."

    _____.

Translate to English:

6. 저는 핸드폰을 보고 있어요.

    _____.

7. 이미 가고 있어요?

    _____.

8. 내일 영어 선생님에게 물어보세요.

    _____.

Progressive Tense

Chapter 1

9. 돈을 가지고 있어요?

_____.

10. 지금 하고 있지만 내일까지 끝낼 수 없어요.

_____.

New Phrases

오래간만이에요.	"Long time, no see."
무슨 뜻이에요?	"What does it mean?"

New Vocabulary

잔소리	"nagging"
잔소리(를) 하다	"to nag"
점	"dot," "point," "period"
공	"zero"
제로	"zero"
꼬리	"tail"
퍼센트	"percent"
프로	"percent"
쇼핑(을) 하다	"to go shopping"
밧줄	"rope"
줄	"cord," "line"
끈	"string"
신발 끈	"shoestring," "shoelaces"
뜻	"meaning"
전공	"a major (study)"
부전공	"a minor (study)"
피에로	"clown"
그네	"a swing"
인사(를) 하다	"to say hello," "to bow," "to greet"
낮	"day(time)"

Chapter 1: Progressive Tense

낮잠	"(daytime) nap"
낮잠(을) 자다	"to take a (daytime) nap"
비다	"to be blank," "to be empty"
빈칸	"a blank space"
칸	"(tin) can"
통	"container"
물통	"water container"
물병	"water bottle"
아저씨	"(unmarried) man," "(middle-aged) man"
아줌마	"(married) woman," "(middle-aged) woman"
아가씨	"(unmarried) lady," "(young and single) lady"
총각	"(unmarried) man," "(single) man"
시집(을) 가다	"to get married" (used for females)
장가(를) 가다	"to get married" (used for males)
싱겁다	"to be bland (tasting)"
바퀴	"wheel"
바퀴벌레	"cockroach"
개미	"ant"

If and When

Chapter 2

Conversation

성아:	시간이 있을 때 저를 조금 도와줄 수 있어요?
민철:	그래요. 무슨 일이 있어요?
성아:	내일 로스앤젤레스로 이사가요.
민철:	아, 맞아요!
성아:	오늘 밤까지 짐을 싸고 싶어요.
민철:	조금 이따 시간이 있으면 도와줄 수 있어요.
성아:	정말 고마워요.

In English, the words "if" and "when" are easy to tell apart – we know that using "if" means that something *might* or *might not* happen, and we also know that using "when" means that something *will* happen, but we simply don't know the time that it will happen. In Korean, it's not as easy to tell "if" and "when" apart if you are translating something – and this confusion is caused specifically when translating to and from English. To avoid this confusion, it's important to learn what each grammar form means in *Korean* before thinking of the translation in *English*.

Let's learn how to say "if" and "when" in Korean. There are two grammar forms we will need to learn.

Chapter 2: If and When

Verb Stem + (으)면

Take a verb stem and add 으면 if it ends in a *consonant*, or 면 if it ends in a *vowel*.

This form can mean either "when" or "if," depending on the context. It is used for talking about something that *might* or *might not* happen. Before we talk more about when to use this form, let's look at a few conjugated examples.

먹다 → 먹 + 으면
→ 먹으면

결혼하다 → 결혼하 + 면
→ 결혼하면

비싸다 → 비싸 + 면
→ 비싸면

어렵다 → 어려우 + 면
→ *어려우면

*As we learned in the previous book, some types of verbs can have unique ways of conjugating, such as when conjugating the 요 form. In addition, some types of verbs can also have different ways of conjugating when they are used with certain grammar forms as you can see above. Fortunately, there are only a few additional rules to learn – 3 to be exact.

While these rules apply here (with the 면 form), they will also be reused in many other grammar forms later. Learn them here once, and you'll be able to use them again.

Rule 1: Ends in ㅂ (Descriptive Verb)

When the verb stem ends in a single ㅂ, first remove the ㅂ. Then add 우. Then, add the rest of the grammar form. This rule only applies to *descriptive verbs*.

어렵다 → 어려 + 우 → 어려우 + 면
→ 어려우면

차갑다 → 차가 + 우 → 차가우 + 면
→ 차가우면

맵다 → 매 + 우 → 매우 + 면
→ 매우면

If and When

Rule 2: Ends in ㅎ (Descriptive Verb)

When the verb stem ends in a single ㅎ, remove the ㅎ. Then, add the rest of the grammar form. This rule only applies to *descriptive verbs*.

그렇다 → 그러 + 면
→ 그러면

빨갛다 → 빨가 + 면
→ 빨가면

이렇다 → 이러 + 면
→ 이러면

These type of verbs are much less common than the other two types of verbs listed in these rules.

Rule 3: Ends in ㄹ

For verbs that end in a single ㄹ, add the rest of the grammar form as if it ended in a *vowel* instead.

살다 → 살 + 면
→ 살면

멀다 → 멀 + 면
→ 멀면

드물다 → 드물 + 면
→ 드물면

> **Adv**: There are a few common exceptions to this, such as the verb 듣다 ("to listen"), which becomes 들으면 (and also becomes 들어요 in the 요 form). You'll learn other exceptions along the way, but there's no need to worry about them yet as they're not common. I'll point out any more that come up on the way.

When the grammar form happens to begin with another ㄹ, the two ㄹ's will combine together into one. We've already learned this same rule in the previous book, when we learned about the grammar for "can" and "can't."

살다 → 살 + (을/ㄹ) 수 있다
→ 살 수 있다

Chapter 2
If and When

Up until now we simply haven't needed these additional rules, so you won't need to re-learn anything. Simply add these to your memory and use them each time we learn a new grammar form from now on. I'll remind you along the way as we need them.

Going back to the grammar form, I mentioned that it can mean either "when" or "if," depending on the context. Here is an example of what I mean.

시간이 있으면 도와주세요.
"Please help me if/when you have time."

In the above sentence, using either "when" or "if" would be correct in English. That's because this grammar form is used for talking about things that *might* or *might not* happen. It's best to not translate it to "if" or "when" until you've first completely understood the Korean sentence.

Sometimes, either "if" or "when" will be a better translation in English, depending on the Korean sentence.

오늘 비가 오면 밖에 안 나가요.
"If it rains today, I won't go outside."

You can see how in the above sentence, translating this grammar form in English as "when" would actually be a bit strange. Here's one more, much longer sentence.

부모님에게 친절하면 생일 선물을 많이 받을 수 있어요.
"If you are nice to your parents, you can get many birthday presents."

Although I translated this sentence as "if," it would be equally grammatically correct to use "when."

> **Adv**
> You can also add 만약(에), which means "in case" or "if," to the beginning of a sentence that uses the (으)면 form. This does not change the meaning of the sentence, but simply adds more *emphasis* to the meaning of "if."
>
> 만약에 비가 오면 영화관에 가요.
> "In case it rains we'll go to the movie theater."

Now that we know how to say that something might or might not happen, let's learn the second grammar form we'll need to know.

If and When

Verb Stem + (을/ㄹ) 때

Take a verb stem and add 을 때 if it ends in a *consonant*, or ㄹ 때 if it ends in a *vowel*.

This form can also mean either "when" or "if," depending on the context. It is used for talking about something that *will* happen; specifically, it's used for talking about the *time* that something happens. Let's look at a few conjugated examples before we talk more about this grammar form.

먹다 → 먹 + 을 때
→ 먹을 때

결혼하다 → 결혼하 + ㄹ 때
→ 결혼할 때

비싸다 → 비싸 + ㄹ 때
→ 비쌀 때

어렵다 → 어려우 + ㄹ 때
→ *어려울 때

*Notice how this grammar form also uses the same additional rules as before.

The word 때, which is used in this grammar form, means "time" (however, it's not interchangeable with the word 시간). Therefore, when using this form you're talking specifically about the *time* that something happens or happened.

학교에 있을 때 공부해요.
"I study when I am at school."

In the above sentence, 학교에 있을 때 literally translates as "the time that I am at school." You can see how in English, this can translate to either "when I am at school" or "if I am at school."

오빠가 밥을 먹을 때 시끄러워요.
"When my older brother eats, he is noisy."

You can also think of this sentence as meaning "The time(s) when my brother eats, it's noisy."

If and When

시간이 있을 때 도와주세요.
"Please help me if/when you have time."

This sentence should look similar to one we recently learned, but this time the grammar form is different from before. Although both 시간이 있을 때 and 시간이 있으면 are correct, and both "if" and "when" are correct too, their meanings in Korean are slightly different. Let's talk for a moment about how they are different.

Comparing the Forms

Take the following two sentences:

A. 결혼하면 요리를 많이 하고 싶어요.
B. 결혼할 때 요리를 많이 하고 싶어요.
"When I get married, I want to cook a lot."

Both of these sentences are grammatically correct, but one of them is a bit ridiculous. Before going any further, take a moment on your own to think about which sentence this could be. Did you get it? No worries if you didn't. Let's go over each of them.

A. This form is used when talking about something that *might* or *might not* happen. This sentence means that, if or when I *might* or *might not* get married, I want to cook a lot. This seems natural, because I don't know when it will happen, or even *if* it will happen – but if it does happen, I certainly want to cook a lot.

B. This form is used for talking about the *time* that something happens. This sentence means that, at the time that I get married, I want to cook a lot. But hold on a moment – at the actual *time* that I get married, I will be wearing a tuxedo and standing in the wedding hall. Perhaps it is your lifelong dream to put on a Teppanyaki show for all of your guests on your wedding day (I won't judge you), but most likely you didn't mean that you wanted to cook during the actual *time* of your wedding.

28

If and When

Chapter 2

"If" and "When" in Past Tense

You can also use these forms for things that *might* or *might not* have happened in the past, or for talking about the *time* that something happened in the past. In this case, first conjugate the verb as if you were going to make the past tense.

하다 → 해 + ㅆ → 했 + 어요 or 습니다

But instead of adding 어요 or 습니다 to the end, attach 으면 or 을 때.

숙제를 했으면....
숙제를 했을 때....
"If/when I did homework...."

Here are a couple of examples:

제가 어렸을 때 한국말을 못 했어요.
"When I was young, I couldn't speak Korean."

어렸을 때 is the common way of saying "when I was young." 어리다 means "to be young," but young like a *child*. Or you can use the descriptive verb 젊다 instead to mean "to be young" when describing teenagers, or young adults.

어제 학교에 갔으면 숙제를 왜 안 했어요?
"If you went to school yesterday, why didn't you do the homework?"

This kind of conjugation also applies to any other grammatical form which would normally attach to the *verb stem*. You'll see more examples throughout this book, so keep an eye out for them.

Now that we've gone over how to say "if" and "when," let's take a look at the conversation.

성아: 시간이 있을 때 저를 조금 도와줄 수 있어요?
"When you have time can you help me a little?"

Remember here that since 성아 is asking 시간이 있을 때, she is referring specifically to the *time* that 민철 will have time to help, and not whether 민철 *might* or *might not* have time.

29

Chapter 2

If and When

민철: 그래요. 무슨 일이 있어요?

"Okay. What's wrong?"

그래요, in addition to meaning "Really.," can also be used to mean "okay" when you are *agreeing* to something. Since it comes from the verb 그렇다, its *formal* version would be 그렇습니다.

> **Advanced**
>
> Note how 그렇다 conjugates to 그래요. All verb stems ending in ㅎ will conjugate in this same way. For verb stems ending in ㅎ (which aren't very common), remove the ㅎ and attach the vowel *sound* of ㅐ, then add 요.
>
> 빨갛다 – 다 – ㅎ → 빨가
> 빨가 – ㅏ + ㅐ → 빨개요
>
> 까맣다 – 다 – ㅎ → 까마
> 까마 – ㅏ + ㅐ → 까매요
>
> 하얗다 – 다 – ㅎ → 하야
> 하야 – ㅑ + ㅐ → 하얘요
>
> Notice how 하얗다 becomes 하얘요, and not 하얘요. Fortunately, if you were to forget to add the *sound* of the ㅐ, and simply added the actual *vowel* ㅐ, you'd still end up with something that sounds very similar.
>
> To see why this happens, try saying 야, but immediately followed by 애. It should sound like 얘. This is the rule that all verb stems ending in ㅎ follow when conjugating to the 요 form.

"무슨 일이 있어요?" is a common way of asking what is wrong, or asking if there is anything wrong. Here, this 일 is different from the one that we previously learned which means "work," or "job;" instead, this 일 means "a matter" (or "a concern").

As we learned in the previous book in Chapter 11, 무슨 is the *adjective* version of "what," so 무슨 일 literally means "what matter," and asking "무슨 일이 있어요?" literally means "What matter is there?"

Another way of asking the same thing is with the verb 이다 instead of 있다 – "무슨 일이에요?" This is a more direct way of asking *what* the matter is, instead of asking *if* there is something wrong. Both ways are fine.

성아: 내일 로스앤젤레스로 이사가요.

"I'm moving to Los Angeles tomorrow."

The verb 이사(를) 가다 means "to move" to somewhere else, and is only used when you are moving to a different place to *live*. Its opposite is 이사(를) 오다, which means "to move" when someone is *coming* from somewhere (you could say this if someone is moving to the same area as you). The difference between 이사(를) 가다 and 이사(를) 오다 comes from the verbs attached to the end – 가다 ("to go") and 오다 ("to come").

If and When

Toward – (으)로

You might be thinking, "But wait a minute, if the English translation says '*to* Los Angeles' then why don't we just use 에?" While 에 means "to," (으)로 means "toward" (such as "in the direction of"). Some types of verbs that show *movement* (including 이사가다) prefer using "toward," and will sound awkward when used with 에 ("to"). For a more natural translation in English, I've kept the translation as "to Los Angeles" in the conversation. I'll point out other verbs showing movement that prefer "toward" as we meet them.

To say "toward," take a location and attach 으로 if it ends in a *consonant*, or attach 로 if it ends in a *vowel*. Locations ending in ㄹ will also simply add 로.

집으로
학교로

Let's take a look at a few example sentences.

저는 지금 집으로 가고 있어요.
"I'm going (toward) home now."

학교로 오세요.
"Please come to school."

Notice how the above sentences use the regular verbs 가다 and 오다, with which we've previously been using 에 to show the location. Using 에 would be equally correct for these sentences too, but know that all verbs showing *movement* (such as 가다, 오다, etc.) *can* also use "toward" instead. Here are a few more examples:

어제 밤에 병원으로 들어갔어요.
"He went in to the hospital yesterday night."

제 방으로 옮겨주세요.
"Please move it to my room."

침대 밑으로 밀었어요.
"I pushed it underneath the bed."

Chapter 2

If and When

(으)로 can only mean "toward" when used with verbs that show *movement*. For example, it cannot be used with 있다 ("to exist"), but it can be used with 가다, 오다, and many other verbs.

However! Although this may literally mean "toward," feel free to translate it into English as "to," as it will most often sound more natural this way.

Although saying "I'm moving toward Los Angeles" sounds awkward in English, it's perfectly normal in Korean.

> 민철: 아, 맞아요!
> "Ah, that's right!"

> 성아: 오늘 밤까지 짐을 싸고 싶어요.
> "I want to pack my luggage by tonight."

We learned in the previous book that 까지 can be used to mean "until." It can also mean "by" when talking about *time*, as it does in the above sentence.

> 3 시까지
> "until 3 o'clock" or "by 3 o'clock"

> 내일까지
> "until tomorrow" or "by tomorrow"

> 민철: 조금 이따 시간이 있으면 도와줄 수 있어요.
> "When I have time after a little while I can help."

이따(가) means "after a while" or "later." Adding 조금 before 이따 means "after a *little* while" or "a *little* later."

The opposite of 이따(가) is 아까, which means "a while ago," or "earlier."

> 성아: 정말 고마워요.
> "Thanks a lot."

Remember that the verb 고맙다 is a little less polite than 감사하다, but it's fine to use either one. Because of this, 고맙다 is more commonly used between friends. Both 고맙다 and 감사하다 can be used with a wide variety of *adverbs* – for example, here 정말 ("really").

If and When

Chapter 2

Practice

Conjugate the following verbs using (으)면:

1. 춥다

   _____.

2. 길다

   _____.

3. 덥다

   _____.

4. 팔다

   _____.

5. 가르치다

   _____.

Translate to Korean:

6. "If you really like movies, please watch this movie too."

   _____.

7. "When you go to the park today, please bring water."

   _____.

8. "When I graduate, I want to go to eat sushi together."

   _____.

If and When

Chapter 2

9. "When I graduated, I ate sushi."

_____.

10. "When I was young, I liked cats."

_____.

Translate to English:

11. 오늘 시간이 있으면 도와줄 수 있어요.

_____.

12. 오늘 시간이 있을 때 도와줄 수 있어요.

_____.

13. 무슨 일이 있어요? 왜 다른 도시로 이사가고 싶어요?

_____.

14. 내일 2시까지 하세요.

_____.

15. 제가 8살이었을 때 매일 학교에 갔어요.

_____.

New Phrases

무슨 일이 있어요?	"What's wrong?"
무슨일이에요?	"What's wrong?"
생일 축하합니다.	"Happy Birthday."

If and When

Chapter 2

New Vocabulary

로스앤젤레스	"Los Angeles"
이따(가)	"after a while," "later"
아까	"a while ago," "earlier"
짐	"luggage"
짐(을) 싸다	"to pack luggage"
일	"a matter," "something (to do)"
이사(를) 가다	"to move (away)"
이사(를) 오다	"to move (here)"
생일	"birthday"
시끄럽다	"to be noisy," "to be annoying (to hear)"
어리다	"to be young (like a child)"
젊다	"to be young (and youthful)"
늙다	"to be old"
밀다	"to push"
당기다	"to pull"
순간	"a moment," "an instant"
인기(가) 많다	"to be very popular"
레시피	"recipe"
요리사	"chef"

Chapter 2
If and When

Future Tense

Conversation

진원:	잘 먹겠습니다!
시경:	네. 많이 드세요. 아, 민수 씨는 어디 있어요?
진원:	친구를 만나러 나갈 거예요. 지금 준비하고 있어요.
시경:	왜 지금 나가요? 벌써 8 시예요.
진원:	그 친구가 밤에만 시간이 돼요.
시경:	전화로 이야기할 수 없어요?
진원:	그 친구는 핸드폰이 없어요.
시경:	아, 알겠어요.
진원:	잘 먹었습니다!
시경:	네.

Future Tense

So far we've learned the *present tense* (to talk about things currently happening) and the *past tense* (to talk about things that already happened). Now it's time to learn about the *future tense*, which can be used to talk about things that will happen.

In English, we only need to add one word word – "will" – in order to speak in the future tense. Here's an example:

"I *will* go to school tomorrow."

Chapter 3: Future Tense

Using the future tense in Korean isn't much more difficult, but there are two ways to do it. You can use either way. Let's learn them one at a time.

1. Verb Stem + 겠다

Take a verb stem and attach 겠다. This 겠다 will then be conjugated any way that you'd like. So far, we've learned two popular ways to conjugate it at the *end* of a sentence – using the 요 form and the 니다 form. When it's not at the end of a sentence, you can also use it with other forms, such as 고 ("and" – 겠고), 지만 ("but" – 겠지만), and more.

하다 → 하
하 + 겠다 → 하겠다
하겠다 → 하겠어요 or 하겠습니다

내일 숙제를 하겠습니다.
"I will do the homework tomorrow."

먹다 → 먹
먹 + 겠다 → 먹겠다
먹겠다 → 먹겠어요 or 먹겠습니다

그런 음식을 왜 먹겠습니까?
"Why will you eat that kind of food?"

놀다 → 놀
놀 + 겠다 → 놀겠다
놀겠다 → 놀겠어요 or 놀겠습니다

저는 학교에서 놀겠습니다.
"I will play at school."

춥다 → 춥
춥 + 겠다 → 춥겠다
춥겠다 → 춥겠어요 or 춥겠습니다

한국은 겨울에 정말 춥겠습니다.
"Korea will be really cold in the winter."

It's simple to use the future tense with *negative sentences* as well.

하지 않겠습니다.
안 하겠습니다.
"I won't do it."

Future Tense

In addition, the future tense can also be combined with the *progressive tense*.

내일 도서관에서 하루 종일 공부하고 있겠습니다.
"Tomorrow I will be studying all day at the library."

> **Advanced**
>
> In addition to 하루 ("one day") and 이틀 ("two days"), you might also hear 사흘 ("three days") and 나흘 ("four days"). There are also Pure Korean words for days farther than this, but they're not commonly used, if ever – with two exceptions.
>
> You can use 보름 for "15 days," or to say "the 15th day of the month." Or, you can simply say 15 일. You can also use 그믐 for "the last day of the month." Or, you can simply say 30 일, or 31 일 (or however many days February has, if it ever decides to make up its mind).
>
> Two more useful words to learn are 석 달 ("three months") and 넉 달 ("four months"), which come after the regular 한 달 or 1 개월 ("one month"), and 두 달 or 2 개월 ("two months"). Months beyond these are not commonly used either.

2. Verb Stem + (을/ㄹ) 것이다

Take a verb stem and attach 을 if it ends in a *consonant*, or attach ㄹ if it ends in a *vowel*. Then attach 것이다, which is a combination of 것 ("thing") and 이다 ("to be"). 이다 will then be conjugated any way that you'd like. Here are a few examples.

하다 → 하
하 + ㄹ 것이다 → 할 것이다
할 것이다 → 할 것이에요 or 할 것입니다

내일 숙제를 할 것입니다.
"I will do the homework tomorrow."

먹다 → 먹
먹 + 을 것이다 → 먹을 것이다
먹을 것이다 → 먹을 것이에요 or 먹을 것입니다

그런 음식을 왜 먹을 것입니까?
"Why will you eat that kind of food?"

놀다 → 놀
놀 + ㄹ 것이다 → 놀 것이다
놀 것이다 → 놀 것이에요 or 놀 것입니다

저는 학교에서 놀 것입니다.
"I will play at school."

Chapter 3

Future Tense

While the 겠다 form acts the same for every type of verb, this 것이다 form uses the three special additional rules we learned in Chapter 2.

Remember that verb stems ending in ㄹ (a *consonant*) will conjugate as if they ended in a *vowel* instead.

춥다 → 춥
춥 → 추우
추우 + ㄹ 것이다 → 추울 것이다
추울 것이다 → 추울 것이에요 or 추울 것입니다

> 한국은 겨울에 정말 추울 것입니다.
> "Korea will be really cold in the winter."

Also remember that *descriptive verb* stems ending in ㅂ will conjugate differently, just as we learned in Chapter 2.

Just like with the 겠다 form, this form can also be used with *negative sentences*.

> 하지 않을 것입니다.
> 안 할 것입니다.
> "I won't do it."

It can also be used with the *progressive tense*.

> 내일 도서관에서 하루 종일 공부하고 있을 것입니다.
> "Tomorrow I will be studying all day at the library."

When to Use Future Tense

We've already learned that for most situations, the *present tense* can be used to talk about things that are going to happen in the future. Here's a quick example:

> 내일 학교에 가요.
> "I'm going to school tomorrow."

The future tense has an advantage over the present tense when talking about things that haven't happened yet. Using the future tense emphasizes that something *will* happen. Take the following two sentences:

> 학교에 갑니다.
> "I go to school."

Future Tense

학교에 가겠습니다.
"I will go to school."

The second sentence adds more emphasis that the person *will* go to school, while the first sentence simply states something that happens – it could be now, or it could be in the future. The second sentence is clear that it will happen in the *future*.

This emphasis is useful when you want to, well... emphasize that something *will* happen. It can be used to show that you are intending to do something, or that you are certain something will happen.

15 일에 엘비스가 우리 학교에 옵니다.
"On the 15th, Elvis comes to our school."

15 일에 엘비스가 우리 학교에 올 것입니다.
"On the 15th, Elvis *will* come to our school."

내일 비가 옵니다.
"Tomorrow it rains."

내일 비가 오겠습니다.
"Tomorrow it *will* rain."

Two Future Tenses: 겠다 and 것이다

"So what's the difference between the two?" Both have the same meaning, but using 겠다 is a bit more *formal* than using 것이다. However, even though it's a bit more polite, you don't have to worry about this when using them; you can use whichever form that you'd like. If you're still unsure of which form to use, I would recommend using 것이다 when speaking in the 요 form, and 겠다 when speaking in 니다 form (since it is a bit more formal).

> **Advanced**
>
> There is one more additional (small) difference between using 겠다 and 것이다. Using 겠다 puts more emphasis on the *verb* in a sentence, while using 것이다 puts more emphasis on the *subject* of that verb in a sentence. Here's an example of what I mean:
>
> 제가 하겠습니다.
> "I will **do** it."
>
> This sentence emphasizes the verb, "do" (하다) – as opposed to another verb.
>
> 제가 할 것입니다.
> "**I** will do it."
>
> This sentence emphasizes the subject of the verb, "I" (제가) – as opposed to another subject.
>
> The difference between these two forms is small, but I've exaggerated it here to show it to you.

Chapter 3: Future Tense

Let's go over the conversation.

> 진원: 잘 먹겠습니다!
> "Let's eat!"

잘 먹겠습니다 literally means "I will eat well," but is used as a polite way to say that you're thankful for the meal. It can be used to say thanks to the person who cooked the food, to the person who bought it for you, or just to the food in general for being there.

Note that this phrase is 잘 먹겠습니다, and not 잘 먹겠어요 or 잘 먹을 것입니다. This is an example of a common phrase that is used so often that it is only used in one way – 잘 먹겠습니다. Another example is the phrase 안녕하세요 (and not 안녕해요). Since 잘 먹겠습니다 is formal, we'll learn another less-formal way of saying this (such as with friends) in Chapter 13.

> 시경: 네. 많이 드세요. 아, 민수 씨는 어디 있어요?
> "Okay. Enjoy. Ah, where is 민수?"

We previously learned that 많이 is an adverb that means "a lot." 드세요 comes from the *honorific* verb 드시다, which we'll learn about in Chapter 8 of this book. All that you need to know now is that 드세요 is a polite *command* that means, "Please eat."

많이 드세요 therefore means "Please eat a lot." It's a polite way to tell someone to eat a lot, and to enjoy their meal.

Culture Notes

Korea hasn't always been a first world country. In Korea's past when food was more scarce than it is today, being able to eat enough food was a sign of health and prosperity. Contrast that with now; if you visit Korea today, you might find it difficult to not get full when eating, as Koreans can be more than generous when feeding guests (especially foreigners). However, the culture of food being a scarcity has stayed, and you can still see it today in phrases such as 많이 드세요. We'll learn a few more phrases related to food in the upcoming chapters, so keep an eye out for them.

Future Tense

> 진원: 친구를 만나러 나갈 거예요. 지금 준비하고 있어요.
> "He will leave to meet a friend. He is getting ready now."

In addition to meaning "to prepare," 준비(를) 하다 can also mean "to get ready."

Verb Stem + (을/ㄹ) 거다

Although we just learned 것이다 as one of the two forms of future tense, using 거다 is much more common. However, know that 것이다 is the original form that it comes from. 것이다 and 거다 work in the same way. 거 is a shortened version of 것.

Take a verb stem and attach 을 if it ends in a *consonant*, or attach ㄹ if it ends in a *vowel*. Then attach 거다 (the 다 comes from 이다), and conjugate it any way that you'd like. Here is an example:

하다 → 하
하 + ㄹ 거다 → 할 거다
할 거다 → 할 거예요 or 할 겁니다

> 내일 숙제를 할 거예요.
> 내일 숙제를 할 겁니다.
> "I will do the homework tomorrow."

Remember that 이다 becomes 입니다. In this case, the ㅂ니다 sound will attach directly to 거, becoming 겁니다 (and not 거입니다). This is an exception. In other cases, 입니다 will remain separate, and will not combine with the word it follows.

In addition, although 거 is a shortened version of 것, it cannot be substituted for 것 in every situation. We will learn more about how to use 거 in place of 것 in Chapter 10.

> 시경: 왜 지금 나가요? 벌써 8 시예요.
> "Why is he leaving now? It's already 8 o'clock."

벌써 and 이미

In the previous book, we learned that we can use 이미 to mean "already." There is one additional way to say "already" – 벌써 – and it's used slightly differently.
이미 is the normal way to say "already."

> 저는 이미 숙제를 했어요.
> "I already did the homework."

Chapter 3
Future Tense

벌써 also means "already," but is used when you want to express that you are *surprised*.

벌써 숙제를 했어요?
"You already did the homework?"

Use 벌써 to say "already" when you want to express that you are surprised, and use 이미 all other times. Simple, right? Here are two more examples:

이미 시작했어요.
"It already started."

벌써 시작했어요.
"It already started (... and I'm surprised that it did)."

진원: 그 친구가 밤에만 시간이 돼요.
"That friend can only meet at night."

시간(이) 되다

While literally meaning "to become time," 시간(이) 되다 is used to mean "to have time." It's used when asking if someone is *available* at a certain time, or if a certain time is *convenient* for someone.

언제 시간이 됩니까?
"When do you have time?"
"When would be convenient?"

저는 내일 10시에 시간이 될 거예요.
"I'll have time tomorrow at 10 o'clock."
"I'll be available tomorrow at 10 o'clock."

Because 시간(이) 되다 adds the meaning of a time being *available*, it's different from simply using 시간(이) 있다 ("time exists"), which doesn't specify that a time is *convenient*.

There are many other phrases that use this (이/가) 되다 form, and we'll cover more of them later in this book.

시경: 전화로 이야기할 수 없어요?
"Can't they talk on the phone?"

Future Tense

Using: Noun + (으)로

In the last chapter we learned that (으)로 can be used to mean "toward." It has one more usage, to mean "using."

Although (으)로 here literally means "using," depending on the sentence you might also see it translated as "by," "with," "as," or "on" as in the conversation, among other possible translations. Let's take a look at a few examples.

펜으로 쓰고 싶어요.
"I want to write with a pen."

저는 매일 자전거로 학교에 갑니다.
"I go to school everyday by bicycle."

핸드폰으로 전화했어요.
"I called him using a cell phone."

선물로 받았어요.
"I got it as a present."

Note how 선물로 translates to "as a present" – it might be easiest to simply memorize this one separately.

When using (으)로 after a noun ending with ㄹ, simply attach 로.

편지를 연필로 썼어요.
"I wrote a letter in pencil"

You'll know whether (으)로 is being used to mean "toward" or "using" depending on the context of the sentence.

진원: 그 친구는 핸드폰이 없어요.
"That friend doesn't have a cell phone."

시경: 아, 알겠어요.
"Ah, okay."

In the previous book, we learned the phrase 알겠습니다 on its own. Now we can see how 알겠습니다 comes from the verb 알다 ("to know") and the future tense 겠다. 알겠어요 or 알겠습니다 can be used to mean "I see" or "I understand," or simply as a polite way to say "Okay."

| Chapter 3 | **Future Tense** |

However, 알다 cannot be used in this way with the 것이다 form; 알 것입니다 would simply mean "I will know," and doesn't have the same meaning.

> 진원: 잘 먹었습니다!
> "Thank you!"

잘 먹었습니다 is the *past tense* version of 잘 먹겠습니다, which we learned before. It's used as a polite way to say that you're thankful *after* finishing a meal.

You might also see this phrase as 잘 먹었어요 (the less formal version). The meaning is the same.

> 시경: 네.
> "Okay."

Culture Notes

In Korea, a 학원 ("academy") is a cram school, or an institute, where people will take classes in addition to their regular schedule at school. These classes can be on any subject that they want to improve in school such as mathematics and English, or for recreational subjects such as martial arts or learning to play instruments. As a typical Korean high school student will already be at school from morning until late afternoon (and I thought 8 to 2 was tiring enough in the U.S.), with the addition of after-school academies Koreans will often be studying until late in the evening or even past midnight, returning home only to sleep (if they have any time left for sleep).

Future Tense

Chapter 3

Animal Group Counter – 떼

We previously learned how to use 마리 when counting animals. There is one more counter that we need to learn for animals. 떼 means "a group," and is used when talking about a *group* of animals. We learned this in the previous book, but in English we have to use many different words to count groups of animals, such as the following:

"a swarm of bees" / "a pack of wolves" / "a herd of buffalo" / "a flock of geese"

In Korean, you can use 떼 to replace "swarm," "pack," "herd," "flock," and any other *group counter* for animals. To use it in a sentence, place the animal's name first, followed by 떼.

하늘에 새 떼가 지나가고 있어요.
"A flock of birds are passing by in the sky."

강에서 물고기 떼를 봤어요.
"I saw a school of fish in the river."

Practice

Translate to Korean:

1. "I will not go."

2. "Will you work on the 23rd this month?"

3. "I will have 25 dollars by tomorrow."

4. "Today I did the laundry, and tomorrow I will do the dishes."

5. "If you are available at 5 o'clock, please let me know."

Chapter 3
Future Tense

6. "I left to go to work by car."

_____.

Translate to English:

7. 언제 할 거예요?

_____.

8. 지금 시작하겠습니다.

_____.

9. 잘 먹겠습니다!

_____.

10. 벌써 밥을 먹었어요?

_____.

11. 계약서에 연필로 사인하세요.

_____.

12. 시작하지 않았지만 내일 할 거예요.

_____.

New Phrases

잘 먹겠습니다.	"Thank you (for the food)."
많이 드세요.	"Eat a lot (and enjoy)."

New Vocabulary

하루 종일	"all day" (adverb)

Future Tense

벌써	"already" (surprised)
이미	"already"
시간(이) 되다	"to have time"
시작	"start"
녹차	"green tea"
홍차	"black tea" (literally, "red tea")
층	building floor counter
떼	animal group counter
지나가다	"to pass by," "to go by"
동아리	"club," "group"
1 층	"first floor"
위층	"upper floor," "upstairs"
아래층	"lower floor," "downstairs"
지하	"basement"
학원	"academy"
알려주다	"to tell," "to let (someone) know"
계약	"contract"
계약서	"contract (paper form)"
사인	"signature"
사인(을) 하다	"to sign"
줄이다	"to decrease (something)"
늘리다	"to increase (something)"
맛(을) 보다	"to taste (something)"
구름	"cloud"

Chapter 3

Future Tense

Complex Sentences

Chapter 4

Conversation

철수:	서울에서 하고 싶은 것이 있어요?
현지:	네, 있어요. 저는 영어를 못 하는 사람을 만나고 싶어요.
철수:	영어를 잘하는 사람이 아니고요?
현지:	네, 영어를 못 하는 사람을 만나고 그 사람과 친구가 되고 싶어요.
철수:	정말 특이해요. 아무튼....
현지:	저는 한국어를 더 연습하고 싶어요. 같이 연습할 사람이 필요해요.
철수:	지금도 한국어로 말하고 있지 않아요? 이것은 연습이 아니에요?
현지:	아.... 그러게요.

Turning Action Verbs into Adjectives

We've already learned a few different ways to use verbs; we can put them at the end of a sentence (by conjugating them to the 요 form, for example), and we can also use them to connect sentences together (such as by using 고 – "and"). We've also learned how to turn a *descriptive verb* into an adjective in Chapter 10 of the previous book. Now there's one more important usage that we need to learn – turning an *action verb* into an adjective.

So far, we have no way of saying the following sentence in Korean:

"I bought the book *that he wrote*."

Chapter 4
Complex Sentences

The best that we could do so far would be the following:

저는 책을 샀어요.
"I bought the book."

The piece that's missing – "that he wrote" – *describes* the book, and is being used as an adjective.

On its own, this is the best that we can currently do to express "that he wrote" in Korean:

그분이 썼어요.
"He wrote it."

Notice the "that" meaning isn't here, but don't worry. We'll talk about how to connect this with the rest of the sentence shortly. In fact, the Korean language does not need the word "that," and it's only used in English translations.

First we need to change 그분이 썼어요 into an *adjective*, so that we can add it before 책 to complete the sentence. In order to do this, we'll need to learn the conjugation rules for changing an action verb into an adjective.

Past Tense:
Action Verb Stem + (은/ㄴ)

Take an action verb stem and attach 은 if it ends in a *consonant*, or attach ㄴ if it ends in a *vowel*.

쓰다 → 쓰
쓰 + ㄴ → 쓴

Already with this we can complete our sentence – "I bought the book that he wrote." First let's make "that he wrote."

그분이 쓴
"(that) he wrote"

Remember that the "that" is not used in Korean, but is only used in the English translation.

Now we can add "(that) he wrote" before 책, and combine it together with the rest of the sentence.

Complex Sentences

저는 그분이 쓴 책을 샀어요.
"I bought the book that he wrote."

먹다 → 먹
먹 + 은 → 먹은

오늘 (제가) 먹은 밥이 정말 맛있었어요.
"The food I ate today was really delicious."

In the above sentence, 제가 is *optional*, and would only be necessary if you wanted to clarify that you're talking about the food that *you* ate, as opposed to someone else.

Also remember from the previous book that *pronouns* (such as "I," "you," etc.) in Korean are *optional* and are only used to clarify the subject.

Let's continue with another example.

공부하다 → 공부하
공부하 + ㄴ → 공부한

어제 도서관에서 3 시간 동안 공부한 사람이 누구였어요?
"Who was the person who studied at the library yesterday for 3 hours?"

In the above sentence, you can see how "that" not being necessary in Korean makes things much simpler for us. The above sentence translated to English would use "who" instead of "that" because it's referring to a *person*, but in Korean there's no need to worry about adding "who," "that," or any extra connecting words.

We also learned in Chapter 2 that some verbs (ones ending in ㄹ or ㅎ) can conjugate differently depending on the grammatical form. When changing action verbs to adjectives, those same extra rules are necessary.

> **Adv**
>
> You might be curious about combining the *progressive tense* (고 있다) with this form in the *past tense* to express "*was* (verb)ing." However, 고 있은 would be grammatically *incorrect*.
>
> There is a different form that we must use for expressing continuous past actions, which we will learn later on.

Chapter 4: Complex Sentences

Present Tense:
Action Verb Stem + 는

Take an action verb stem and attach 는. Let's look at some examples.

연습하다 → 연습하
연습하 + 는 → 연습하는

> 한국어를 매일 연습하는 사람들은 빨리 배워요.
> "People who study Korean everyday learn quickly."

먹다 → 먹
먹 + 는 → 먹는

> 김치를 많이 먹는 사람들도 한국어를 빨리 배워요.
> "People who eat a lot of kimchi also learn Korean quickly."

Remember to keep in mind the additional rules that we learned in Chapter 2.

알다 → 알
알 – ㄹ → 아
아 + 는 → 아는

> 여기 철수 씨를 아는 사람이 있어요?
> "Is there someone here who knows Chul-soo?"

Future Tense:
Action Verb Stem + (을/ㄹ)

Take an action verb stem and attach 을 if it ends in a *consonant,* or attach ㄹ if it ends in a *vowel*.

수영하다 → 수영하
수영하 + ㄹ → 수영할

> 오늘은 바다에서 수영할 사람이 없어요.
> "There is nobody who will swim in the ocean today."

받다 → 받
받 + 을 → 받을

Complex Sentences

Chapter 4

친구에게 받을 돈이 있을 거예요.
"I'll have some money that I will get from a friend."

놀다 → 놀
놀 – ㄹ → 노
노 + ㄹ → 놀

내일 같이 놀 사람이 있어요?
"Is there someone who will play together (with me) tomorrow?"

We'll learn more about using 같이 in this chapter's conversation.

We'll also need to know how to conjugate this future tense form as it's used in many grammar forms, such as ㄹ 때, and ㄹ 수 있다, which we've learned previously, and others that we have yet to learn.

Using 것

There are a few additional uses of conjugating action verbs using past, present, and future tense. When these new *adjectives* are combined with 것 ("thing") they can take on an additional meaning.

Something one did: (은/ㄴ) 것

Using the *past tense* and 것, we can say "something one (did)."

제가 먹은 것은 비빔밥이에요.
"What I ate is bibimbap."

Culture Notes

비빔밥 literally means "mixed rice," and is a combination of rice with various vegetables and meats – often including shredded beef, red pepper paste, and sesame oil, among other ingredients. There are many different kinds, including hot and cold varieties. It's served in a metal or stone bowl and mixed by yourself before eating.

Chapter 4

Complex Sentences

제가 한 것이 아니에요.
"It's not something that I did."
"I didn't do it."

It would also be grammatically correct to say 제가 안 했어요 to mean "I didn't do it."

제가 만든 거예요.
"It's something that I made."
"I made it."

Something one does: 는 것

Using the *present tense* and 것, we can say "something one (does)."

김치가 먹는 거예요.
"Kimchi is something that you eat."

피자는 제가 좋아하는 거예요.
"Pizza is something that I like."

철수 씨가 매일 하는 것이 뭐예요?
"What it is that Chul-soo does everyday?"

Something to: (을/ㄹ) 것

Using the *future tense* and 것, we can say, "something to (verb)."

오늘 할 것이 없어요.
"There is nothing to do today."

Note that the above sentence literally means, "There is not something to do today."

집에 먹을 것이 있어요?
"Is there something to eat at home?"

도서관에 읽을 것이 많아요.
"There are many things to read at the library."

Now that we've covered how to change action verbs into adjectives, let's go over the conversation.

Complex Sentences

철수: 서울에서 하고 싶은 것이 있어요?
"Is there something you want to do in Seoul?"

Remember that the above rules we learned only apply to action verbs. 싶다, as seen in the sentence – 하고 싶은 – is a *descriptive verb*, and simply conjugates normally.

현지: 네, 있어요. 저는 영어를 못 하는 사람을 만나고 싶어요.
"Yes, there is. I want to meet someone who can't speak English."

못 and 지 못하다

We previously learned that we can use 못 before *Pure Korean verbs* to mean "can't."

갈 수 없어요.
못 가요.
"I can't go."

There is also a way to use 못 with *Sino Korean verbs*, by attaching 지 못하다 to the verb stem. This works in the same way as attaching 지 않다.

요리할 수 없어요.
요리하지 못해요.
"I can't cook."

잘 이해하지 못했어요.
"I couldn't understand it well."

Just like 지 않다, this form can also be used with *Pure Korean verbs* as well.

가지 못했어요.
"I couldn't go.

> **Advanced**
>
> We've previously learned that the *descriptive verb* 잘생기다 ("to be handsome") is only used in the *past tense*. There are also two more common verbs which are only used in the *past tense* – 못생기다 ("to be unattractive," "to be ugly") and 못되다 ("to be mean," "to be bad").
>
> 저 원숭이는 정말 못생겼어요.
> "That monkey is really ugly."
>
> 저 남자는 사실 못된 사람이에요.
> "That man is in fact a bad person."

| Chapter 4 | **Complex Sentences** |

철수: 영어를 잘하는 사람이 아니고요?
"Not someone who can speak English well?"

This sentence ends in 아니고요, which is the verb 아니다 ("to not be") combined with 고 ("and") and the informal 요 ending.

Ending Sentences With 고요

This is the same grammar that we've learned previously using 고 ("and"). Simply take a verb stem and attach 고. However, when using this at the end of a sentence, it's polite to add 요 after – becoming 고요. You can remove the 요 when speaking *casually*, which we'll learn about in Chapter 10.

There are two main purposes for ending a sentence with 고요, whether a statement or a question.

1.   It shows that the sentence is not yet finished.

Just like when using 고 in the middle of a sentence, using it at the end also means that you're probably going to say something else afterward.

저는 김치를 좋아하**고** 매일 먹고 있어요.
"I like kimchi *and* I eat it everyday."

저는 김치를 좋아하**고요**.
"I like kimchi...."

2.   It makes a sentence sound *softer*.

Sometimes speaking directly can sound a bit harsh, in Korean or in English. Take the following two sentences:

A.   저는 미국 사람이에요.
B.   저는 미국 사람이고요.

Sentence A is a direct sentence – "I am an American."

Sentence B, however, is slightly less direct. Ending the sentence with 고요 gives it a softer feeling. If you have to translate this, you could write it in English as "Well, I'm an American, for one."

Complex Sentences

Chapter 4

By making the sentence sound like it isn't yet finished, you also make the sentence sound a bit softer.

Going back to the conversation, let's take a look specifically at 아니고요.

Noun + (이/가) 아니고요

When used in this form, like in the conversation, 아니고요 has an additional meaning all on its own – "not." You can use 아니고요 to make sentences that would, in English, *begin* with "not." Let's look at a few examples.

개를 키우고 싶어요? 고양이가 아니고요?
"You want a dog? Not a cat?"

생선이라고요? 쇠고기가 아니고요?
"You said fish? Not beef?"

이것이 그림이에요? 사진이 아니고요?
"This is a drawing? Not a picture?"

> 현지: 네, 영어를 못 하는 사람을 만나고 그 사람과 친구가 되고 싶어요.
> "Yes, I want to meet someone who can't speak English and become friends with them."

More About 고

In the conversation, notice how although the meaning is "Yes, I want to meet someone who can't speak English and (I want to) become friends," the expression "want to" (고 싶다) is only included once in the sentence in *both* English and Korean. This is to avoid repetition. The following type of sentence would therefore be repetitive, and should be avoided:

네, 영어를 못 하는 사람을 만나고 싶고 그 사람과 친구가 되고 싶어요.
"Yes, I want to meet someone who can't speak English and I want to become friends."

> 철수: 정말 특이해요. 아무튼....
> "That's really unusual. Anyway...."

아무튼 is an expression that means "anyway." It can be used to change the subject of a conversation, and it shows that you're about to talk about something different. Two more equally common expressions that also have the same meaning as 아무튼 are 하여튼 and 어쨌든. Feel free to use whichever one you'd like.

59

Chapter 4: Complex Sentences

현지: 저는 한국어를 더 연습하고 싶어요. 같이 연습할 사람이 필요해요.
"I want to practice Korean more. I need someone to practice together with."

같이

같이 is an *adverb* that means "together," so it can be used anytime you want to say that someone is doing something *together* with someone else. Earlier in this chapter we saw the following example sentence:

내일 같이 놀 사람이 있어요?
"Is there someone who will play together (with me) tomorrow?"

Literally this sentence means, "Tomorrow is there someone who will play together?" The meaning of "with me" is *assumed* from the context, but it could mean "with another person" as well. In order to clarify that you mean "with me," you could add in 저와 ("with me") before 같이 in the sentence.

내일 저와 같이 놀 사람이 있어요?
"Is there someone who will play together with me tomorrow?"

However, it's not necessary to do this unless you're worried that someone might not understand that you mean "with *me*."

You can also use the adverb 따로 ("separately") in the same way as 같이.

따로 주세요.
"Give them to me separately."

따로 살 거예요.
"I'll buy it separately."

필요하다

In the previous book we learned that 필요하다 means "to be necessary." 필요하다 is a *descriptive verb*, and therefore does not use the Object Marker (을/를) to mark what it is that you need. Most of the time, the Subject Marker (이/가) will be used to mark what is necessary.

저는 돈이 필요해요.
"I need money."

60

Complex Sentences

뭐가 필요해요?
"What do you need?"

> 철수: 지금도 한국어로 말하고 있지 않아요? 이것은 연습이 아니에요?
> "Aren't we speaking in Korean now too? Is this not practice?"

지금도 is a combination of 지금 with 도, meaning "even now" or "now too."

> 현지: 아.... 그러게요.
> "Ah.... Yeah."

그러게요 is a phrase that can be used when you're *agreeing* with what someone else has said. It can be translated to English as either "that's right" or simply as "yeah."

> **Advanced**
>
> If you read through the example sentences in this chapter, you might notice that most of the example sentences – with action verbs turned into adjectives – use the *Subject Marker* (이/가) in the phrase that is turned into an adjective. You will most commonly see the Subject Marker used, but *not* the Topic Marker (은/는).
>
> 제가 만든 영화...
> "The movie that I made..."
>
> 저는 만든 영화 would translate as "As for me, the movie that (someone) made..." and would be *incorrect*. If you choose to use a pronoun when changing action verbs into adjectives, I'd highly recommend using the Subject Marker after it (and not the Topic Marker).
>
> 어제 만든 김치가 정말 맛있었어요!
> "The kimchi (I/you/etc.) made yesterday was really delicious!"
>
> 어제 (철수 씨가) 만든 김치가 정말 맛있었어요!"
> "The kimchi Chul-soo made yesterday was really delicious!"

Practice

Translate to Korean:

1. "This is the computer that I bought."

    _____.

2. "A book is something that you can read."

    _____.

Complex Sentences

3. "I need a book to read."

_____.

4. "I have no friends that I can hang out together with."

_____.

5. "I need a little more time."

_____.

6. "The kimchi that I made was more delicious than the kimchi that Chul-soo made."

_____.

Translate to English:

7. 그것이 소설이라고요? 사전이 아니고요?

_____.

8. 그분이 말한 것을 들었어요?

_____.

9. 같이 할 수 있는 것이 있어요?

_____.

10. 도와줄 사람이 있어요?

_____.

11. 이 영화를 만든 사람이 누구예요?

_____.

Complex Sentences

Chapter 4

12. 지금 먹을 것이 필요해요.

_____.

New Phrases

그러게요	"That's right.," "Yeah."
아무튼	"Anyway...," "In any case..."
하여튼	"Anyway...," "In any case..."
어쨌든	"Anyway...," "In any case..."

New Vocabulary

비빔밥	"bibimbap"
같이	"together" (adverb)
따로	"separately" (adverb)
특이하다	"unusual," "odd"
특별하다	"to be special"
기름	"oil," "gas(oline)"
주유소	"gas station"
역	"(train/subway) station"
버스 정류장	"bus station," "bus stop"
정류장	"station," "stop"
편의점	"convenience store"
태우다	"to give (someone) a ride"
고치다	"to repair"
고장(이) 나다	"to break down," "to malfunction"
깨다	"to break (something)," "to smash (something)"
정리(를) 하다	"to organize," "to put (something) in order"
방문	"visit"
방문(을) 하다	"to visit"
들르다	"to stop by," "to drop by"
머무르다	"to stay," "to remain"

63

Chapter 4
Complex Sentences

날짜	"a date," "a day"
따라하다	"to imitate," "to copy"
따라가다	"to (go) follow"
따라오다	"to (come) follow"
베개	"pillow"
이불	"blanket"
뚜껑	"lid"
세탁기	"washing machine"
식기	"dishes"
식기 세척기	"dish washer"
숟가락	"spoon"
수저	"spoon and chopsticks"
왕	"king"
왕자	"prince"
여왕	"queen"
공주	"princess"
병	"disease," "sickness"
정보	"information"
얻다	"to get," "to obtain"
회장님	"president (of a company)"
소설	"novel," "fiction story"
사실	"(in) fact," "(in) truth" (noun/adverb)
실제로(는)	"in reality," "actually" (adverb)

More Complex Sentences

Chapter 5

Conversation

브래드:	저... 혹시 이 책에 대해서 알고 있어요?
민호:	어떤 책이에요?
브래드:	한국어를 공부하기 위한 책이에요.
민호:	몰라요. 하지만 저는 한국 사람이라서 그런 책이 필요 없어요.
브래드:	하하. 아, 맞아요.

This chapter will cover a few more essential grammar forms that you can use in your sentences, including how to say "about" and "for." Let's cover both of these before we go into the conversation.

About:
Noun + 에 대한 + Noun
Noun + 에 대해(서) + Verb

In order to say "about," take a noun (what it is *about*) and attach 에 대한. Then attach another *noun*.

Or alternatively, take a noun and attach 에 대해(서) when it's followed by a *verb*. The 서 at the end is completely *optional*.

To give a bit more information, when "about" is followed by a noun in Korean, it's being used as an *adjective*. When it's being followed by a verb, it's being used as an *adverb*.

65

Chapter 5: More Complex Sentences

The form you use will therefore depend on whether "about" is being used as an *adjective* or an adverb. Here's an example of each of these in English:

A. "I read a book about Korea."
B. "I read about Korea."

Sentence A shows "about" being used as an *adjective*, since "about" is describing "book." Sentence B shows "about" being used as an *adverb*, since "about" is used to modify the verb "read."

> **Adv** Both forms of "about" come from the same verb – 대하다 ("to face"), which you don't need to learn on its own. We've already learned the rules for how this verb could change to become 대한, and we'll learn how it can change to become 대해(서) later in this chapter.

저는 한국에 대한 책을 읽었어요.
"I read a book about Korea."

This sentence uses "about" as an *adjective*, since 책 (a noun) follows directly after it.

저는 한국에 대해서 읽었어요.
"I read about Korea."

This sentence uses "about" as an *adverb*, since 읽다 (a verb) follows directly after it. Let's look at a few more example sentences.

저는 사랑에 대한 노래를 불렀어요.
"I sang a song about love."

저는 미국 미술에 대해 공부했어요.
"I studied about American art."

뭐에 대해서 배우고 싶어요?
"What do you want to learn about?"

고빌리에 대해 알고 있어요?
"Do you know about Billy Go?"

저는 한국 역사에 대한 영화를 봤어요.
"I saw a movie about Korean history."

More Complex Sentences

Chapter 5

For (After Noun):
Noun + (을/를) 위한 + Noun
Noun + (을/를) 위해(서) + Verb

Just like with "about," the form of "for" that you will use depends on whether it's followed by a noun or a verb (whether it's being used as an *adjective* or as an *adverb*); but it will also depend on whether you're using it after a *noun* or after a *verb*.

Although this sounds like twice the effort, it actually works the same way as "about," since "about" can only be placed after a noun anyway. With "for," we will often want to also use it after verbs; I'll explain this shortly. First we'll learn how to say "for" when it's used *after a noun*.

In order to say "for" as an *adjective*, take a noun (what it is *for*) and attach 을 after a *consonant*, or 를 after a *vowel*. Then use 위한, followed by another noun.

저를 위한 선물이 있어요?
"Is there a present for me?"

감기 회복을 위한 약을 먹었어요.
"I took medicine for recovering from a cold."

약(을) 먹다 literally means "to eat medicine," but is the normal way to say "to take medicine."

In order to say "for" as an *adverb*, take a noun and attach 을 after a *consonant*, or 를 after a *vowel*. Then use 위해(서), followed by a verb. The 서 at the end is completely *optional*.

에디 씨를 위해 선물을 샀어요.
"I bought a present for Eddie."

엄마를 위해 집을 청소했어요.
"I cleaned the house for mom."

"But the above sentence has 집 (a noun) used after 위해. Shouldn't it be 위한?" Although it's true that 위해 is directly followed by 집 (a noun), the sentence would only make sense this way. Let's try using 위한 in this sentence instead, and looking at what the meaning would become.

엄마를 위한 집을 청소했어요.

67

Chapter 5: More Complex Sentences

I should first point out that this sentence is *grammatically* correct, and could be used in another context. However, the meaning will likely be different from what we are trying to say.

엄마를 위한 means "for mom," so we're doing okay so far. The next part of the sentence, 집, is where the meaning changes.

엄마를 위한 집 means "a house for mom," or "a house that is for the purpose of mom." Basically this would mean that the house is going to be presented or given to the mother, since it's "for" her.

Continuing with the sentence, adding 청소했어요 would then mean "I cleaned the house that is for mom." While this sentence is still grammatically correct, it is most likely not what you would want to say.

Using 위해(서) instead shows that the *action* of cleaning the house was for mom (this is what it means to use it as an *adverb*), instead of showing that the *house* itself was for mom.

Let's continue and learn how to say "for" when it's used with a *verb*, instead of a noun.

For (After Verb):

Verb Stem + 기 위한 + Noun

Verb Stem + 기 위해(서) + Verb

Now we'll learn how to say "for" when it's used *after a verb*. In order to say "for" as an *adjective*, take a verb stem and attach 기. Then use 위한, followed by another noun.

한국어를 배우기 위한 책이에요.
"It's a book for learning Korean."

저녁을 요리하기 위한 재료가 필요해요.
"I need ingredients for cooking dinner."

In order to say "for" as an *adverb*, take a verb stem and attach 기 like before. Then attach 위해(서). The 서 at the end is completely *optional*.

저는 공부하기 위해서 학교에 갔어요.
"I went to school for studying."

집을 사기 위해 돈이 많이 필요해요.
"I need a lot of money for buying a house."

More Complex Sentences

Chapter 5

In addition, this grammar form has one additional translation – "in order to." It can be used in the same way, and translated as either "for" or "in order to," depending on your preference.

저는 공부하기 위해서 학교에 갔어요.
"I went to school in order to study."

집을 사기 위해 돈이 많이 필요해요.
"I need a lot of money in order to buy a house."

돈을 벌기 위해서 일을 구했어요.
"I looked for a job in order to earn money."

사람들은 행복할 수 있기 위해 돈이 필요해요.
"People need money in order to be happy."

Now that we've covered how to say "about" and "for," let's start going over the conversation.

브래드: 저... 혹시 이 책에 대해서 알고 있어요?
"Uh... do you know about this book by chance?"

민호: 어떤 책이에요?
"What kind of book is it?"

브래드: 한국어를 공부하기 위한 책이에요.
"It's a book for studying Korean."

민호: 몰라요. 하지만 저는 한국 사람이라서 그런 책이 필요 없어요.
"I don't know. But I don't need that kind of book because I'm a Korean."

In order to understand 한국 사람이라서, we're going to need to learn a new grammar form – 서.

69

Chapter 5 More Complex Sentences

Cause and Effect: Verb Stem + 아/어/etc. + 서

CAUSE → EFFECT

There's a simple form that you can use when you want to show that one thing is or was *caused* by something else. Before going into detail about how this form can be used, let's cover how to make it.

Take a verb and conjugate it the same way as you would conjugate the 요 form. Then, instead of attaching 요 to the end, attach 서. Here are a couple of conjugated examples:

하다 → 해
해 + 서 → 해서

먹다 → 먹어
먹어 + 서 → 먹어서

There is an exception for the verb 이다 ("to be"). 이다 conjugates simply as 이라서 when used after a *consonant*, or 라서 when used after a *vowel*. The same applies to the verb 아니다, which becomes 아니라서.

이다 → (이)라서
아니다 → 아니라서

This form is used to show a *cause* and *effect* in a sentence – it can be translated to English as either "because," or "so." Let's take a look at a quick example sentence.

밥을 많이 먹어서 배가 불러요.

The literal translation of this sentence would be "I ate a lot of food *so* I am full." The *cause* of the sentence is shown *before* 서 (밥을 많이 먹어서), and the *effect* of that is shown *after* 서 (배가 불러요). Another translation of the sentence could be "I am full *because* I ate a lot of food."

Also notice that even though the English sentence uses the past tense ("I ate"), the Korean sentence does not. When making sentences using this 서 form, it's not necessary to change the sentence to past tense, unless the *effect* of the sentence is in the past tense. Here's an example of what I mean:

More Complex Sentences

Chapter 5

밥을 많이 먹어서 배가 불렀어요.
"I ate a lot of food so I was full."
"I was full because I ate a lot of food."

Notice how the verb 먹다 stays the same (먹어서) in the present tense and the past tense example sentences; it does not become 먹었어서. The only verb that is in the past tense is the one at the end of the sentence. Most of the time when using 서, the verb it attaches to will remain in the present tense, such as in every example in this chapter. Let's look at a few more examples.

잠을 조금만 자서 아주 피곤해요.
"I slept only a little so I'm very tired."

역시 숙제를 안 해서 시험에 떨어졌어요.
"I didn't do the homework so I failed the test just as expected."

저는 언어에 관심이 있어서 한국어를 공부하고 있어요.
"I'm interested in languages so I'm studying Korean."

Note that 관심(이) 있다 is used with 에 to mean "interested in." For *people*, remember to use 에게 instead.

저는 남자라서 18 살이 되면 군대에 갈 거예요.
"I will go to the military when I'm 18 years old because I am a man."

18 살이 되면 literally means "when I become 18 years old," but the verb 되다 is used in this sentence because the speaker is not yet 18. Saying 18 살이면 instead would mean "if I were 18 years old," and would have a different meaning than using 되면.

Culture Notes

In Korea, all men aged 19 or older (in Korean age, which we'll cover in Chapter 10) are required to register for the military and serve for approximately two years. This of course excludes people with certain health or mental issues, but avoiding this mandatory military service for any other reason would be illegal.

비가 와서 소풍을 못 갔어요.
"It rained so I couldn't go on a picnic."

Remember that the first part of the sentence (before 서) will show the *cause*, and the second part of the sentence (after 서) will show the *effect* of the action.

Chapter 5: More Complex Sentences

One more common use of this 서 form is in the word 그래서, which comes from 그렇다 ("to be so") and means "so" or "therefore." You can use 그래서 at the beginning of a sentence.

그래서 제가 학교에 갔어요.
"So I went to school."

그래서 뭘 먹고 싶어요?
"So what do you want to eat?"

뭘 is a shortened version of 무엇을 – 뭐를 is simply not used.

> **Advanced**
>
> Just as the first verb will stay the same when using the 서 form – such as with the previous example using 먹어서 – the same thing applies when using the 고 ("and") form as well. Let's look at a couple of examples.
>
> 오늘 쇼핑하고 집에서 요리했어요.
> "Today I went shopping and cooked at home."
>
> 밥을 먹고 학교로 갈 거예요.
> "I'll eat and go to school."
>
> You're still free to conjugate the verb any way that you'd like, but know that it's not necessary.
>
> 오늘 쇼핑했고 집에서 요리했어요.
> "Today I went shopping and cooked at home."
>
> 밥을 먹을 거고 학교로 갈 거예요.
> "I'll eat and go to school."
>
> Note that 거고 is the shortened way of saying 것이고.

Going back to the conversation, let's take a look at one more thing – 필요(가) 없다. We previously learned how to say that something is necessary with 필요하다. You can use 필요(가) 없다 to say that something is unnecessary; literally it means "there is no necessity." It works in the same way as 필요하다.

저는 돈이 필요해요.
"I need money."

저는 돈이 필요 없어요.
"I don't need money."

Another alternative is to use the negative form of 필요하다 – 필요하지 않다.

저는 돈이 필요하지 않아요.
"I don't need money."

More Complex Sentences

Chapter 5

브래드: 하하. 아, 맞아요.
"Haha. Ah, that's right."

Practice

Translate to Korean:

1. "I bought a present for my English teacher."

   _____.

2. "I sang a song for my friend."

   _____.

3. "I bought a car for my mother."

   _____.

4. "That camera is not for children."

   _____.

5. "Yung-hee bought that book in order to study Korean."

   _____.

6. "I exercise everyday in order to be healthy."

   _____.

Translate to English:

7. 철수 씨를 위한 음식은 누가 먹었어요?

   _____.

More Complex Sentences

Chapter 5

8. 그것이 필요한 거예요.

   _____.

9. 그것이 필요 없는 거예요.

   _____.

10. 유럽으로 가기 위한 준비를 했어요?

    _____.

11. 한국어를 잘하기 위해 연습이 많이 필요해요.

    _____.

12. 제가 도와주기 위해서 필요한 것들이 많아요.

    _____.

New Phrases

(사)실은...	"Actually...," "In fact..."

New Vocabulary

서점	"bookstore"
청소(를) 하다	"to clean (the house)," "to vacuum"
청소기	"vacuum cleaner"
재료	"ingredient"
구하다	"to look for," "to seek"
배(가) 부르다	"to be full"
군대	"the military"
소풍	"picnic"
소풍(을) 가다	"to go on a picnic"
산책	"a walk," "a stroll"
산책(을) 하다	"to take a walk"

More Complex Sentences

Chapter 5

그래서	"So...," "Therefore..."
그러나	"However..."
필요(가) 없다	"to be unnecessary"
약(을) 먹다	"to take medicine"
역시	"(just) as expected" (adverb)
(시험에) 떨어지다	"to fail (a test)"
(시험[을]) 통과하다	"to pass (a test)"
(수업[을]) 듣다	"to take (a class)"
휴지	"tissue," "toilet paper"
새우	"shrimp"
랍스타	"lobster"
굴	"oyster"
연어	"salmon"
오징어	"squid"
문어	"(large) octopus"
낙지	"(small) octopus"
조개	"clam," "shellfish"
해물	"seafood"
상어	"shark"
악어	"alligator"
하마	"hippopotamus"
기린	"giraffe"
호랑이	"tiger"
표범	"panther," "leopard"
곰	"bear"
오리	"duck"
동물원	"zoo"
끼	meal counter
장(을) 보다	"to shop for groceries"
교과서	"textbook"
관심	"an interest"
관심(이) 있다	"to be interested"
관심(이) 없다	"to not be interested"
회복	"recovery"

More Complex Sentences

Chapter 5

회복(을) 하다	"to recover," "to get well"
흥미롭다	"to be interesting," "to be amusing"
심하다	"to be severe," "to be harsh"
얼음	"ice"
먼지	"dust"
아몬드	"almond"

Adverbs

Chapter 6

Conversation

호준:	빨리 와요. 지금 바로 시작할 거예요.
선경:	호준 씨는 축구를 너무 많이 보고 있어요.
호준:	저는 축구 없이 못 살아요.
선경:	알아요. 알아요.... 아, 그 선수가 괜히 뛰었어요.
호준:	실수로 너무 멀리 뛰었어요. 공이 다시 엑스 팀으로 갔어요.
선경:	이 경기는 못 이길 거예요.
호준:	아! 진지하게 채널을 바꾸고 싶어요.

Adverbs in Korean

Although we've been using adverbs for a while, we haven't yet learned how to create our own. Before going further, let's review what an adverb is, and how to use it.

First, an *adjective* is a word that describes a *noun*.

중요한 책
"an important book"

An *adverb*, however, is a word that describes a *verb*.

빨리 읽다
"to read quickly"

77

Chapter 6: Adverbs

Adverbs can give more life to a simple verb by describing *how* something happens.

In addition to verbs, an adverb can also describe other *adverbs*.

빨리 읽으세요.
"Please read it quickly."

더 빨리 읽으세요.
"Please read it more quickly."

어제 피자를 많이 먹었어요.
"I really ate a lot of pizza yesterday."

어제 피자를 너무 많이 먹었어요.
"I really ate too much pizza yesterday."

Just as adjectives are used before the noun that they're describing, adverbs are used before the verb that they're describing.

We've learned several adverbs already, and there are still more to learn, but instead of cramming vocabulary, let's learn how to create our own adverbs.

Descriptive Verb Stem + 게

Adverbs in Korean can be created from *descriptive verbs*.

For example, take the descriptive verb 행복하다 – "to be happy." Knowing that it's a descriptive verb, we can change it to an *adverb* – "happily."

To make an adverb from a descriptive verb, take its verb stem and attach 게. Let's take a look at a few examples.

행복하다 → 행복하
행복하 + 게 → 행복하게

저는 돈이 많기 때문에 행복하게 살 수 있어요.
"Because I have a lot of money, I can live happily."

Just as saying 돈이 있다 ("to exist") means "I have money," saying 돈이 많다 means "I have a lot of money."

맵다 → 맵
맵 + 게 → 맵게

Adverbs

엄마가 김치를 너무 맵게 만들었어요.
"Mom made the kimchi too spicy."

While 너무 맵게 in the above sentence literally means "too spicily," the English translation would simply be "spicy." This is because in Korean, in order to describe an action verb (such as 만들다), a descriptive verb *must* be changed into an adverb first; 맵다 is describing *how* the mother made the kimchi.

크다 → 크
크 + 게 → 크게

철수 씨는 항상 크게 말해요.
"Chul-soo always talks loudly."

Note that 크다 can mean "to be big" or "to be loud," depending on the sentence it's being used in.

빠르다 → 빠르
빠르 + 게 → 빠르게

선생님은 책을 빠르게 읽었어요.
"The teacher read the book quickly."

Unique Adverbs

"But didn't we learn that 빨리 meant quickly?" It does, and 빠르게 does too. This is because some adverbs in Korean are completely unique – they were not created by adding 게. We've already learned many examples of adverbs that don't end in 게, such as 더, 덜, 빨리, 잘, 많이, and others. These adverbs exist on their own, and can simply be memorized.

This means that some adverbs will have two versions of themselves – such as 빨리 and 빠르게 which both mean "quickly." In this case, which do you use? The answer is simple: either one is fine.

It's often more common for Koreans to use the unique adverb over the 게 adverb (when both versions exist), but both have the same literal meaning.

There is no trick to creating your own unique adverbs; you'll have to memorize them.

Chapter 6

Adverbs

히 Adverbs

Many descriptive verbs that end in 하다 can also be changed to an adverb by changing 하다 to 히. Here are a few examples:

조용하다 → 조용히
안전하다 → 안전히
급하다 → 급히

This does not apply to all descriptive verbs.

심심하다 → 심심하게 (not 심심히)
위험하다 → 위험하게 (not 위험히)

Sometimes, the version using 게 will be preferred, and other times the version using 히 will be preferred (when there are both options).

Because of this, it's still best to simply *memorize* adverbs in Korean, and to use these tips only as guides to help you along the way. When you have a descriptive verb that ends in 하다 and you're not sure which method is best (between 히 or 게), use the first method with 게.

Adverbs in Phrases

When we change a descriptive verb into an adverb, it's *usually* obvious what the adverb's meaning will be – we can guess that 행복하다 ("to be happy") will mean "happily" as an adverb (행복하게). However, there are times when the meaning will not be obvious to an English speaker. Here are just a few common examples that you should be aware of.

재미있게 보다 (literally, "to watch entertainingly")
"to enjoy (watching)"

영화를 재미있게 보세요!
"Please enjoy (watching) the movie!"

재미있게 읽다 (literally, "to read entertainingly")
"to enjoy (reading)"

책을 재미있게 읽었어요.
"I enjoyed (reading) the book."

Adverbs

재미있게 놀다 (literally, "to play entertainingly")
"to enjoy (playing)," "to have fun"

오늘 친구들과 재미있게 놀았어요.
"I enjoyed playing with my friends today."
"I had fun with my friends today."

맛있게 먹다 (literally, "to eat deliciously")
"to enjoy (eating)"

영희 씨가 만든 라면을 맛있게 먹었어요.
"I enjoyed the ramen that Yung-hee made."

There are more adverbs used in phrases which we'll learn along the way, but be aware of these ones first before going on.

Culture Notes

Eating in Korea

Here are a few quick tips about eating in Korea:

- Allow the oldest person in the room to sit down first, as well as to begin eating first.
- Use chopsticks only for eating, and not for pointing. Also avoid using chopsticks for poking food, except when picking up the item would be too difficult otherwise.
- Avoid blowing your nose at the table. This should be done away from the table.
- Pour drinks for people who are older than you, and use two hands when pouring. This will win you big points as a non-Korean. You can then pour your own drink afterward.
- Typically, it's considered impolite to refuse a drink (such as alcohol) when it's offered to you, but this does not mean that you need to drink alcohol in order to be accepted. Koreans will understand if you have a strong reason for not drinking (such as a medical condition, or a religious reason), so it will be more polite to explain the reason than to simply refuse a drink.

In addition, although I don't think there would be a reason for you to do this anyway, avoid putting chopsticks directly into a bowl of rice and leaving them sticking up. Sticking chopsticks directly upright in white rice is done as part of a Buddhist offering for deceased relatives.

Exceptions

Although *grammatically* you can take any descriptive verb and turn it into an adverb using 게, there are some cases where the resulting adverb will not be used in Korean.

Adverbs

A common example is the verb 천천하다 ("to be slow"). Saying 천천하게 would be *understood*, but would sound strange. In this case, 천천히 ("slowly") is preferred.

The more Korean that you learn, the more exceptions that you'll find to the rules, just as you would when learning any foreign language. This is why it's best to simply memorize each adverb; but remember that using 게 to create an adverb will still be understood, even if it sounds strange.

Now that we've learned the general rules for adverbs as well as how they work, let's go over the conversation.

호준: 빨리 와요. 지금 바로 시작할 거예요.
"Come quickly. It'll start right now."

Informal Commands Using 요

Previously we learned that we can make polite commands in Korean by attaching (으)세요 to the end of a verb stem.

내일 우리 집으로 오세요.
"Please come to my house tomorrow."

You can also make commands by using the regular 요 form. Making a command this way is less polite than (으)세요, but is acceptable when used between people who know each other well.

내일 우리 집으로 와요.
"Come to my house tomorrow."

However, it still should not be used with people who you are not familiar with, or with people who you would normally want to show respect to (such as a boss, or teacher), or in any formal situation.

Adverbs

To make it, simply conjugate the 요 form as usual, and use it as a command.

빨리 숙제를 해요.
"Do your homework quickly."

Although 빨리 means "quickly," it can also be translated as "hurry up and," or "right away," in order to sound more natural. The above sentence could therefore also be more naturally translated as "Hurry up and do your homework."

우리 집으로 빨리 와요.
"Hurry up and come to my house."
"Come to my house right away."

선경: 호준 씨는 축구를 너무 많이 보고 있어요.
"You're watching soccer too much."

Versus & To: 대

A simple word you can use with sports (or events) is 대. It is used with *Sino Korean numbers*.

대 can mean "versus" (or "vs.") when used between teams, or sides.

어제 미국 대 한국의 경기를 봤어요.
"I saw the America vs. Korea game yesterday."

대 can also mean "to" when used between scores.

우리 팀이 5 대 1 로 이기고 있어요.
"Our team is winning at 5 to 1."

호준: 저는 축구 없이 못 살아요.
"I can't live without soccer."

Without – 없이

The verb 없다 has its own unique adverb – 없이. Using 없게 would be *incorrect*.

When using 없이, the normally-added Subject Marker (이/가) is *not* added.

Chapter 6

Adverbs

저는 선생님 없이 한국어를 배울 수 없어요.
"I can't learn Korean without a teacher."

친구 없이 보내는 주말은 너무 지루해요.
"A weekend spent without friends is too boring."
"It's too boring to spend a weekend without friends."

> **Advanced**
>
> Saying "with" can be done differently from saying "without." When speaking about *people* you can either use (와/과) 함께 or (와/과) 같이 ("together with") instead, as we've learned previously. Or, much less commonly you can use 있게, or even 있이 when speaking about *things*.
>
> 함께 갈 거예요.
> 같이 갈 거예요.
> "We'll go together."
>
> 케첩 있게 주세요.
> 케첩 있이 주세요.
> "Please give it to me with ketchup."
>
> However, here's a more common way to ask for ketchup:
>
> 케첩과 같이 주세요.
> "Please give it to me with ketchup."

Remember that in English sports are "played," but in Korean sports are "done" (하다). "To play soccer" in Korean would be 축구(를) 하다 – and not 축구(를) 놀다.

선경: 알아요. 알아요.... 아, 그 선수가 괜히 뛰었어요.
"I know. I know.... Ah, that player ran for nothing."

괜히

괜히 is an *adverb* that translates to "in vain." In English, "in vain" isn't commonly used in conversation, but in Korean it's perfectly normal. While it literally means "in vain," it can also translate more naturally as "pointlessly" or "for nothing," depending on the context.

어제 괜히 숙제를 했어요.
"Yesterday I did my homework in vain."
"Yesterday I pointlessly did my homework."
"Yesterday I did my homework for nothing."

This sentence could be used after finding out that the assignment was cancelled, after having already finished it.

김치를 괜히 더 샀어요. 집에 이미 많아요.
"You bought more kimchi for nothing. There's already a lot at home."

Adverbs

Chapter 6

뛰다 and 달리다

In the previous book we learned the verb 달리다 ("to run"). Here is an additional word that you can use to mean "to run" – 뛰다.

While 달리다 simply means "to run," 뛰다 can mean either "to run" or "to jump," depending on the context of the sentence.

수업에 늦어서 학교로 뛰었어요.
"I ran to school because I was late for class."

사진을 찍기 위해 높이 뛰었어요.
"I jumped high in order to take a picture."

호준: 실수로 너무 멀리 뛰었어요. 공이 다시 엑스 팀으로 갔어요.
"He ran too far by mistake. The ball went back to team X."

실수로 and 일부러

실수로 is an *adverb* that means "by mistake." Its opposite is 일부러, which is an *adverb* that means "on purpose." 실수로 can also be translated as "accidentally," and 일부러 as "intentionally."

실수로 숙제를 안 했어요.
"I didn't do my homework by mistake."

일부러 숙제를 안 했어요.
"I didn't do my homework on purpose."

Adv
Note that while 실수 means "mistake" or "accident," it is not the word to use for a *traffic* accident (or other work-related accident). For that, use 사고 ("accident") instead.

Adverbs

선경: 이 경기는 못 이길 거예요.
"They won't be able to win this match."

While we've already learned 이기다 ("to win") and 지다 ("to lose"), there's also 비기다 ("to draw," "to tie").

미국과 영국이 0 대 0 으로 비겼어요.
"America and England tied at 0 to 0."

호준: 아! 진지하게 채널을 바꾸고 싶어요.
"Ah! I seriously want to change the channel."

Place: 위 or 등

In competitions (and sports games), you can use 위 with *Sino Korean numbers* to say "first place," "second place," and so on.

1 위
"first place"

2 위
"second place"

3 위
"third place"

You can also use 등 in the same way (also with *Sino Korean numbers*).

1 등
"first place"

2 등
"second place"

3 등
"third place"

> 위 sounds a bit more *official* than 등 – you're more likely to see 위 used on official broadcasts, but both 위 and 등 are fine for conversation.

Adverbs

Chapter 6

Culture Notes

화이팅 comes from the word "fighting," and is probably related to the words "fighting spirit." It's used in Korea as a chant to encourage someone to do their best. A natural translation could be either "Break a leg!" or "Good luck!" depending on the situation.

Although it's a bit less common, you might also see this written as 파이팅. They are the same thing.

Practice

Translate to Korean:

1. "Did you enjoy reading my book?"

   _____.

2. "I accidentally made the pizza too hot."

   _____.

3. "I can't jump high without expensive exercise shoes."

   _____.

4. "Please speak a little more loudly."

   _____.

Adverbs

Chapter 6

5. "I enjoyed eating the steak that my mother made."

_____.

6. "Chul-soo ran slow on purpose."

_____.

Translate to English:

7. 도서관에서 조용히 말하세요.

_____.

8. 제 친구와 재미있게 놀고 점심을 맛있게 먹었어요.

_____.

9. 제 친구는 멀리 이사갔어요.

_____.

10. 제 카메라를 괜히 꺼냈어요.

_____.

11. 경기가 5 대 5 로 비겨서 재미있게 못 봤어요.

_____.

12. 실수로 케첩 없이 먹었어요.

_____.

New Phrases

화이팅!	"Good luck!," "Break a leg!"

Adverbs

Chapter 6

New Vocabulary

스포츠(를) 하다	"to play sports"
(소리[가]) 크다	"to be loud"
(소리[가]) 작다	"to be quiet"
깨끗이	"cleanly"
천천히	"slowly"
안전하다	"to be safe"
안전하게	"safely"
위험하다	"to be dangerous"
급하다	"to be urgent"
급히	"urgently"
너무 많이	"too much" (adverb)
재미있게 보다	"to enjoy (watching)"
재미있게 읽다	"to enjoy (reading)"
재미있게 놀다	"to enjoy (playing)," "to have fun"
맛있게 먹다	"to enjoy (eating)"
라면	"ramen"
괜히	"in vain" (adverb)
실수	"mistake," "accident"
실수로	"by mistake," "accidentally" (adverb)
일부러	"on purpose," "intentionally" (adverb)
가까이	"closely" (adverb)
멀리	"far" (adverb)
없이	"without" (adverb)
소스	"sauce"
케첩	"ketchup"
마요네즈	"mayonnaise"
겨자	"(spicy) mustard"
머스터드	"(yellow) mustard"
(시간[을]) 보내다	"to spend (time)"
주말	"weekend"
평일	"weekday"
공휴일	"holiday"

89

Chapter 6

Adverbs

주로	"mainly" (adverb)
지금 바로	"right now (immediately)" (adverb)
바로 지금	"right this second" (adverb)
선수	"player," "athlete"
뛰다	"to run," "to jump"
높이	"high" (adverb)
경기	"match," "game"
진지하다	"to be serious"
장난	"prank," "joke"
장난감	"toy"
인형	"doll," "plush toy"
결국	"in the end," "ultimately" (adverb)
꺼내다	"to take/pull out"
들다	"to pick up," "to carry"
처음에	"at first"
마지막	"last" (noun)
마지막에	"at the end"
원래	"original," "originally"
아래	"the bottom," "under"
전체	"the whole thing"
점수	"score"
대	"versus," "to"
위	place counter
등	place counter
꼴찌	"last place"
성공	"success"
실패	"failure"
성공(을) 하다	"to succeed"
실패(를) 하다	"to fail"
비기다	"to draw," "to tie"
운동화	"tennis shoes," "exercise shoes"
간장	"soy sauce"
진하다	"to be strong," "to be thick," "to be dark"
연하다	"to be weak," "to be thin," "to be pale"

Adverbs

Chapter 6

교통	"traffic"
사고	"accident"
교통 사고	"traffic accident"
완전하게	"completely"

Chapter 6
Adverbs

Comparisons

Chapter 7

Conversation

지원:	저도 언젠가 병현 씨같이 영어를 잘하고 싶어요!
나라:	저도요! 하지만 병현 씨는 매일 8시간 정도 공부하고 있어요.
지원:	저는 그만큼은 못 해요!
나라:	병현 씨는 학생들 중에 공부를 제일 열심히 하는 사람이에요.
지원:	저는 병현 씨처럼 영어를 잘할 수 없지만, 그만큼 공부를 하지도 않아요.
나라:	지원 씨는 영어 공부를 얼마만큼 하고 있어요?
지원:	공부는.... 자주 하지 않아요. 나라 씨는요?
나라:	헤헤. 저도 오늘은 아직 공부하지 않았어요.
지원:	그래서 우리가 영어를 잘 못 해요.

Someone, Something, Somewhere, and Sometime

While I could simply teach you these four words in Korean in the vocabulary section of this chapter, I think that they each deserve a more detailed explanation of how they work.

Someone → 누군가
Something → 뭔가 (or 무엇인가)
Somewhere → 어딘가
Sometime → 언젠가

| Chapter 7 | **Comparisons** |

You'll probably notice right away that these words look very similar to words that we've previously learned. Specifically, 누구 ("who"), 뭐 ("what"), 어디 ("where"), and 언제 ("when").

Here is an example of each one.

오늘 뭔가 먹었어요?
"Did you eat something today?"

나중에 어딘가에 갈 거예요.
"Later I will go somewhere."

누군가가 이미 했어요.
"Someone did it already."

Note the additional Subject Marker (가) after 누군가; 누군가 on its own is a noun, so you would still add whatever particles that you would normally add when using it.

누군가를 만났어요.
"I met someone."

> **Advanced**
>
> Although 누군가, 뭔가, and 어딘가 are the standard words for "someone," "something," and "somewhere," they are not the most commonly used versions. More often Koreans will simply use the original words in these situations – 누구/누가, 뭐, and 어디.
>
> In order to use 누구/누가, 뭐, and 어디 in this way, you will need to change the spoken *emphasis* of your sentence – that is, you'll need to *remove* emphasis from 누구/누가, 뭐, or 어디 in the sentence and instead emphasize the *verb*. Here are a few examples of what I mean, with the spoken emphasis shown in **bold**. You can add this emphasis by saying the word a little bit *longer*, just as you would when emphasizing something in English.
>
> 뭐했어요?
> "What did you do?"
>
> 뭐**했어요?**
> "Did you do something?"
>
> 어디 갔어요?
> "Where did you go?"
>
> 어디 **갔어요?**
> "Did you go somewhere?"

Comparisons

Chapter 7

For "someone," use 누가 when it's the *subject* of a sentence, and 누구 in all other cases. This is explained in detail Chapter 8 of the previous book.

누가 했어요?
"Who did it?"

누가 **했어요.**
"Someone did it."

누구 만났어요?
"Who did you meet?"

누구 만났어요?
"Did you meet someone?"

언제, however, cannot be substituted for 언젠가.

지원: 저도 언젠가 병현 씨같이 영어를 잘하고 싶어요!
"I also want to speak English well just like Byung-hyun sometime!"

Like: Noun + 같이

Previously we learned how to use the verb 같다 ("to be the same," "to be like") to say that something is "like" or "as" something else. When using 같다 in this way, adding 와 or 과 is *optional*. Here are a couple of examples:

저와 같은 사람을 싫어할 수 없어요.
"I can't dislike a person like me."

이것은 그것과 같아요.
"This is the same as that."

However, so far we're limited to using 같다 as either an *adjective* (in the first sentence) or as a *verb* (in the second sentence). If we could use it as an *adverb*, we'd be able to use it in more places. Here's an example of "like" being used as an *adverb*:

저는 철수 씨같이 노래를 부를 수 있어요.
"I can sing *like* Chul-soo."

In order to say "like" or "as" as an *adverb*, use 같이 after a noun (without 와 or 과). Then finish the rest of the sentence.

95

Chapter 7

Comparisons

저같이 노래를 잘 부르는 사람을 알고 있어요?
"Do you know a person who sings well like me?"

우리 학교에 사자같이 무서운 선생님이 있어요.
"There's a teacher in our school who is as scary as a lion."

Remember that you will simply use the verb 같다 if you want to say that something is "like" or "the same as" something else when you're not using it as an *adverb*.

제 이름과 같아요.
"It is the same as my name."

The above sentence would not use 같이 with the verb 이다 ("to be"), but uses the verb 같다 on its own. Saying 제 이름같이예요 would therefore be *incorrect*.

나라: 저도요! 하지만 병현 씨는 매일 8 시간 정도 공부하고 있어요.
"Me too! But Byung-hyun is studying about 8 hours everyday."

About: 정도

Making approximations (guessing) can be done using the *noun* 정도. It can translate as either "about" or "approximately."

500 원 정도예요.
"It's about 500 Won."

매일 6 시간 정도만 자요.
"I'm sleeping about only 6 hours everyday."

As you'll notice in the above sentence, the particle 만 is added *after* 정도, and not after 시간. This is because using 만 after 시간 would have a different, and slightly strange meaning; look at the following (*incorrect*) example sentence:

Comparisons

Chapter 7

1 시간만 정도 공부했어요.
"I studied about only 1 hour."

Although speaking this way this would be understood, it sounds a bit odd as "about" will generally come directly *before* what it is referring to in English, and the same applies in Korean. Here is the correct version of this sentence:

1 시간 정도만 공부했어요.
"I studied only about 1 hour."

> **Adv**
> Another word that you can use is 쯤, which works in the same way as 정도 and has a similar meaning. However, 쯤 is placed *directly* after the word, without using a space.
>
> 1 시간쯤 공부했어요.
> "I studied about 1 hour."

지원: 저는 그만큼은 못 해요!
"I can't do that much!"

As Much As: 만큼

만큼 means "as much as" and can be used to talk about an *amount*. It is attached directly *after* the word that you want to talk about, without a space.

철수 씨만큼은 술을 못 마셔요.
"I can't drink alcohol as much as Chul-soo."

한국어 선생님만큼은 한국어를 잘할 수 없어요.
"I can't speak Korean as well as the Korean teacher."

저만큼 예쁜 사람은 없어요.
"There is no person as pretty as me."

Another useful way to use 만큼 is as a *noun*, after an adjective. In this way, you can think of 만큼 as "amount" – such as in the conversation, where 그만큼 means "that much" or "that amount."

When using 만큼 in this way, add a *space* between it and the adjective that it follows.

철수 씨가 마실 수 있는 만큼은 술을 못 마셔요.
"I can't drink as much alcohol as Chul-soo can drink."
"I can't drink the amount of alcohol that Chul-soo can drink."

97

Chapter 7

Comparisons

할 수 있는 만큼만 하세요.
"Only do what you can do."
"Only do the amount that you can do."

저는 공부하는 만큼 놀고 있어요.
"I'm playing as much as I study."
"I am playing the amount that I study."

> **Advanced**
>
> **약간**
>
> 약간 is an *adverb* that means "slightly," or "a slight/little amount."
>
> 약간 더워요.
> "It's slightly hot."
>
> 약간 배가 고파요.
> "I'm slightly hungry."

나라: 병현 씨는 학생들 중에 공부를 제일 열심히 하는 사람이에요.
"Byung-hyun studies the hardest among all of the students."

Among – 중

중 ("center") can be used with 에(서) to mean "among." The 서 at the end is completely *optional*.

이 책들 중에서 뭘 읽고 싶어요?
"What do you want to read among these books?"

작년에 본 영화들 중에서 뭐가 재미있었어요?
"Among the movies you saw last year, what was entertaining?"

100 명 중에 1 명을 고르세요.
"Select one person among 100 people."

Pure Korean and Sino Korean

고르다 is a verb that means "to choose," or "to select." You might notice that this has the same meaning as 선택(을) 하다, which we learned in the previous book. 선택(을) 하다 is a *Sino Korean verb* (it originally comes from the Chinese language), and 고르다 is a *Pure Korean verb*.

Comparisons

Chapter 7

Often, you will find that there will be more than one verb in Korean that you can use to say the exact same thing – for example, 고르다 and 선택(을) 하다. This is because the Korean language originally borrowed many additional words from Chinese.

"So what's the difference?" There is no significant difference in meaning, so feel free to use whichever one you'd like. Sino Korean verbs will most often use the Object Marker (을/를) with the verb 하다, while Pure Korean verbs will simply end in 다 and therefore cannot be split apart.

> **Adv**: The only (small) difference between using a Sino Korean verb or a Pure Korean verb, such as between 고르다 and 선택(을) 하다, is that using the Sino Korean verb will sound *slightly* more formal than the Pure Korean verb. This is the reason why we learned previously that 감사하다, a Sino Korean verb, is slightly more polite than 고맙다, a Pure Korean verb.

This also applies to Sino Korean *nouns* and Pure Korean *nouns*. The word for "adult" can be 어른 in Pure Korean, and 성인 in Sino Korean. In short, don't be surprised to learn two or more words in Korean for the same one word in English; this is only due to the influence of the Chinese language on the Korean language, and will actually help you by giving you a much larger vocabulary in Korean.

Most & Best – 제일

Another useful word to know is 제일, which is an adverb that means "most," or "(the) best."

제일 맛있는 음식이 뭐예요?
"What's the most delicious food?"

작년에 본 영화들 중에서 뭐가 제일 재미있었어요?
"Among the movies you saw last year, what was most entertaining?"

엄마가 세상에서 제일 좋아요.
"Mom is the best in the world."

세상에서 is a common expression that means "in the world."

이 도서관은 제일 유명한 건물 중에 하나예요.
"This library is one of the most famous buildings."

Take care to read the above sentence again slowly, as it incorporates both 중에(서) and 제일. It literally can also translate to "As for this library, it is one among the most famous buildings."

Comparisons

제일 is also commonly combined with the verb 좋아하다 ("to like"). 제일 좋아하는 translates as "favorite."

제가 제일 좋아하는 음식은 피자예요.
"My favorite food is pizza."

제일 좋아하는 영화가 뭐예요?
"What's your favorite movie?"

뭘 제일 좋아했어요?
"What did you like best?"

Although in English we say "*my* favorite," Korean prefers 제가 제일 좋아하는, such as in the above sentence – 저의 제일 좋아하는 would be *incorrect*.

> **Adv** An alternative for 제일, which is a *Sino Korean adverb*, is the *Pure Korean adverb* 가장, which also means "most" or "(the) best." 가장 is used in the same way as 제일.
>
> 가장 좋아하는 영화가 뭐예요?
> "What's your favorite movie?"

지원: 저는 병현 씨처럼 영어를 잘할 수 없지만, 그만큼 공부를 하지도 않아요.
"I can't speak English well like Byung-hyun, but I don't even study that much."

Like: Noun + 처럼

Using 처럼 works the same way as 같이, but 처럼 is more commonly used.

우리 학교에 사자처럼 무서운 선생님이 있어요.
"There's a teacher in our school who is as scary as a lion."

바보처럼 행동했어요.
"He acted like an idiot."

영희 씨는 천사처럼 친절한 여자예요.
"Yung-hee is a girl who is as nice as an angel."

집처럼 편한 곳이 없어요.
"There is no place comfortable like home."

Be aware of 같이, but know that 처럼 is used more often.

Comparisons

지도 않다

지도 않다 is simply 지 않다 together with the particle 도. To compare 지 않다 and 지도 않다, take a look at the following two sentences:

내일 학교에 가지 않을 거예요.
"I will not go to school tomorrow."

내일 학교에 가지도 않을 거예요.
"I will not even go to school tomorrow."

While the meaning of both sentences is similar, adding 도 to 지 않다 emphasizes that you are not *even* doing the verb that it's used with.

지는 않다

In addition to 도, you might also see 지 않다 used with 는 (지는 않다). This also has the same meaning as 지 않다, but is used to *emphasize* that you will not be doing the verb that it's used with.

Remember that the Topic Marker (은/는) can be translated as "as for." With this in mind, take a look at the following two sentences:

내일 학교에 가지 않을 거예요.
"I will not go to school tomorrow."

내일 학교에 가지는 않을 거예요.
"As for going to school tomorrow, I won't."

Another way to think of the above sentence is as meaning "I will not *go* to school tomorrow (but I might do something else)."

> **Adv**
> You can also add 도 or 는 when using 지 못하다.
>
> 물을 마시지도 못했어요.
> "I couldn't even drink water."

나라: 지원 씨는 영어 공부를 얼마만큼 하고 있어요?
"How much are you studying English?"

| Chapter 7 | **Comparisons** |

How Much: 얼마만큼 and 얼마나

얼마만큼 means "how much," or "to what extent," and can be shortened to 얼마큼.

얼마나 can also be used in the same way, and has a similar meaning.

한국어를 얼마큼 할 수 있어요?
한국어를 얼마나 할 수 있어요?
"How much Korean can you speak?"

피자를 얼마나 먹었어요?
"How much pizza did you eat?"

돈이 얼마큼 필요해요?
"How much money do you need?"

> **Adv** Another common shortening of 얼마만큼 is 얼만큼; however, this is actually an *incorrect* spelling of the word. Although it's *incorrect*, you may find that Koreans will use it much more often than the correct versions, 얼마만큼 and 얼마큼. Just to note, the above conversation sentence could have also been written as the following:
>
> 지원 씨는 영어를 얼만큼 공부하고 있어요?
> "How much are you studying English?"

지원: 공부는…. 자주 하지 않아요. 나라 씨는요?
"Well… I don't often. And you?"

나라: 헤헤. 저도 오늘은 아직 공부하지 않았어요.
"He, he. I also didn't study today yet."

Still and Yet: 아직

아직 can mean either "still" or "(not) yet," depending on the sentence that it's used in.

Comparisons

Chapter 7

In *positive* sentences (sentences that don't end with a verb using 안 or 지 않다), 아직 translates as "still."

아직 공부하고 있어요?
"Are you still studying?"

아빠는 아직 집에 있어요.
"Dad is still at home."

In *negative* sentences, 아직 can translate as "(not) yet."

점심을 아직 안 먹었어요.
"I didn't eat lunch yet."

아직 안 나갈 거예요.
"I won't leave yet."

> **Adv**
> You can also use 아직도 in the same way as 아직, in order to *emphasize* "still" or "(not) yet." 아직도 is a combination of 아직 with the particle 도 and means "even still."
>
> 아직도 공부하고 있어요?
> "Are you *still* studying?"

지원: 그래서 우리가 영어를 잘 못 해요.
"That's why we don't speak English well."

"Can't do well" – 잘 못 하다

We learned that we can use 잘하다 to mean "to do well" and 못 하다 to mean "to be unable to do," so it should make sense that combining the two gives the meaning of "to be unable to do well."

한국어를 잘 못 해요.
"I can't speak Korean well."

요리를 잘 못 해요.
"I can't cook well."

"That's why..." – 그래서

We previously learned that 그래서 can mean "so" or "therefore," and is used at the *beginning* of a sentence. It also has one more translation – "That's why..."

Chapter 7: Comparisons

It can only be used in this way after you've just finished *explaining* something.

그래서 집에 못 갔어요.
"That's why I couldn't go home."

그래서 김치를 좋아해요.
"That's why I love kimchi."

Remember that 그래서 still only means "so" or "therefore" literally. It only takes on the translation of "That's why..." when used in sentences after you've just finished explaining something.

Which: 어느

Another useful word for sentences with *comparisons* is 어느, which means "which."

어느 책을 읽고 싶어요?
"Which book do you want to read?"

어느 영화를 봤어요?
"Which movie did you see?"

어느 선생님이 있었어요?
"Which teacher was there?"

Practice

Translate to Korean:

1. "What is your favorite book?"

_____.

2. "I like that book the best."

_____.

3. "I still like this shirt."

_____.

Comparisons

Chapter 7

4. "How much did you study English?"

   _____.

5. "He doesn't have a friend like me."

   _____.

6. "He doesn't have a friend who's nice like me."

   _____.

7. "Which is my sandwich?"

   _____.

8. "That's why I study Korean."

   _____.

Translate to English:

9. 제일 좋아하는 영화가 뭐예요?

   _____.

10. 저는 그런 영화를 좋아하지도 않아요.

    _____.

11. 아직 안 왔어요.

    _____.

12. 철수 씨만큼은 잘하지 못해요.

    _____.

Chapter 7

Comparisons

13. 철수 씨가 말할 수 있는 만큼은 잘 못 해요.

_____.

14. 오늘 뭔가를 했어요?

_____.

15. 언젠가 한국에 갈 거예요.

_____.

16. 그 가게에서 파는 샌드위치만큼 맛있는 음식이 없어요.

_____.

New Phrases

| 헤헤. | "He, he." |
| 그래서... | "That's why..." |

New Vocabulary

누군가	"someone"
뭔가	"something"
무엇인가	"something"
어딘가	"somewhere"
언젠가	"sometime"
같이	"like," "as" (adverb)
정도	"about," "approximately"
만큼	"as much as"
중에서	"among"
제일	"most," "(the) best" (adverb)
세살	"the world"
세상에서	"in the world"
바보	"idiot," "fool"

Comparisons

행동(을) 하다	"to act," "to behave"
천사	"angel"
악마	"devil"
얼마(만)큼	"how much," "to what extent" (adverb)
얼마나	"how much," "to what extent" (adverb)
아직	"still," "(not) yet" (adverb)
아직도	"even still," "(not) yet" (adverb)
열쇠고리	"keychain"
어느	"which" (adjective)
변태	"pervert"
고르다	"to choose," "to select"
자랑(을) 하다	"to boast," "to brag"
성인	"adult"
어린이	"child"
인생	"(one's) life"
심장	"heart"
신뢰(를) 하다	"to trust"
진실하다	"to be honest"
거짓말쟁이	"liar"
상식	"common knowledge," "common sense"
남	"others," "other people"
도둑	"thief," "burglar"
오락실	"arcade"
투명하다	"to be transparent"
불투명하다	"to be opaque"
분명하다	"to be clear," "to be plain (to see/understand)"

Chapter 7: Comparisons

Honorific Speech

Chapter 8

Conversation

웨이터:	어서 오세요! 몇 분이세요?
철수:	2 명이요.
웨이터:	네, 들어오세요.
철수 & 영희:	감사합니다.
웨이터:	이 쪽으로 앉으시겠어요?
철수 & 영희:	네.
웨이터:	음료는 뭘 드시겠어요?
철수:	저는 물이요.
영희:	저는 와인 1 잔을 주세요.
웨이터:	네, 그럼 물 1 잔과 와인 1 잔을 갖다 드리겠습니다.

Honorifics can be a difficult topic to grasp for the first time. Don't feel bad if you have to read through this chapter more than once in order to understand these concepts. There's no need to rush through things, so take your time; this is a fairly long chapter.

What is Honorific Speech?

While we've covered *formal* and *informal* speech, the 니다 and 요 forms being our two main examples, we haven't yet talked about *honorific speech*. Honorific speech is something different from formal and informal speech. It is different in that we can use honorific speech in a formal or informal sentence (we'll learn more about this soon).

Chapter 8

Honorific Speech

Honorific speech is used to show respect when speaking *about* someone else, and not only when speaking *to* someone else.

For example, let's first look at a normal sentence that you could say to an older classmate, using informal speech (요 form):

혹시 오늘 선생님이 있어요? 아직 못 봤어요.
"By chance is the teacher here today? I didn't seen him yet."

Notice that the speaker is using the 요 form because they're speaking to an older classmate. While you could also use the 니다 form, it's probably not necessary unless the older classmate is someone who you wish to be extra polite to – the 요 form is enough.

However, the speaker is also talking about the teacher (선생님). A teacher is someone who you would normally want to show respect to, right? Yes. Although asking "선생님이 있어요?" is *grammatically* correct and acceptable, this sentence could be improved by adding honorific language to show respect to the teacher.

혹시 오늘 선생님이 **계세요**? 아직 못 봤어요.
"By chance is the teacher here today? I didn't see him yet."

Notice how we switched 있어요 to 계세요 (we'll cover this soon). This is because 있다 ("to exist") is used to talk *about* the teacher. The end of the second sentence, 봤어요, stays the same, because it is only used to talk about the speaker ("*I didn't see him yet.*"). Here is another example:

어디 가요?
"Where are you going?"

어디 **가세요**?
"Where are you going?"

Looking at these two sentences, we can assume that the second one is being used to ask a question to someone the speaker wants to show respect to, such as a teacher or a stranger.

Remember that honorific speech is used for the *person* who you are talking about, and not specifically for the person you are talking to (unless you are asking someone a question directly, in which case you are talking about them). Let's take a look at another example of this:

지금 어디 있어요?
"Where are you now?"

110

Honorific Speech

Chapter 8

This same question, if asked to someone who you would want to show respect to (such as a teacher, or boss, etc.) would be better asked like this:

지금 어디 **계세요**?
"Where are you?"

We can use honorific speech to show respect to a person who we are talking about – whether we are talking about the person who we're directly asking a question to (such as in the above example), or about someone else (such as in the earlier example with the teacher).

Now that we have a basic introduction to what honorific speech is, let's learn our first honorific grammar form.

(으)세요

You might recognize this form from Chapter 17 in the first book. This form is actually the most basic way to use honorific speech.

In order to make it, take a verb stem and attach 으세요 if it ends in a *consonant*, or add 세요 if it ends in a *vowel*.

We previously learned that we can use this form to make polite commands – similar to using "please." Here are two examples of using it in that way:

집에 가세요.
"Please go home."

숙제를 하세요.
"Please do the homework."

But polite commands aren't the only thing that (으)세요 can be used for; it can also be used for regular sentences – such as ones where you would normally use the 니다 or 요 forms – when you want to show respect to the person you are talking *about*.

김 씨가 뭐하세요? 알아요?
"What is Mr. Kim doing? Do you know?"

Notice that in the above sentence, (으)세요 is only used when talking about Mr. Kim, and not when the speaker asks a question to the *listener*. Speaking in this way only shows additional respect to Mr. Kim.

Honorific Speech

Chapter 8

Advanced

When asking simple direct questions to *strangers* – such as ones that would normally end with the 요 form – it's much more polite to use this honorific (으)세요 form. In fact, using the 요 form to ask questions to strangers can be impolite. While using the 요 form for regular sentences can be acceptable, *questions* tend to sound much more appropriate with honorific speech, especially to strangers.

For example, instead of asking 철수 씨를 알아요? to a stranger (which sounds a bit impolite), use 철수 씨를 아세요? instead.

한국어를 잘하세요!
"You speak Korean well!"

The above sentence is also showing additional respect, but to the person being complimented (here, "you").

For verb stems that end in ㄹ, remove the ㄹ before attaching 세요.

철수 씨를 아세요?
"Do you know Chul-soo?"

Advanced

An alternative to using (으)세요 for making polite commands is using (으)십시오. This form is even more formal than (으)세요, but because of that is also less commonly used.

To make it, simply take a verb stem and attach 으십시오 if it ends in a *consonant*, or 십시오 if it ends in a *vowel*. Verb stems ending in ㄹ will remove the ㄹ before adding 십시오.

집에 가십시오.
"Please go home."

저를 믿으십시오.
"Please believe me."

However, 십시오 can *only* be used for making polite *commands*, and not for other kinds of sentences.

Honorific Verbs: (으)시다

We learned that we can use (으)세요 to use normal verbs in *honorific* sentences. However, (으)세요 originally comes from the form (으)시다. You will need to know this form in order to conjugate different tenses (past tense, etc.), and to use honorific speech in different types of sentences.

To make this form, take a verb stem and attach 으시다 if it ends in a *consonant*, or attach 시다 if it ends in a vowel.

가다 "to go" (regular) → 가시다 "to go" (honorific)
하다 "to do" (regular) → 하시다 "to do" (honorific)
예쁘다 "to be pretty" (regular) → 예쁘시다 "to be pretty" (honorific)

Honorific Speech

Chapter 8

Just as with (으)세요, verb stems ending in ㄹ will drop the ㄹ before adding 시다.

팔다 "to sell" (regular) → 파시다 "to sell" (honorific)

As we learned in Chapter 8, (으)시다 becomes (으)세요; this form can be used for polite commands, regular sentences, and questions.

오늘 뭐하세요?
"What are you doing today?"

요리를 자주 하세요?
"Do you cook often?"

In *formal* speech, (으)시다 can become either (으)십니다 or (으)십니까.

오늘 뭐하십니까?
"What are you doing today?"

요리를 자주 하십니까?
"Do you cook often?"

Attaching (으)시다 to a verb is the most basic way of turning it into an honorific verb. We'll see examples of this form in sentences soon.

Honorific Tenses

What if you want to use honorific speech in the *past tense* or the *future tense*? Both of these can be done easily. First, take an *honorific verb*, and get its verb stem. Let's look at 가시다 as an example.

가시다 – 다 → 가시

Let's conjugate the *past tense* of 가시다. We can conjugate this to the past tense in the same way as we would conjugate any other verb. We learned how to conjugate the past tense in Chapter 20 of the first book.

가시 + 어 → 가셔
가셔 + ㅆ → 가셨
가셨 + 어요 → 가셨어요

Now let's conjugate the *future tense* of 가시다. This can also be done in the same way as we would conjugate any other verb.

113

Honorific Speech

가시 + ㄹ 것이다 → 가실 것이다
가시 + 겠다 → 가시겠다

언제 가시겠습니까?
언제 가실 거예요?
"When will you go?"

There are more tenses that we can use, such as the progressive tense, but we'll learn these along the way.

More Honorific Verbs

Using verbs with (으)시다 is not the only way to show respect to someone who you are talking about; there are also other verbs that you can use instead of the regular ones we've learned. Some verbs will have their own unique honorific version as well. There are not many of them, but they are commonly used, and important to know. Whenever a verb has its own unique honorific version, you *must* use that verb in honorific speech instead of adding (으)시다. Let's take a look at the most common honorific verbs.

먹다 → 드시다 "to eat"

Since 먹다 has its own honorific version, using 먹으시다 would be *incorrect*.

뭘 드실 거예요?
"What will you eat?"

맛있게 드세요!
"Enjoy (the food)!"

> **Adv** Another even more honorific verb for "to eat" is 잡수시다. This is used commonly in the (으)세요 form as 잡수세요 ("Please eat."). For most situations, 드시다 is acceptable.

있다 → 계시다 "to exist"
없다 → 안 계시다 "to not exist"

Using 있으시다 or 없으시다 would be *incorrect* when talking about a person.

회장님이 사무실에 계세요?
"Is the president in the office?"

선생님이 지금 여기 안 계셔서 제가 전화를 받았어요.
"I answered the phone because the teacher isn't here now."

Honorific Speech

Chapter 8

Advanced

Although 있으시다 and 없으시다 are *incorrect* when talking about a person (계시다 and 안 계시다 need to be used), they can still be used as honorific versions of "to have" and "to not have." These are only used when you are speaking to someone who you also want to show respect to.

You would not hear 선생님이 있으세요?, but you could use 숙제가 있으세요? when speaking directly to someone who you want to show respect to.

시간이 있으세요?
"Do you have any time?"

In addition, 이시다 (the honorific verb for 이다 – "to be") can also be used in the same way, when directly speaking with someone who you want to show respect to.

만 원이세요.
"That'll be 10,000 Won."

자다 → 주무시다 "to sleep"

Using 자시다 would be *incorrect*.

아버지는 지금 주무시고 계세요.
"Father is sleeping now."

Notice how we replaced 있다 with 계시다 in the above sentence, which uses the *progressive tense*. It would be strange (and *incorrect*) to leave the sentence half-finished as 주무시고 있어요, or as 자고 계세요.

Advanced

You do not have to use the honorific verb with the 고 계시다 form *if* the verb does not have its own unique honorific verb. While you must use 주무시다 (since it is the unique honorific verb for 자다), you do not need to change 가다 to 가시다 to use it with 고 계시다. Having 고 계시다 on its own will be enough. Here are a few examples:

지금 집으로 가고 계세요.
"He's going home now."

Note that it would be fine to use 가시다 (가시고 계시다), but it isn't necessary.

아버지는 뭐하고 계세요?
"What's father doing?"

Saying 뭐하시고 계세요 would be correct as well, but is unnecessary. Again, remember that this is only acceptable when the verb does not have its own unique honorific verb. Using 먹고 계시다 would therefore be *incorrect* (it must be 드시고 계시다).

Honorific Speech

죽다 → 돌아가시다 "to die," "to pass away"

Using 죽으시다 would be *incorrect*.

할아버지가 작년에 돌아가셨어요.
"My grandfather passed away last year."

돌아가시다 comes from the verb 돌아가다 ("to go back"), but has a different meaning when used with 시다 – "to pass away." When using 돌아가다 (or 돌아가시다) to mean "to go back," be careful that your sentence is clear *where* the person will be going back to, or people might misunderstand it to mean that the person has died.

집으로 이미 돌아가셨어요.
"He went back home."

이미 돌아가셨어요.
"He already passed away."

There are other honorific verbs, but these are the most common ones to be aware of.

Honorific Nouns

As well as using unique *verbs* in honorific speech, there are also honorific *nouns* that you will need to learn. These nouns simply act as replacements for their normal versions when you want to show more respect to the person who you are talking *about*. Fortunately for us, like honorific verbs, there are not many of them. Here are the most common ones to be aware of:

사람 → 분 "person"

아주 친절한 분들이세요.
"They're very nice people."

Note that this is also where the word 그분 ("that person") originally comes from.

집 → 댁 "house"

내일 할머니 댁에 놀러 가요.
"Tomorrow I'm going to play at my grandmother's house."

집, as well as 댁, are often used directly after the owner, and do not need the Possessive Marker (의), such as in the above example.

Honorific Speech

나이 → 연세 "age"

연세가 어떻게 되세요?
"How old are you?"

This is a much more polite way to ask someone's age than by using 나이 ("나이가 어떻게 돼요?"), which can come across as rude when asked to someone who appears much older than you are. However, note that asking a person's age can be impolite on its own, so be careful when using this phrase to strangers.

이름 → 성함 "name"

성함이 어떻게 되세요?
"What is your name?"

It's much more polite to ask a person's name using 성함. Using 이름 ("이름이 어떻게 되세요?") is appropriate when asking the name of someone who appears to be similar in age with yourself, or in a situation where you do not feel the need to be extra respectful.

Honorific nouns are important to know and use, but feel free to use the non-honorific versions if you happen to forget the honorific versions. It's much more important to use honorific verbs than to worry about honorific nouns in the beginning.

Now that we've learned about honorific verbs, honorific nouns, and how to use them, let's go over the conversation.

웨이터: 어서 오세요! 몇 분이세요?
"Welcome! How many people?"

Quickly: 어서

어서 is an *adverb* that means "quickly" or "promptly." It's commonly used together with the verb 오다 ("to come"), but it can also be used in place of 빨리 for verbs such as 먹다 or 자다.

어서 오세요 is a common phrase used for inviting people inside. It literally means "Please come quickly."

> **Adv** In addition to 어서 오세요, you might also hear 어서 오십시오.

Chapter 8 — Honorific Speech

Note About (이)세요

이세요 comes from the verb 이다 ("to be"). When it's used after a *vowel*, 이세요 will simply become 세요.

한국 사람이세요?
"Are you a Korean?"

아, 할머니의 친구세요?
"Ah, are you a friend of my grandmother?"

철수: 2 명이요.
"2 people."

웨이터: 네, 들어오세요.
"Okay, come in."

철수 & 영희: 감사합니다.
"Thank you."

웨이터: 이 쪽으로 앉으시겠어요?
"Will you sit on this side?"

Side: 쪽

쪽 means "side," but it can have a few different meanings depending on how it is being used, such as "direction" or "way."

저 쪽으로 갔어요.
"He went that way."

왼쪽을 보세요.
"Please look at the left side."

오른쪽으로 갔어요.
"He went to the right."

쪽 can also be used with north, south, east, and west (known as "cardinal directions"). In Korean, these are ordered 동 (east), 서 (west), 남 (south), and 북 (north) – 동서남북.

Honorific Speech

해가 동쪽에서 떴어요.
"The sun rose from the east."

북쪽으로 가면 추워요?
"Is it cold if I go north?"

Although the future tense (here, 겠다) means "will," because it is combined with an honorific verb (here, 앉으시다, which means "to sit"), a more natural English translation is "would."

> 철수 & 영희: 네.
> "Okay."

> 웨이터: 음료는 뭘 드시겠어요?
> "What would you like to drink?"

Eat & Drink: 드시다

We learned that 드시다 is the honorific version of 먹다 ("to eat"), but it's also the honorific version of 마시다 ("to drink").

물을 드세요.
"Please drink water."

김치를 드시고 싶으세요?
"Would you like to eat kimchi?"

Notice how 고 싶다 will become 고 싶으시다 (conjugated as 고 싶으세요) when used in honorific speech – in honorific speech, all verbs about the person who you want to show respect to will become honorific verbs.

The above sentence in the conversation would literally translate to "As for a beverage, what will you drink?" However, "What would you like to drink?" is a more natural way to translate this question into English.

> 철수: 저는 물이요.
> "I'll have water."

Since the Topic Marker (은/는) can mean "as for," this sentence could literally translate as "As for me, water."

Chapter 8

Honorific Speech

영희: 저는 와인 1 잔을 주세요.
"I'll have a glass of wine."

잔 is the counter for a "glass" (or "cup") of something, such as a beverage. It is used with *Pure Korean numbers*.

옥수수차를 2 잔 마셨어요.
"I drank 2 cups of corn tea."

Advanced

A common way to order *food* in quantities is by using 인분, which means "a portion for a person." 인분 is a *counter* that is used with *Sino Korean numbers*.

밥을 2 인분 주세요.
"Please give me enough rice for 2 people."
"Please give me 2 portions of rice."

햄버거 세트 9 인분이 얼마예요?
"How much is a hamburger set for 9 people?"

Remember that you can still continue using regular counters (병, 잔, etc.) when ordering *drinks*.

콜라 한 병을 주세요.
"Give me a bottle of cola."

웨이터: 네, 그럼 물 1 잔과 와인 1 잔을 갖다 드리겠습니다.
"Alright, then I'll bring you water and a glass of wine."

Humble Verbs

While honorific verbs are used to show *respect* to a person who you are talking about, a humble verb is used by the speaker to show his or her own *humility*. Specifically, you will want to use humble verbs whenever you would also use honorific verbs; they will go together in sentences.

Fortunately, there are only *two* humble verbs that we need to learn, and you will use them frequently.

주다 → 드리다 "to give"

내일 드릴 거예요.
"I will give it to you tomorrow."

Use 드리다 whenever you are giving something to someone who you want to show respect to. For example, the above sentence could be used when speaking to a teacher or a boss.

Honorific Speech

If a teacher or boss is giving something to you, then you would not use a humble verb; you would use 주시다 (the honorific verb for 주다 – "to give").

선생님이 내일 주실 거예요.
"The teacher will give it to me tomorrow."

If it helps you to remember, you can imagine *humble verbs* as if the speaker is bowing down while doing something for someone else. You wouldn't want to make a sentence where your teacher or boss is bowing down to you while giving you a present (no matter how much you might enjoy seeing that), so make sure to only use humble verbs when appropriate. To restate, whoever is using a humble verb (such as 드리다) is showing that they are lowering themselves to whoever they are speaking *about*. Here's an example:

제가 이 선물을 정말로 드리고 싶었어요.
"I really wanted to give you this present."

The above example could be used by a student to a teacher, since the student is talking *about* the teacher (in this case, also speaking directly to the teacher).

저도 선물을 드리고 싶었어요.
"I also wanted to give them a present."

The above example could be used by one student to another – notice how it simply ends in the 요 form – while still talking *about* a teacher (or boss, etc.). For all other situations, such as when talking *about* a classmate (or anyone else who you do not need to show extra respect to), using 주다 is fine.

내일 줄 거예요.
"I will give it to you tomorrow."

보다 → 뵙다 "to see" (also 뵈다)

보다 is either 뵙다 or 뵈다; either is fine.

그럼 내일 뵙겠습니다.
"Well then, I will see you tomorrow."

Adv When using *humble speech*, there is also one additional way to say "we" – 저희.

Let's go back to the conversation.

Chapter 8

Honorific Speech
"To Bring"

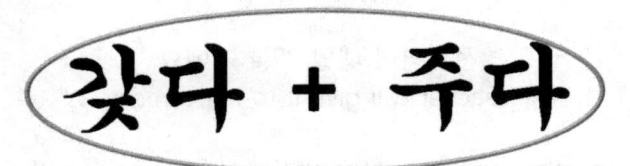

갖다 + 주다

갖다 드리다 is a combination of two verbs – 갖다 which is short for 가지다 ("to have"), and 드리다 which is the *humble verb* for 주다. Combined, 갖다 주다 (or 갖다 드리다) literally means "to get and give." It is used to mean "to (get and) bring," and is used when you are talking about bringing (or getting) an item for someone.

펜을 빨리 갖다 주세요.
"Please hurry and bring me a pen."
"Please hurry up and get me a pen."

펜을 갖다 드렸어요.
"I brought them a pen."

The above sentence could be used when giving the pen to a teacher (or boss, etc.), since it uses 드리다.

Advanced

Honorific and Humble Particles

When using honorific or humble speech, there are three common particles that can (and usually) change to different versions. These particles are *only* used after a person who you want to show respect to (and not after *yourself*, for example).

Note that all three of these particles keep their original meaning. Only their spelling (and pronunciation) is different.

에게(서) → 께

We learned in Chapter 17 of the first book that 에게(서) means "to and from (a person)." 께 works in the same way, and can mean both 에게 or 에게서.

할머니께 말했어요.
"I told it to my grandmother."

선생님께 선물을 받았어요.
"I received a present from the teacher."

선생님께 선물을 드렸어요.
"I gave a present to the teacher."

While 선생님에게 선물을 드렸어요 would make sense, using 께 is preferable, and is a better match for the tone of the sentence (since it uses the *humble verb* 드리다 anyway).

Subject Marker (이/가) → 께서

Although 께서 appears similar to 께, they're not the same. 께서 can replace both 이 and 가 as the Subject Marker in a sentence.

Honorific Speech

선생님께서 주셨어요.
"The teacher gave it to me."

할머니께서 지금 주무시고 계세요.
"My grandmother is sleeping now."

Topic Marker (은/는) → 께서는

께서는 can replace both 은 and 는 as the Topic Marker in a sentence.

선생님께서는 언제 졸업하셨어요?
"When did you (sir) graduate?"

할아버지께서는 뭘 드시고 싶으세요?
"Grandfather, what do you want to eat?"

Remember that while using these three particles isn't absolutely necessary, they're preferred when using honorific or humble speech.

While you can make grammatically correct sentences without using honorifics, not using them in certain situations can be seen as *impolite*. As a beginner in the Korean language, you will be forgiven when you make mistakes. However, the more Korean that you know – and you'll know a lot more by the end of this book – the more you will be expected to correctly use honorific speech. Don't stress about this for now, but know that ultimately, you will need to understand the concepts in this chapter in order to avoid speaking impolitely.

Practice

Change the following verbs to honorific verbs:

1. 하다
2. 먹다
3. 자다
4. 있다
5. 없다
6. 가다
7. 죽다
8. 알다

Translate to Korean using honorific speech:

9. "By chance are you American?"

Chapter 8

Honorific Speech

10. "Why didn't you go together yesterday?"

_____.

11. "What do you want to eat?"

_____.

12. "What is your name?"

_____.

13. "Please come this way."

_____.

14. "When can you give it to me?"

_____.

Translate to English:

15. 댁이 어디세요?

_____.

16. 연세가 어떻게 되세요?

_____.

17. 저 분은 누구세요?

_____.

18. 아직 드리지는 못했어요.

_____.

Honorific Speech

19. 내일 갖다 주세요.

_____.

20. 다음에 뵙겠습니다.

_____.

New Phrases

어서 오세요.	"Welcome.," "Come in."
식사하셨어요?	"Have you eaten anything?"
맛있게 드세요!	"Enjoy (the food)!"
좋은 하루 되세요.	"Have a nice day."
좋은 하루 보내세요.	"have a nice day."
환영합니다.	"Welcome."
(곳)에 오신 것을 환영합니다.	"Welcome to (place)."

New Vocabulary

드시다	"to eat," "to drink" (hon.)
잡수시다	"to eat" (hon.)
계시다	"to exist" (hon.)
주무시다	"to sleep" (hon.)
돌아가시다	"to die," "to pass away" (hon.)
돌아가다	"to go back"
돌아오다	"to come back"
말씀	"word" (hon.)
댁	"house" (hon.)
연세	"age" (hon.)
성함	"name" (hon.)
따님	"daughter" (hon.)
아드님	"son" (hon.)
어서	"quickly," "promptly" (adverb)
드리다	"to give" (hum.)

Chapter 8: Honorific Speech

뵈다	"to see" (hum.)
뵙다	"to see" (hum.)
메뉴	"menu"
쪽	"side"
오른쪽	"right (side)"
왼쪽	"left (side)"
동	"east"
서	"west"
남	"south"
북	"north"
동쪽	"east (side)"
서쪽	"west (side)"
남쪽	"south (side)"
북쪽	"north (side)"
양쪽	"both sides"
한쪽	"one side"
뜨다	"to rise (the sun/moon)"
지다	"to set (the sun/moon)"
음료	"beverage"
식사	"a meal"
식사(를) 하다	"to have a meal"
와인	"wine"
잔	"glass (counter)"
옥수수	"corn"
옥수수차	"corn tea"
보리	"barley"
보리차	"barley tea"
꿀차	"honey tea"
갖다 주다	"to (get and) bring"
갖다 드리다	"to (get and) bring" (hon.)
환영(을) 하다	"to welcome"
졸업식	"graduation (ceremony)"
졸업(을) 하다	"to graduate"
장소	"location," "place"

Verb Endings

Chapter 9

Conversation

제레미:	안녕하세요.
할머니:	안녕하세요. 아이고! 한국말을 참 잘하시네요!
제레미:	아, 아니에요. 저는 아직 잘 못 해요.
할머니:	어디서 배우셨어요?
제레미:	독학으로 배웠어요.
할머니:	한국이 어때요? 좋아하세요?
제레미:	당연히 좋아하죠!
할머니:	오! 좋아요!
제레미:	전 한국을 사랑해요.
할머니:	뭘 제일 좋아하세요? 한국 음식도 잘 드시나요? 안 매워요? 너무 맵죠?
제레미:	하하. 아니요. 안 매워요. 한국 음식을 잘 먹고 좋아해요.
할머니:	그렇군요. 아이고! 정말 훌륭하세요.

What is a Verb Ending?

We've learned several types of *verb endings* already in this book and in the first book – one example is the 요 form. But repeating the same verb ending (such as the 요 form) can be a bit... well, boring. Here's an example conversation showing what I mean:

Chapter 9

Verb Endings

A. 김치를 자주 드세**요**?
"Do you eat kimchi often?"

B. 아니요. 먹으면 배가 아파서 자주 못 먹어**요**.
"No. I can't eat it often because my stomach hurts when I eat it."

A. 그래요? 정말 안됐어**요**.
"Yeah? That's really too bad."

B. 네, 그래**요**.
"Yeah, it is."

Notice how every sentence ends with 요; there's nothing wrong with the grammar, but the conversation seems a bit dull. Neither A nor B are expressing their emotions in their speech. In a real conversation, A might be surprised after hearing that B can't eat kimchi, but there's no surprise shown in the conversation – the 요 form does not contain any specific emotion, good or bad. This conversation could easily be improved by using different verb endings.

"Does this mean I'll have to learn new rules, like with the 요 form?" Fortunately, not at all! The verb endings that we'll be learning in this chapter are all simple to use and attach easily onto verb stems. This chapter will cover *four* of the most common verb endings that we can use to add more emotion to our conversations, and help to make our speech sound much more natural and lively.

Note that none of these four verb endings has a direct translation into English, but simply add different emotions to your sentences. You're free to translate them any way that you'd like, and any way that would seem natural, depending on the context of the sentence.

Expressing Surprise – 네요

You can use the 네요 verb ending when you want to add the feeling of being *surprised* to your sentence.

To use this form, take a verb stem and attach 네요.

하다 → 하
하 + 네요 → 하네요

먹다 → 먹
먹 + 네요 → 먹네요

Verb Endings

Chapter 9

For verb stems that end in ㄹ, remove the ㄹ before attaching 네요.

살다 → 살
살 – ㄹ → 사
사 + 네요 → 사네요

Here are some example sentences, along with natural English translations:

맛있네요.
"Wow, it's delicious."

While this could be translated as "Wow," among other words, know that there is no direct English translation, and you can feel free to translate it (or not) to English in any way that you'd like to fit the situation.

정말 빨리 먹네요!
"Wow, you eat really fast!"

한국말을 잘하시네요!
"You speak Korean well!"

"Right?" – 죠

You can use the 죠 verb ending when you want to add the meaning of "right?" or "isn't it?" or "aren't you?," for example, to your sentence. It's used in this way as if you are asking someone to *confirm* what you are saying. Another way to think of this ending is like the stereotypical "eh?" used by Canadians (If you're a Canadian reading this, I'm sorry).

To use this form, take a verb stem and attach 죠.

맛있죠?
"It's good, isn't it?"

It's often used with questions, but it can be used in regular sentences as well, just like "isn't it?" in spoken English.

맛있죠!
"It's good, isn't it!"

어제 학교에 안 갔죠?
"You didn't go to school yesterday, did you?"

Verb Endings

고양이는 물을 싫어하죠?
"Cats hate water, right?"

Showing Curiosity – 나요

You can use the 나요 verb ending when you want to add the feeling of being especially *curious* when asking a question.

In addition, using 나요 can make your sentence sound a bit more *gentle* (making a sentence that sounds softer, and less dry).

To use this form, take a verb stem and attach 나요. For verb stems that end in ㄹ, remove the ㄹ before attaching 나요.

맛있나요?
"Is it delicious?"

영어를 잘할 수 있나요?
"Can you speak English well?"

혹시 식사하셨나요?
"By chance did you eat something?"

Realizing Something – 군요/는군요

You can use the 군요 verb ending in a sentence when you want to add the feeling of *realizing* something.

To use this form, take a verb stem and attach 군요.

There is one additional step to learn for using this form: when using this form with an *action verb* in the *present tense*, attach 는군요 instead.

맛있군요!
"Oh, it's really good!"

지금 나가는군요.
"Oh, he's leaving now."

미국 사람이시군요!
"Wow, you're an American!"

Verb Endings

> Chapter 9

김치를 좋아하는군요.
"Wow, he likes kimchi."

Since 는군요 is only used when an *action verb* is in the *present tense*, in other cases simply attach 군요.

이미 나갔군요.
"Oh, he already left."

A Quick Review of Verb Endings

Now that we've covered the four most common verb endings, let's go back to the conversation with A and B, and see if we can improve it a bit.

A. 김치를 자주 드시나요?
"Do you eat kimchi often?"

B. 아니요. 먹으면 배가 아파서 자주 못 먹어요.
"No. I can't eat it often because my stomach hurts when I eat it."

A. 그렇군요. 정말 안됐네요.
"Oh, I see. That's really too bad."

B. 네, 그렇죠.
"Yeah, it is, huh?"

While the first conversation between A and B was still acceptable and correct, this one shows much more emotion, and is a bit more interesting.

Now let's begin covering the chapter conversation.

제레미: 안녕하세요.
"Hello."

할머니: 안녕하세요. 아이고! 한국말을 참 잘하시네요!
"Hello. Oh my! You speak Korean really well!"

참 is an adverb that can be used to mean "really" and is similar 정말, though it sounds a bit more formal than 정말.

131

Chapter 9 — Verb Endings

Since the conversation sentence ends with 시네요, we can know that the elderly lady is talking about someone else – here, Jeremy. And since she's using (으)시, we can also know that she is showing *respect* to Jeremy. By 네요 at the end, she's also showing *surprise* that Jeremy is able to speak Korean so well.

> 제레미: 아, 아니에요. 저는 아직 잘 못 해요.
> "Ah, no. I still can't speak it well yet."

You're likely to receive compliments when you begin speaking Korean with a Korean person. A good response is to stay humble, and to reply with 아니에요 (literally, "I'm not."). 아니에요 can be used in this way to *deny* what someone has said. By using 아니에요, Jeremy is politely denying the woman's compliment. While this could seem rude in English (it might be more polite in English to say "Oh, no, but thank you."), it is polite to deny a compliment in Korean.

> 할머니: 어디서 배우셨어요?
> "Where did you learn it?"

> 제레미: 독학으로 배웠어요.
> "I learned by self study."

We learned that (으)로 can be used to mean "by" or "using," among others. Here, 독학으로 means "by self-study."

> 할머니: 한국이 어때요? 좋아하세요?
> "How is Korea? Do you like it?"

> 제레미: 당연히 좋아하죠!
> "Of course I like it!"

당연히 is an *adverb*, and comes from the descriptive verb 당연하다 ("to be reasonable," "to be natural"). It can be used in many situations.

> 당연하죠!
> "Of course!"
> "Naturally!"

> 당연한 거예요.
> "It's only natural."

Verb Endings

Chapter 9

> **Culture Notes**
>
> **"It's a carrot!"**
>
> Since 당연 sounds similar (slightly) to the word 당근 ("carrot"), a common joke is to use 당근 with the verb 이다 ("to be") when saying "of course."
>
> 당근이죠!
> "Of course!"
> "Naturally!"
>
> This literally means "It's a carrot, huh!"

할머니: 오! 좋아요!
"Oh! Good!"

제레미: 전 한국을 사랑해요.
"I love Korea."

Shortened Korean

The Korean language is full of shortened words. We've already learned a few examples such as 거예요 (것이에요), and 얼마큼 (얼마만큼). Another common word is 전 (저는).

Although I'd recommend avoiding this for now (since it's slightly less formal than using 저는), you'll find in some cases in which the Topic Marker (specifically, 는) can be shortened to ㄴ when used after a *vowel*. Later on in this book I'll cover more examples of when this happens; for now, knowing 전 should be enough.

할머니: 뭘 제일 좋아하세요? 한국 음식도 잘 드시나요? 안 매워요? 너무 맵죠?
"What do you like most? Do you eat Korean food? Isn't it spicy? It's too spicy, right?"

Enjoying Food: 잘 먹다

We learned that the phrase 잘 먹겠습니다, and 잘 먹었습니다, can be used before and after a meal to say thanks for the food. We also learned that 잘 먹겠습니다 literally means "I will eat well," and 잘 먹었습니다 means "I ate well."

You can also use 잘 먹다 (or the honorific version, 잘 드시다) in other situations as well. It can translate as "to enjoy (eating)," and can be used in the same way as 맛있게 먹다 (taught in Chapter 6).

Chapter 9

Verb Endings

Adv 잘 can also mean 자주 ("often"), so 잘 먹다 at the same time can also mean "to eat often." 잘 안 먹다 can therefore also mean "to not eat often." Keep this in mind if you hear a sentence using 잘 먹다 which does not seem to mean "to enjoy (eating)."

> 제레미: 하하. 아니요. 안 매워요. 한국 음식을 잘 먹고 좋아해요.
> "Haha. No. It's not spicy. I eat Korean food and enjoy it."

Since we just learned that 잘 먹다 can mean "to enjoy (eating)," the speaker is actually saying "I enjoy eating Korean food and like it," but "enjoy it" is a more natural English translation for this sentence.

> 할머니: 그렇군요. 아이고! 정말 훌륭하세요.
> "Oh, I see. Oh my! That's really wonderful!"

그렇군요 is a commonly used phrase, and can translate as "Oh, I see." It can be used when you have *realized* that someone said something that was correct.

Although the woman is using 훌륭하세요 (literally, "*you* are wonderful"), a more natural translation could be "*That* is really wonderful!"

Practice

Translate to Korean using the 네요 verb ending:

1. "You really like kimchi!"

   _____.

2. "Chul-soo can't eat hamburgers."

   _____.

Translate to Korean using the 죠 verb ending:

3. "You're studying Korean a lot, aren't you!"

   _____.

Verb Endings

4. "Korean is simple, isn't it?"

_____.

Translate to Korean using the (는)군요 verb ending:

5. "Oh, they're not an American."

_____.

6. "Oh, Chul-soo can't eat steak either."

_____.

Translate to Korean using the 나요 verb ending:

7. "Is that correct?"

_____.

8. "Do you like Korean music?"

_____.

Translate to English:

9. 지금은 조금 바쁘네요.

_____.

10. 여기는 처음이죠?

_____.

11. 이제 집에 가겠군요.

_____.

Chapter 9 — Verb Endings

12. 혹시 이 학교에서 수학 가르치시는 선생님을 아시나요?

_____.

New Phrases

그렇군요.	"Oh, I see."

New Vocabulary

안됐다	"to be sorry (to hear)," "to be too bad" (past tense)
참	"really" (adverb)
독학	"self study"
당연히	"of course," "naturally" (adverb)
당연하다	"to be reasonable," "to be natural"
물론	"of course," "it goes without saying" (adverb)
좁다	"to be narrow," "to be cramped"
두껍다	"to be thick"
얇다	"to be thin (not thick)" (pronounced 얄따)
넓다	"to be wide," "to be spacious" (pronounced 널따)
궁금하다	"to be curious (to know)" (descriptive verb)
긴장(을) 하다	"to be nervous," "to be tense"
칭찬	"compliment"
칭찬(을) 하다	"to compliment," "to praise"
칭찬(을) 받다	"to receive a compliment," "to be praised"
단어	"vocabulary word"
문장	"a sentence"
예문	"example sentence"
문법	"grammar"
동사	"verb"

Verb Endings

Chapter 9

형용사	"adjective"
부사	"adverb"
명사	"noun"
번역	"(written) translation"
통역	"(spoken) translation"
번역가	"(written) translator"
통역사	"interpreter"
번역(을) 하다	"to translate (writing)"
통역(을) 하다	"to translate (speaking)"
페이지	"page (of writing)"
안경	"glasses"
안경(을) 쓰다	"to wear glasses"
일터	"workplace"

Chapter 9: Verb Endings

Introduction to Casual Korean

Chapter 10

Conversation

현정:	안녕! 잘 지냈어?
지혜:	응! 잘 지냈어. 현정이도 잘 지냈어?
현정:	응! 나 지금 뭔가 좀 먹으러 갈 거야. 같이 갈래?
지혜:	그래. 뭘 먹고 싶어?
현정:	떡볶이랑 김치찌개 어때?
지혜:	아, 그럼 안 돼. 난 요즘 매운 걸 잘 못 먹어.
현정:	너 매운 걸 못 먹어? 진짜?
지혜:	매운 걸 먹으면 배가 아프니까 못 먹어. 미안해.
현정:	아니, 괜찮아. 그럼 난 불닭 먹을래!
지혜:	야, 이 바보! 그게 더 맵잖아!

What is Casual Korean?

Casual Korean is different from honorific, formal, and informal Korean – it's a new kind that we haven't learned about yet. Before we go further, first let's do a brief review of each of these. If you'd like a more in-depth review I'd also recommend re-reading each of those lessons.

Honorific Korean is used when you want to show respect to a person who you are speaking about.

Chapter 10 — Introduction to Casual Korean

Formal Korean (such as when using the 니다 or 니까 endings) is used in these situations:

1. Meeting people for the first time
2. Business-related conversation
3. Whenever you want to sound extra polite

Informal Korean (such as the 요 form) is used in all other situations – except when using casual Korean is more appropriate.

Let's do a quick review of honorific speech. We learned that honorific Korean works differently from formal and informal Korean, because it's used when you are speaking *about* someone who you want to show respect to – honorific Korean is unrelated to who you are currently speaking *to*. You could use informal Korean (such as by ending your sentences in the 요 form) when speaking *to* someone you know while talking about your grandfather, but you would use honorific verbs for speaking about your grandfather. If this seems a bit confusing, I'd recommend reading over the previous chapter again to make sure you have a good understanding of the essential basics of honorific Korean before moving on to this chapter.

Casual Korean works similarly – you can have a sentence that uses casual Korean (we'll learn how to do this soon), but that also uses honorific verbs. Whether you use casual Korean or not depends on who you are speaking *to*, and not on who you are speaking *about*.

So when do we use casual Korean? Casual Korean, known as 반말 (literally "half words"), is actually a type of informal Korean. It's not used when you would use formal Korean – if you use casual Korean, it will no longer be formal. Let's learn when it's appropriate.

Casual Korean is appropriate in these situations:

1. Talking to a close friend who is the same age as you or younger
2. With a boyfriend or girlfriend
3. To small children
4. To family members
5. To animals
6. When given permission

Among these, the most common time that you will be using casual Korean will be when speaking to friends. Remember that this only applies to friends who are the same age as you or younger, and not to friends who are older than you are – strange how that works, right? We'll talk about this more in a bit.

Introduction to Casual Korean

Chapter 10

When speaking Korean with a boyfriend or girlfriend, it's acceptable to use casual Korean, but some couples will also prefer to speak more politely (such as with the 요 form). This is completely up to the couple.

When speaking to small children, it's acceptable to speak in casual Korean, though it's also acceptable to use polite Korean.

Although it's acceptable to speak in casual Korean with family members, some people will still prefer to speak more politely to their parents.

When speaking to animals (these are really just one-way conversations), only use casual speech. It can actually be impolite if you speak to an animal using polite Korean, and then speak to a person using the same polite Korean.

Finally, you can also speak casually when someone gives you permission, or tells you to. These situations can happen often with non-Koreans – a Korean might ask you to speak casually once you've become acquainted. This can also happen with close friends, especially male and female friends, even when one person is a bit older than the other. However, if you've received permission to speak casually with someone you normally wouldn't speak casually – such as to someone older than you – you should only do so in *private*. When speaking with that person in *public*, it's best to return to polite Korean.

How to Speak 반말

The most basic thing you will need to do when speaking casual Korean (반말) is to say goodbye to 요 ("It's not you, 요. It's me.").

해요. → 해.
먹어요. → 먹어.
계세요. → 계셔.

Remember that 계세요 comes from the *honorific verb* 계시다.

Introduction to Casual Korean

가나요? → 가나?
좋아하죠. → 좋아하지.

Notice in the above example how 죠 changes to 지. This is because the verb ending 죠 is actually a combination of 지 with 요 (지 + 요 → 죠). Removing the 요 leaves 지 alone again.

좋군요. → 좋군.
하세요? → 하셔?

Also notice how (으)세요 becomes (으)셔 and not (으)세. This comes from the original verb form of (으)시다.

이에요/예요 → (이)야.

There is an exception with the verb 이다 ("to be"), which becomes 이야 when used after a *consonant*, or 야 when used after a *vowel*.

미국 사람**이야**.
"I'm an American."

아침 8 시**야**.
"It's 8 o'clock in the morning."

아니에요 → 아니야

The same applies with the verb 아니다 ("to not be"), which simply becomes 아니야.

미국 사람이 **아니야**.
"I'm not an American."

Now that we've learned the most basic way to change our sentences into casual Korean, let's learn some additional grammar and words that we can also use.

Introduction to Casual Korean

Chapter 10

Me and You: 나 & 너

When speaking in 반말, you'll use different words for "me" and "you."

Instead of using 저 ("I," "me"), you can use 나, which has the same meaning, but is only used in casual speech.

And instead of using any other word for "you," you can use 너, which is also only used in casual speech.

Also, just as 저는 can be shortened to 전, 나는 and 너는 can also be shortened to 난 and 넌.

When saying "my," 저의 can either become 나의 or 내.

The word "your" works a bit differently. When *speaking*, you can either say 너의 or 니. When *writing*, however, use 네. The actual shortening of 너의 is 네, but because 네 ("your") sounds so similar to 내 ("my"), in speech it's more commonly said as 니.

> **Adv** 너 also changes when it is *plural* – instead of 너들, use 너희.

When using 나 with the Subject Marker, it becomes 내가. When using 너 with the Subject Marker it becomes 네가 in *writing*, or 니가 when *spoken*.

> **Adv** 너가 is also acceptable for *speaking*, and has the same meaning.

Seem confusing? No worries, as the next grammar point will help make speaking casual Korean a bit easier.

143

Chapter 10
Introduction to Casual Korean

Advanced

You may hear older people who use 나 when referring to themselves, but who end their sentences in the 요 form. While you might think this is a bit strange – "Isn't the 요 form for *informal speech*, and 나 for *casual speech*?" – remember that 나 can be used to people who are younger than you are. If someone uses the 요 form together with 나, they are showing that although they are older, they do not feel they should be speaking *casually* to someone. This is kind of a middle ground between casual speech and informal speech. I would recommend avoiding this middle ground completely until you have a very strong understanding of formal, informal, honorific, and casual speech, as misusing it can be quite awkward. However, be aware of it in case you might hear it, and know that it's acceptable for an older person to speak in this way to someone who is much younger than they are.

Optional Markers

When speaking in 반말, it's fine to not use Topic Markers, Subject Markers, and Object Markers, as long as the meaning can still be understood. Basically what this means is, as long as it would not be confusing what the topic of a sentence is, or the subject or object of a verb is, then it's okay to not use those markers in a sentence.

Remember that this only applies when using 반말, and not when using the 요 form or speaking formally. Let's look at a few examples.

난 가고 싶어.
나 가고 싶어.
"I want to go."

친구와 밥을 먹었어.
친구와 밥 먹었어.
"I ate with a friend."

뭘 먹었어요?
뭐 먹었어?
"What did you eat?"

I'm not saying that it is *necessary* to remove these markers when speaking – I'm only saying that you *can*. Note that if you were to remove all markers in a longer sentence, the meaning could become vague, so practice by removing only one type of particle at a time before doing this yourself when speaking.

Remember to use formal, informal, and casual Korean when each is appropriate. When in doubt, use formal Korean. If you know that formal Korean isn't required but you're not sure whether to use the 요 form or casual, use the 요 form. It's always better to be a bit more polite than to be rude.

We still have more to learn about casual Korean, but let's learn more through this chapter's conversation.

Introduction to Casual Korean

Chapter 10

현정: 안녕! 잘 지냈어?

"Hi! Have you been doing well?"

안녕 is the casual version of 안녕하세요. Note that since this is a standard phrase, saying 안녕해 would be *incorrect*.

The next phrase, 잘 지냈어, comes from the adverb 잘 and the verb 지내다 – together meaning "to be well." We learned in the first book that we can ask people how they are doing by using 잘 지내세요 in a question. 잘 지냈어 is a casual version of this, in the *past tense*.

잘 지내다 can be used in the *past tense* (for example, "잘 지내셨어요?" or "잘 지냈어?"), or in the *present tense* (for example, "잘 지내세요?" or "잘 지내?"). You can also use this with the *progressive tense*, as 잘 지내고 있다 (for example, "잘 지내고 계세요?" or "잘 지내고 있어?"). Feel free to use any of them.

> **Advanced**
>
> While we're talking about casual phrases with 잘, there are two more phrases that we can learn – 잘 가(요) and 잘 있어(요). Although we previously learned 잘 가요, know that in casual speech this can become 잘 가. It can be used in the same way as 안녕히 가세요, but in casual situations. Also, 잘 있어(요) can be used in the same way as 안녕히 계세요.
>
> 잘 가!
> "Bye!"
>
> 잘 있어!
> "Bye!"

지혜: 응! 잘 지냈어. 현정이도 잘 지냈어?

"Yeah! I've been doing well. Have you?"

응 is casual for 네. And although it's written 응, most often it will actually be *pronounced* 어 (since it's easier to say).

Names in Casual Speech

When speaking casually, there's no need to use 씨 or 선생님 (or any similar titles), unless you want to show extra respect (such as to a teacher or boss). Instead, simply use the person's first name.

If the person's name ends in a *consonant*, attach 이 to the end of their name before using it in a sentence.

희진**이**는 숙제했어?
"Did Hee-jin do the homework?"

Chapter 10: Introduction to Casual Korean

If the person's name ends in a *vowel*, you can use it normally without adding anything.

철수도 그렇게 생각해?
"Do you think so too Chul-soo?"

However, you will still use these titles (such as 씨 or 선생님) when talking *about* someone who you want to show respect to, even if he or she is not in the room. Also, remember that honorifics can and will still be used as well when appropriate.

김 선생님이 방금 어디 가셨어?
"Where did Mr. Kim just go?"

방금 is an *adverb* that means "just," and is used when something has *just* happened.

제가 방금 했어요.
"I just did it."

When you're simply *calling out* to a friend, such as to get their attention, attach 아 to the end of their name if it ends in a *consonant*. Or if their name ends in a *vowel*, attach 야.

희진**아**!
"Hee-jin!"

철수**야**!
"Chul-soo!"

Advanced

금방

금방 is often confused with 방금, since they sound similar. While 방금 means "just (happened)," 금방 means "right away."

금방 나갈 거예요.
"I will leave right away."

However, 금방 is not used for *commands* (whereas you can use 빨리 for commands).

빨리 오세요!
"Come right away!"

현정: 응! 나 지금 뭐가 좀 먹으러 갈 거야. 같이 갈래?

"Yeah! I'm kinda gonna go eat something now. Wanna come with me?"

Introduction to Casual Korean

좀 and 조금

좀 is a shortened version of the adverb 조금 ("a little"); it's typically used in casual speech, but is acceptable when using the 요 form as well (but not for formal speech).

아직 조금 있어요?
아직 좀 있어요?
"Is there still a little left?"

좀 has one additional use that 조금 does not; it can also be used as an adverb to *soften* the meaning of a sentence (as it does in this chapter's conversation) – in this way, a good translation for it can be "kinda." Let's take a look at an example sentence:

좀 가고 싶어.
"I kinda want to go."

숙제가 좀 많아요.
"There's kinda a lot of homework."

"Want to" and "Wanna"
Verb Stem + (을/ㄹ) 래(요)

You can use this form as an alternate, more casual version of the 고 싶다 form.

To use it, take a verb stem and attach 을 if it ends in a *consonant*, or attach ㄹ if it ends in a *vowel*. Then attach 래. Finally, you can add a 요 to the end for informal speech.

> **Adv**: Just as with the form 고 싶다, this form can only be used when talking about yourself or someone else who you are *directly* speaking to. It cannot be used to say that someone else (who you're not speaking directly to) "wants" to do something.

하다 → 하
하 + ㄹ래(요) → 할래(요)

한국어 같이 공부할래?
"Do you wanna study Korean with me?"

먹다 → 먹
먹 + 을래(요) → 먹을래(요)

김치 먹을래?
"Do you wanna eat kimchi?"

Chapter 10: Introduction to Casual Korean

살다 → 살
살 – ㄹ → 사
사 + ㄹ래(요) → 살래(요)

난 한국에서 살래.
"I wanna live in Korea."

> **Adv**: This 래(요) form is similar to another form, (으)려고 하다, which we will cover in more detail in Chapter 17.

지혜: 그래. 뭘 먹고 싶어?
"Okay. What do you want to eat?"

현정: 떡볶이랑 김치찌개 어때?
"How about stir-fried rice cakes and kimchi stew?"

Informal Grammar: (이)랑

When using informal speech or 반말, there are also a few extra grammar forms that you can use.

(이)랑 is used in the same way as (와/과), but is only used in informal or casual speech.

To use (이)랑, attach 이랑 directly after a noun that ends in a *consonant*, or attach 랑 after a noun that ends in a *vowel*.

선생님**이랑**
친구**랑**

그 사람이랑 공원에 같이 갔어.
"I went to the park together with that person."

난 지금 친구랑 이야기하고 있어서 좀 바빠.
"I'm kinda busy now because I'm talking with a friend."

Informal Grammar: 한테(서)

한테(서) is used in the same way as 에게(서), and is only used to say "to" and "from" a *person* – not for things. It is also only used in informal or casual speech.

To use 한테(서), attach it directly after a person. The 서 is *optional*, just as it is in 에게(서).

Introduction to Casual Korean

제가 모르는 사람한테서 선물을 받았어요.
"I received a present from someone who I don't know."

철수한테 말했어.
"I told Chul-soo."

Note that the above example translates as "I said to Chul-soo," and not "told." In Korean, 말하다 ("to say") is used to also mean "to tell" when combined with 에게 or 한테. Here's one more example of this:

그 비밀을 제 친구들에게 말하지 않았어요.
"I didn't tell that secret to my friends."

Informal Grammar: 하고

하고 can be used in the same way as (와/과) any time that you're not speaking formally, such as when using informal or casual speech. It's similar to (이)랑.

떡볶이 하나하고 된장찌개 하나 주세요.
"Give me one order of stir-fried rice cakes and one order of bean paste stew."

Culture Notes

찌개 means "stew," and there are many kinds of stews in Korea; 김치찌개 ("kimchi stew") and 된장찌개 ("bean paste stew") are two of the most common types.

떡볶이 ("stir-fried rice cakes") is a spicy snack made from rice cakes mixed in a sauce containing 고추장 ("chili pepper paste"), and a sweetener such as sugar, honey, or corn syrup (or all three). Less-spicy varieties exist as well, but typically it is meant to be a sweet and spicy snack. Additional ingredients, such as hard boiled eggs (my favorite), green onions, and 어묵 ("fish cake"), can be added as well.

어제 친구들하고 같이 밥 먹었어요.
"Yesterday I ate together with friends."

Chapter 10: Introduction to Casual Korean

그 셔츠하고 같은 색깔이에요.
"It's the same color as that shirt."

지혜: 아, 그럼 안 돼. 난 요즘 매운 걸 잘 못 먹어.
"Ah, then no. I can't eat spicy things lately."

More Shortened Words: 거

We previously learned in Chapter 3 that 거 is a shortened version of 것. Furthermore, it can even be used when speaking politely, and not only casually. Let's look at a few more words that we can make using 거, starting with the most basic ones.

이것 → 이거
그것 → 그거
저것 → 저거

Attaching our regular markers (Topic Marker, Subject Marker, Object Marker) also gives us a few new ways to use 거.

거 + (은/는) → 건

안 매운 **건** 맛이 없어요.
"As for things that aren't spicy, I dislike them."

거 + (이/가) → 게

어려운 **게** 제일 재미있어요.
"Difficult things are the most entertaining."

거 + (을/를) → 걸

그런 **걸** 싫어해요.
"I dislike those kind of things."

Of these three, 게 seems to follow its own rules. When used with the Subject Marker, 거 will become 게.

You'll also commonly see 게 used with 이 and 그 (이게 and 그게, from 이것이 and 그것이).

Introduction to Casual Korean

However, 것 cannot be changed to 거 when used together with the particle 도 ("also," "even," "too") – 거도 would be *incorrect*, and it would stay as 것도. It also cannot be changed to 거 when used with the plural particle 들; 거들 would be *incorrect*, and it would stay as 것들.

Shortened Markers: ㄴ and ㄹ

As you've probably now noticed, in casual speech the Topic Marker (은/는) can be shortened to ㄴ, and the Object Marker (을/를) can be shortened to ㄹ when used after a *vowel*. The Subject Marker (이/가), however, only changes when used with 거 (into 게).

난 미국 사람이야.
"I'm an American."

날 좋아해?
"Do you like me?"

| A d v | The verb 하다 can also be shortened in some situations. In *negative* sentences, 하지 can be shortened to 치, as an *adverb* 하게 can be shortened to 케, and 하고 ("and") can be shortened to 코. Here's one example:

난 그렇게 생각치 않아.
"I don't think so." |

현정: 너 매운 걸 못 먹어? 진짜?
"You can't eat spicy things? Really?"

Really: 진짜

진짜 is an informal *adverb* that means "really." It can be used in informal or casual speech, but should not be used when speaking formally. Or, you can continue using the *adverb* 정말(로) ("really") which we learned previously and which is also commonly used.

진짜 있었어?
"He was really there?"

돈이 진짜 많아!
"He really has a lot of money!"

It can also be used as an *adjective* to mean "real."

내 진짜 사진이 아니야.
"It's not my real picture."

151

Chapter 10
Introduction to Casual Korean

네 진짜 목소리야?
"It's your real voice?"

The opposite of 진짜 is 가짜, but it can only be used as an *adjective*.

아니. 가짜 사진이야.
"No. It's a fake picture."

지혜: 매운 걸 먹으면 배가 아프니까 못 먹어. 미안해.
"I can't eat them because if I do my stomach hurts. Sorry."

Informal Grammar: (으)니까

Another useful informal grammar form is (으)니까, which has a meaning similar to 때문 ("because"). This can be used in informal or casual speech, but not in formal speech.

To use it, take a verb stem and attach 으니까 if it ends in a *consonant*, or attach 니까 if it ends in a *vowel*. This form also uses the three special additional rules we learned in Chapter 2.

매일 공부를 하고 있으니까 시험을 잘 봤어.
"I did well on the test because I'm studying everyday."

매운 걸 자주 먹으니까 배가 항상 아프지.
"Your stomach always hurts because you eat spicy things often."

> **Adv** Note that 배가 아프니까 could also have been 배가 아파서, as we learned in Chapter 5, for showing a *cause* and an *effect*. Both sentences are grammatically fine.

내가 미국인이니까 햄버거를 좋아해.
"I like hamburgers because I'm an American."

The above sentence uses the verb 이다 ("to be") with this form (here, 이니까). When used after a *vowel*, 이니까 shortens to 니까.

숙제니까 하고 싶지 않아.
"I don't want to do it because it's homework."

(으)니까 can also be used at the end of a sentence on its own, or by attaching a 요 to the end (to make it more polite).

Introduction to Casual Korean

매일 공부를 하고 있으니까요.
"It's because I'm studying everyday."

매운 걸 자주 먹으니까.
"It's because you eat spicy things often."

수줍은 사람이니까요.
"It's because he's a shy person."

Note that 수줍다 ("to be shy") conjugates to 수줍은 as an *adjective* – 수줍다 is an *irregular* descriptive verb.

현정: 아니, 괜찮아. 그럼 난 불닭 먹을래!
"No, it's okay. Then I wanna eat fire chicken!"

아니 is the casual version of 아니요 ("No.").

아니요 → 아니 "no"

Culture Notes

불닭 (literally "fire chicken") is chicken that is covered in a thick sweet sauce containing large amounts of 고추장 ("chili pepper paste"). It is considered to be one of the spiciest among Korean foods. In addition to being spicy, it's also served at hot temperatures, making it difficult for people who are not used to eating food that is both spicy and hot (but delicious) to consume.

지혜: 야, 이 바보! 그게 더 맵잖아!
"Hey, you idiot! That's spicier!"

야 can be used to call out to someone (or to yell at someone) when using casual speech – it means "Hey." However, this is *only* for casual use, and should never be used in other situations, as it can be considered especially rude.

Chapter 10: Introduction to Casual Korean

바보 means "idiot" and should also only be used when speaking casually, but it's not a strong insult. Friends will often call each other 바보 in a joking manner, so don't feel offended if your friend says this to you when you've made a mistake.

While we learned that 이 means "this," when used before an insult (such as 바보) it translates better into English as "you (insult)." As this can be insulting (that's why it's called an *insult* after all), remember that it should only be used in casual speech, not in other situations.

Informal Grammar: 잖아(요)

잖아(요) is a shortened version of 지 않아(요), the regular negative verb ending we learned; it's used in informal or casual speech. Although 맵잖아 would therefore be a shortened version of 맵지 않아, it's has a unique meaning – 잖아(요) can also be used in *positive* sentences, and not only in negative sentences like 지 않아(요). When you use 잖아(요), you are emphasizing that what you are saying is *correct*; this is similar to saying "Look!" or "See!" in English.

너무 맵잖아!
"See, it's too spicy!"

나도 친구잖아.
"Look, I'm your friend too."

저도 가고 싶잖아요.
"Look, I want to go too."

Although 잖아요 seems like it would be polite (after all, you can use it in informal speech), it's still less polite than using 죠. Avoid using 잖아요 with anyone who you are not well acquainted with, or in any formal situation.

Casual Commands

For a quick note, you can also make casual commands by using the regular 요 form – simply remove the 요 at the end. As you'd expect, making a command this way is for casual use only.

내일 우리 집으로 와.
"Come to my house tomorrow."

Introduction to Casual Korean

Culture Notes

Korean Age vs. American Age

In Korea, age works differently from how it does in other countries. A child in Korea is considered to be already one year old immediately after being born. Also, instead of gaining a year on your birthday, you will only gain a year on the first day of the year (January 1st).

This can get a bit interesting. Imagine a baby born on December 31st (one year old), turning two years old the very next day (January 1st). This is how Korean age is calculated.

Korean age is called 한국 나이, and American age (non-Korean age) is called 미국 나이. Note that even if you're not from America, you will still use 미국 나이 when talking about your age in non-Korean years.

To find your Korean age, take the current year, subtract the year you were born, and then add 1. This means that depending on whether your birthday has passed this year or not, you could be either 1 or 2 years older in your Korean age than your American age (try not to have a mid-life crisis when you calculate this).

You can then use 한국 나이로 ("in Korean age") or 미국 나이로 ("in American age") to say how old you are, such as in these example sentences:

한국 나이로는 29 살이에요.
"In Korean age, I'm 29 years old."

저는 미국 나이로 28 살이에요.
"I'm 28 years old in American age."

Note that it will be assumed that you are talking about 한국 나이 whenever you say your age, so it's not necessary to say this unless you want to be specific.

Chapter 10: Introduction to Casual Korean

Practice

Rewrite the following sentences using casual Korean:

1. 안녕하세요.

   _____.

2. 언제 가세요?

   _____.

3. 맛있네요!

   _____.

4. 잘 지내셨어요?

   _____.

5. 저는 이제 밥을 먹고 싶어요.

   _____.

6. 조금 더워요.

   _____.

7. 누구에게서 받았어요?

   _____.

8. 친구와 놀았어요?

   _____.

Introduction to Casual Korean

Chapter 10

Translate to Korean using casual speech:

9. "See, the stew's too hot!"

_____.

10. "Do you wanna go with me to see a movie?"

_____.

11. "Are you really okay?"

_____.

12. "What's that?"

_____.

13. "Mrs. Kim Yung-hee is very pretty."

_____.

Translate to English:

14. 넌 안 갈래?

_____.

15. 넌 나의 좋은 친구야.

_____.

16. 내가 안 먹을 거니까 네가 먹어.

_____.

17. 진짜 한국 사람이 아니에요? 한국말 너무 잘하세요.

_____.

Chapter 10: Introduction to Casual Korean

New Phrases

안녕.	"Hi." (casual)
잘 가(요).	"Bye." (casual)
잘 있어(요).	"Bye!" (casual)
야!	"Hey!" (casual)
짱!	"Awesome!" (casual)
오랜만이야.	"Long time, no see." (casual)
그럼(요).	"Yeah.," "Of course." (casual)

New Vocabulary

반말	"casual speech"
존댓말	"polite speech"
높임말	"honorific speech"
잘 지내다	"to be well"
응	"yes" (casual)
나	"I," "me" (casual)
너	"you" (casual)
너희	"you" (casual plural)
좀	"a little," "kinda" (informal)
(이)랑	"and," "with" (informal)
하고	"and," "with" (informal)
한테	"to (a person)" (informal)
한테(서)	"from (a person)" (informal)
불량식품	"unhealthy snacks"
김치찌개	"kimchi stew"
찌개	"stew"
된장찌개	"bean paste stew"
떡볶이	"stir-fried rice cakes"
고추	"chili pepper"
고추장	"chili pepper paste"
어묵	"fish cake"
시험(을) 잘 보다	"to do well on a test"

Introduction to Casual Korean

불닭	"fire chicken"
한국 나이	"Korean age"
미국 나이	"American age"
진짜	"real," "really" (informal)
가짜	"fake" (adjective)
국	"soup"
욕	"swear (word)"
모욕	"insult"
모욕(을) 하다	"to insult"
욕(을) 하다	"to swear"
욕(을) 받다	"to be sworn at"
부끄럽다	"to be/feel embarrassing"
창피하다	"to be/feel ashamed"
수줍다	"to be shy"
어색하다	"to be awkward"
놀라다	"to be surprised" (descriptive verb)
놀래다	"to surprise (someone)" (action verb)
깜짝 놀라다	"to be startled" (descriptive verb)
깜짝 놀래다	"to startle (someone)" (action verb)
무료	"free"
무료로	"for free" (adverb)
공짜	"free" (informal)
공짜로	"for free" (adverb) (informal)
국수	"noodles"
불고기	"barbequed meat"
소불고기	"barbequed beef"
돼지불고기	"barbequed pork"
오래간만에	"in a long time" (shortened to 오랜만에)
말(을) 놓다	"to stop speaking politely" (literally, "to put down one's speech")
말(을) 편하게 하다	"to speak without worrying too much about being polite"
방금	"just (happened)" (adverb)

Chapter 10: Introduction to Casual Korean

Shall We?

Conversation

민국:	언제 숙제할까요? 지금 할까요?
현아:	나중에 해요. 오늘은 쉬고 싶어요.
민국:	저도 내일 하고 싶은데 숙제할 시간이 있을까요?
현아:	시간이 있겠죠. 내일 일요일이죠?
민국:	아니요! 월요일이에요! 내일 수업 있어요!
현아:	그래요? 그럼 전 지금 숙제할 거예요.
민국:	저도 지금 할 거예요.

"Shall We?"
Verb Stem + (을/ㄹ) 까(요)?

Making questions using this form is simple, and can be used whenever you want to *suggest* something to someone else, just like "Shall we?" in English. This form can also be used to mean "Shall I?" in the same way, simply depending on the situation in which it is said. To make this meaning more clear, you can add 제가 to your sentence.

To make this form, take a verb stem and attach 을 if it ends in a *consonant*, or attach ㄹ if it ends in a *vowel*. Then add 까 and 요 (this 요 can be removed when speaking casually).

하다 → 하
하 + ㄹ까(요) → 할까(요)?

먹다 → 먹
먹 + 을까(요) → 먹을까(요)?

Chapter 11

Shall We?

같이 운동할까요?
"Shall we exercise together?"

뭘 먹을까요?
"What should we eat?"

누구를 선택할까요?
"Who should we choose?"

공포 영화를 보러 갈까요?
"Shall we go see a horror movie?"

제가 지금 시작할까요?
"Shall I begin now?"

Could & Would

I mentioned that this form is used to *suggest* something to someone else; because of this, it has one additional use – "could" and "would."

By "could" I don't mean "can." Rather, this form can be used for suggesting that something could or would *be* a certain way, or that something could or would *happen*. Let's take a look at a few examples.

내일 눈이 올까요?
"Could it snow tomorrow?"

철수가 집에 있을까?
"Could Chul-soo be at home?"
"Would Chul-soo be at home?"

정말 그럴까요?
"Could it really be so?"

뭐하고 있을까요?
"What could he be doing now?"
"What would he be doing now?"

Now that we've learned the two uses of this form, let's go onto the conversation.

민국: 언제 숙제할까요? 지금 할까요?
"When shall we do our homework? Should we do it now?"

162

Shall We?

> 현아: 나중에 해요. 내일은 어때요? 오늘은 쉬고 싶어요.
> "We'll do it later. How's tomorrow? I want to rest today."

나중에 is an adverb that means "later."

> 나중엔 시간이 없어요.
> "I don't have any time later."

엔 is a shortened version of 에는, but is not used in formal speech.

> 민국: 저도 내일 하고 싶은데 숙제할 시간이 있을까요?
> "I also want to do it tomorrow, though would there be time to do the homework?"

Verb Stem + (은/ㄴ/는) 데

We've already learned a few ways to connect sentences together – 고 ("and"), 지만 ("but"), and others. Let's learn one more useful, and extremely common way – 데. This form has two main uses:

1. *Contrasting* two sentences
2. *Explaining* something

First let's learn how to conjugate it.

For *action verbs*, take a verb stem and attach 는데. If it's being used at the *end* of a sentence, attach 요 as well (unless speaking casually).

For *descriptive verbs*, take a verb stem and attach 은데 if it ends in a *consonant*, or ㄴ데 if it ends in a *vowel*.

하다 → 하
하 + 는데 → 하는데

먹다 → 먹
먹 + 는데 → 먹는데

For *negative sentences*, 지 않다 will become 지 않은데 when attached to a *descriptive verb*, or 지 않는데 when attached to an *action verb*. Remember that a verb's type does not change even when it is negative.

요리하다 → 요리하지 않는데
행복하다 → 행복하지 않은데

Chapter 11

Shall We?

The three additional rules for verbs that we learned in Chapter 2 apply to this form as well.

살다 → 살
살 – ㄹ → 사
사 + 는데 → 사는데

춥다 → 춥
춥 – ㅂ → 추
추 + 우 → 추우
추우 + ㄴ데 → 추운데

The verbs 있다 and 없다 are *irregular verbs*, so they conjugate differently – to 있는데 and 없는데.

In *future tense*, this form will become either 겠는데 or 것인데 (often shortened to 건데), and in *past tense* will become 쓴는데.

Let's look at an example of how this form can be used to *contrast* two sentences.

> 제가 미국 사람인데 한국어도 할 수 있어요.
> "I'm an American, *but* I can speak Korean too."
> "I'm an American, *and* I can speak Korean too."
> "I'm an American, *though* I can speak Korean too."

The above example is a combination of 제가 미국 사람이에요 and 한국어도 할 수 있어요. When it's being used to *contrast* sentences, the 데 form can be translated in English simply as either "and," "but," or "though," among other possible translations.

You might then be wondering how using 데 is different from using 고 ("and") or 지만 ("but") which we learned before, but there's really no need to stress – you can still use 고 and 지만 in the same way as before. Just know that 고 and 지만 are more straightforward, and can only have the meanings of "and" and "but." 데, on the other hand, is more flexible, and also sounds a bit *softer* than using 고 or 지만.

Next, let's look at an example of how it can be used to *explain* something.

When *explaining* something, you can use this form as a way to *set the stage* for what you are going to explain. You can think of it in this way as being similar to saying "So..." at the beginning of a sentence.

> 내일 콘서트에 갈 건데 같이 갈래요?
> "(So...) I'm going to a concert tomorrow; do you want to go together?"

Shall We?

Chapter 11

In the same way, when *asking* for an explanation, you can also use this form. Using this form shows that you are *expecting* someone to explain something to you.

뭐했는데요?
"What did you do?"

어떻게 쓸 수 있는데요?
"How can I use it?"

The difference between using this form and simply asking directly is the *tone* of the sentence – using 데 is *softer* than simply asking the question directly. Asking these questions normally (with "지금 뭐해요?" and "어떻게 쓸 수 있어요?") would also be correct, but are more straightforward, and using 데 shows more that you are really *expecting* to hear the answer.

Since this form is used for both *contrasting* and *explaining*, you might be wondering when you should translate it as "So..." and when you should translate it as "but" or "and." Don't worry – simply choose whichever way fits better in English. The Korean meaning will not change regardless of how you translate it into English.

Let's take a look at a few more examples of the 데 form, along with three example translations for each one.

콘서트에 가고 싶은데 돈이 없어요.
"I want to go to the concert, but I don't have money."
"So... I want to go to the concert, and I don't have money."
"So... I want to go to the concert, though I don't have money."

매운 걸 먹고 싶은데 못 먹어요.
"I want to eat spicy things, but I can't."
"So... I want to eat spicy things, but I can't."
"I want to eat spicy things; I can't."

우산을 안 가져왔는데 비가 왔어요.
"I didn't bring an umbrella, but it rained."
"So... I didn't bring an umbrella, and it rained."
"I didn't bring an umbrella, and it rained."

학교에 갔는데 선생님이 안 계셨어요.
"I went to school, but the teacher wasn't there."
"I went to school, and the teacher wasn't there."
"So... I went to school, and the teacher wasn't there."

Chapter 11

Shall We?

Although the 데 form works quite simply, as you can see, it is often tricky to become comfortable with using because it can translate several ways into English. Remember not to worry about this when you're learning it – continue using 고 ("and") and 지만 ("but") until you feel confident enough to add the 데 form into your sentences.

Time to: Verb Stem + (을/ㄹ) 시간

You can use 시간 with a verb to say "time to."

Take a verb stem and attach 을 if it ends in a *consonant*, or attach ㄹ if it ends in a *vowel*. Then add 시간.

이제 갈 시간이에요.
"It is time to go now."

오늘 만날 시간이 없어요.
"I don't have time to meet today."

쉴 시간도 없네요!
"I don't even have time to rest!"

현아: 시간이 있겠죠. 내일 일요일이죠?
"There'll be time. Tomorrow's Sunday, right?"

민국: 아니요! 월요일이에요! 내일 수업 있어요!
"No! It's Monday! There's class tomorrow!"

현아: 그래요? 그럼 전 지금 숙제할 거예요.
"Really? Well then I'll do the homework now."

Shall We?

Chapter 11

민국: 저도 지금 할 거예요.

"I'll do it now too."

Advanced

Instruments

악기 is the word for "instrument," and each instrument in Korean uses a different verb in order to "play" it (just as we use different verbs in Korean to "wear" different clothes).

Guitar, Piano, Drums – 치다 ("to hit")

제 남자 친구는 기타를 잘 쳐요.
"My boyfriend plays the guitar well."

Stringed instruments – 켜다 ("to bow")

무대에서 바이올린 켜고 있는 사람이 제 친구예요.
"The person playing violin on the stage is my friend."

Wind instruments – 불다 ("to blow")

피리를 부니까 바구니에서 뱀이 나왔어요.
"A snake came out of the basket because I played the pipe."

Harp, 가야금 – 뜯다 ("to pluck")

저기서 하프를 뜯고 있는 여자가 천사와 같아요.
"The girl playing the harp over there is like an angel."

This is the least common of the four verbs, as only includes instruments played by plucking, such as the harp or the 가야금 (a traditional Korean stringed instrument).

Practice

Attach the 데 form to the following verbs:

1. 오다
2. 맛있다
3. 살다
4. 하고 싶다
5. 멀다
6. 뜨겁다
7. 그렇다
8. 좋다
9. 심심하다
10. 이다

Chapter 11

Shall We?

Translate to Korean:

11. "Shall we go to the store?"

_____.

12. "Who could it be?"

_____.

13. "Would there be many people there?"

_____.

14. "So... I bought a new computer, but I can't play games yet."

_____.

Translate to English:

15. 공부할 시간이 있으면 같이 공부할까요?

_____.

16. 이게 어떨까? 철수가 좋아할까?

_____.

17. 제가 좀 도와줄까요?

_____.

18. 아직 먹을 시간이 아니죠?

_____.

New Vocabulary

드라마   "drama"

Shall We?

공포 영화	"horror movie"
액션 영화	"action movie"
S.F. 영화	"sci-fi movie" ("에스 에프")
무협 영화	"martial arts movie"
코미디 영화	"comedy movie"
재난 영화	"disaster movie"
다큐멘터리	"documentary"
로맨스 영화	"romance movie"
예능 프로그램	"variety show," "variety program"
사극	"historical drama"
자막	"subtitles"
더빙	"dubbing," "voiceover"
장르	"genre"
재난	"disaster," "calamity"
예고편	"movie trailer," "movie advertisement"
연예인	"celebrity"
쉬다	"to (take a) rest"
나중에	"later" (adverb)
콘서트	"concert"
만화	"comic," "cartoon"
배우	"actor"
간단하다	"to be simple"
복잡하다	"to be complicated"
순수하다	"to be pure"
성	"castle"
해외	"overseas," "abroad"
내국	"domestic," "within the country"
외국인	"foreigner"
날씬하다	"to be slim"
뚱뚱하다	"to be fat"
조그마하다	"to be tiny"
거대하다	"to be gigantic"
추천(을) 하다	"to recommend"
피아노	"piano"

Chapter 11: Shall We?

기타	"guitar"
바이올린	"violin"
무대	"(performance) stage"
피리	"(musical) pipe"
플루트	"flute"
바구니	"basket"
하프	"harp"
규칙	"rule(s)"
약속	"promise," "appointment"
지키다	"to protect," "to keep (a rule, promise, etc.)"
어기다	"to break (a rule, promise, etc.)"
징그럽다	"to be gross," "to be disgusting"

Let's

Conversation

Chapter 12

박주영:	가자!
이혜원:	음... 조금만 기다리세요.
박주영:	그래.
이혜원:	불을 끄고 창문을 닫을까요?
박주영:	시간도 늦었는데 그냥 나가자.
이혜원:	오케이. 가요.

Korean has several ways of saying "let's" – which one you use will mostly depend on whether you are using casual, informal, or formal speech. Fortunately, all of them are simple to use. This chapter will focus on the two most common and useful ways.

Casual "Let's" – Verb Stem + 자

To make this form, take a verb stem and attach 자. This form should only be used in casual speech.

하다 → 하
하 + 자 → 하자

먹다 → 먹
먹 + 자 → 먹자

171

Chapter 12

Let's

살다 → 살
살 + 자 → 살자

밖에서 놀자.
"Let's play outside."

한국어를 매일 5시간 동안 공부하자.
"Let's study Korean everyday for 5 hours."

나중에 밥 한 번 먹자.
"Let's eat together sometime."

While 한 번 means "one time" or "once," it can also be used to mean "sometime."

Informal "Let's" – (같이) + 요 form

To make this form, use the 요 form of a verb. *Optionally*, you can add 같이 before the verb. Since this form uses the 요 ending, it is appropriate for any *informal* situation, but not for formal situations.

하다 → (같이) 해요
먹다 → (같이) 먹어요
살다 → (같이) 살아요

같이 가요.
"Let's go together."

다 같이 밥 먹어요.
"Let's eat all together."

같은 수업을 등록해요.
"Let's register for the same class."

Let's

Advanced

Although it is less commonly used, there is an additional way to say "let's" for *formal* situations (such as speaking to a boss).

Formal "Let's" – Verb Stem + 시죠

To make this form, take a verb stem and attach 시 (like you would when making honorific verbs). Then attach 죠 (the same verb ending that we learned in Chapter 9).

식사하러 가시죠.
"Let's go eat."

시작하시죠.
"Let's begin."

This form is actually a *command* – you're telling someone to do something, with 죠 ("isn't it?") attached on the end. In this way, it is similar to the (으)세요 ending. However, because this form uses the honorific ending, it can *also* be used as a polite way to say "let's."

먼저 드시죠.
"Please eat first."

함께 보시죠.
"Let's watch together."

Quick Summary of "Let's"

There are only *two* forms of "let's" that we need to worry about for most situations. Whenever you're speaking casually use the 자 form, and whenever you're not use the (같이) 요 form.

Once you're comfortable with these two forms, read over the "Advanced Notes" for this chapter to learn more, but know that these forms will not be as important for everyday Korean as 자 and (같이) 요.

Advanced

Here is one additional form that you should be aware of. Many resources will teach that this form is a polite way to say "let's," but actually this form is *informal*. While it can be appropriate for a boss to use this form to employees (some bosses might speak informally to their employees), it is not a polite form to use to anyone who you would not normally speak informally with – it can also even sound *awkward* when used in casual speech. It should therefore be avoided.

Verb Stem + (읍/ㅂ) 시다

To make this form, take a verb stem and attach 읍시다 if it ends in a *consonant*, or ㅂ시다 if it ends in a *vowel*.

갑시다.
"Let's go."

밥 먹읍시다.
"Let's eat."

Let's go over the conversation.

173

Chapter 12

Let's

> 박주영: 가자!
> "Let's go!"

> 이혜원: 음... 조금만 기다리세요.
> "Hm... Wait just a little bit."

We learned that 조금만 means "only a little," but here it sounds more natural to translate it as "just a little bit."

Notice how although 박주영 is speaking *casually*, 이혜원 replies using honorific speech (기다리세요). This is probably because 박주영 is older than 이혜원, and 이혜원 wants to be respectful – even if they are close.

> 박주영: 그래.
> "Okay."

> 이혜원: 불을 끄고 창문을 닫을까요?
> "Should we turn off the light and close the window?"

> 박주영: 시간도 늦었는데 그냥 나가자.
> "It's late, so let's just leave."

Late: 시간(이) 늦다

시간(이) 늦다 means "to be late," but specifically is for talking about the *time of day* (not for being late to an appointment, etc.). Using 도 adds *emphasis* in the original Korean sentence; this emphasis does not translate well to English – "Even the time is late."

The opposite of 시간(이) 늦다 would be 이르다 ("to be early"), and can be used when talking about both the time of day, *or* being early for something.

Let's

Just: 그냥

그냥 is an *adverb* that can be used in informal or casual speech. It can translate as "just," like the expression "just as it is." Most of the time 그냥 will be used in this way.

그냥 줘요.
"Just give it to me (as it is)."

그냥 책이에요.
"It's just a book."

그냥 can also have the meaning of "nothing special."

그냥 괜찮았어요.
"It was just alright."

그냥.
"Nothing special."

그냥 있어요.
"I'm just here."
"I'm not doing anything special."

이혜원: 오케이. 가요.
"Okay. Let's go."

This sentence is an example of using the 요 form to mean "let's" without adding 같이.

Let's

Chapter 12

Advanced

Both of these verbs can mean "to cut," but each is a bit different. 자르다 means that you are cutting something *off* – such as cutting your hair, cutting down a tree, or *severing* a wire. 베다 means that you are cutting *into* something (making a cut) – such as cutting your finger on a sharp object.

Be careful not to tell your friend that you accidentally 잘랐어요 your finger while preparing lunch (베었어요 would be much more appropriate). If you accidentally *did* cut off your finger, well... maybe you should be more careful next time.

Culture Notes

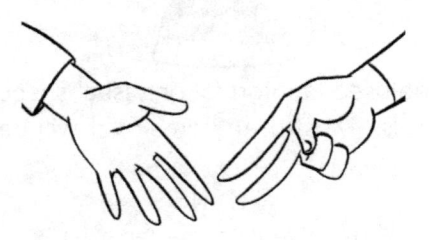

"가위, 바위, 보!"

The Korean version of rock-paper-scissors is 가위 ("scissors") 바위 ("rock," "boulder") 보 ("cloth"). While 보 means "cloth," 보 is not used outside of the name of this game – 천 ("cloth") is used instead.

가위바위보 is played with only one hand (without using your other hand as a "floor," or to make a rhythm).

Practice

Translate to Korean using the 자 form:

1. "Let's do the homework first."

_____.

2. "Let's go together to Korea."

_____.

Let's

Chapter 12

3. "Let's go to see a movie tonight."

_____.

Translate to Korean using the (같이) 요 form:

4. "Let's start."

_____.

5. "Let's eat lunch."

_____.

6. "Let's play until night."

_____.

Translate to English:

7. 집에 가자.

_____.

8. 한국어를 같이 연습해요.

_____.

9. 우리 집으로 같이 가요.

_____.

10. 볼링치러 가자.

_____.

11. 이제 시간이 없으니까 빨리 나가자.

_____.

Chapter 12

Let's

12. 설거지를 하고 청소도 하자.

_____.

New Phrases

오케이.	"Okay."

New Vocabulary

한 번	"one time," "once," "sometime" (adverb)
다 같이	"all together" (adverb)
등록(을) 하다	"to register"
불	"a light"
불(을) 켜다	"to turn on the light"
불(을) 끄다	"to turn off the light"
시간(이) 늦다	"to be late (at night)"
이르다	"to be early"
지각(을) 하다	"to be tardy"
그냥	"just (as it is)" (adverb)
빛	"light"
햇빛	"sunlight," "sunshine"
방향	"direction"
방향으로	"in/toward a direction"
화장품	"makeup"
화장(을) 하다	"to put on makeup"
배추	"cabbage"
상추	"lettuce"
선풍기	"electric fan"
부채	"paper folding fan"
도구	"tool"
기계	"machine"
가리키다	"to point," "to indicate"
밀가루	"flour"
던지다	"to throw"

Let's

닦다	"to wipe," "to dry," "to clean (by wiping)"
손(을) 닦다	"to wash one's hands"
시장	"(outdoor) marketplace"
시골	"countryside"
기본	"the basics," "fundamentals"
기본적이다	"to be basic," "to be fundamental"
끓이다	"to boil (something)"
썰다	"to chop," "to slice"
볶다	"to pan fry"
튀기다	"to deep fry"
찌다	"to steam"
섞다	"to mix"
재다	"to measure"
자	"(measuring) ruler"
지우개	"eraser"
저울	"scale (for weighing)"
베다	"to cut (into)"
자르다	"to cut (off)"
막대기	"stick," "bar," "rod"
가위바위보	"rock-paper-scissors"
바위	"rock," "boulder"
볼링	"bowling"
볼링(을) 치다	"to bowl"
심부름	"errand"
심부름(을) 하다	"to do errands"
원어민	"native speaker"
우체국	"post office"
우표	"postage stamp"
택배	"(mail) package," "parcel"

Chapter 12

Let's

Doing and Asking Favors

Chapter 13

Conversation

백찬일:	지민 씨, 저 좀 도와줄 수 있어요?
전지민:	뭐?
백찬일:	이 문제를 풀어 주세요. 전 못 하겠어요.
전지민:	난 수학은 잘 몰라. 그 문제 하나는 그냥 안 해도 되지 않아?
백찬일:	안 돼요. 도와주세요. 108 나누기 30 이 뭐예요?
전지민:	계산기를 써도 되지?
백찬일:	네, 써도 괜찮아요.
전지민:	그래. 그럼 도와줄게.
백찬일:	다음에 제가 맛있는 요리를 해 줄게요.
전지민:	아싸! 저번에 만들어 준 게 정말 맛있었어.
백찬일:	이번에 더 맛있게 해 줄게요.

"I'll do it for you"
Verb Stem + (을/ㄹ) 게(요)

You can use this form to say that you will do something for someone – like saying "I'll do it for you." Although this form will translate to English in a similar way as the regular future tense – "I *will*" – you can only use this when you, the speaker, are saying that you will do something for someone else; it can't be used to say that someone else will do something for someone (for that, use the regular *future tense*).

Chapter 13
Doing and Asking Favors

This form can be used in *informal* or *casual* speech, but should be avoided in formal situations. We'll cover how to use this in formal situations later in this chapter.

To make this form, take a verb stem and attach 을게 if it ends in a *consonant*, or attach ㄹ게 if it ends in a *vowel*. Then attach 요 (except when speaking casually).

하다 → 하
하 + ㄹ게요 → 할게요

먹다 → 먹
먹 + 을게요 → 먹을게요

Verb stems ending in ㄹ will simply attach 게요 (since the ㄹ goes away during the conjugation).

팔다 → 팔
팔 - ㄹ → 파
파 + ㄹ게요 → 팔게요

This form is pronounced differently from how it looks. The 게 at the end is *pronounced* 께, although it is still spelled 게. 할게요 would be pronounced 할께요, and 먹을게요 would be pronounced 먹을께요. Let's take a look at a few example sentences using this form.

제가 낼게요.
"I'll pay for it."

내가 밥 살게.
"I'll treat (you)."
"I'll buy (you) food."

나중에 쓸게요.
"I'll write it (for you) later."

Although this form means that you're doing something for someone else, it doesn't need to be an actual favor – it can be something so small that nobody would call it a favor.

잘 먹을게!
"Let's eat!"

The above sentence is a casual version of 잘 먹겠습니다, and can be used with or without a 요 at the end. Even though you're not doing anyone a favor by eating their food, you're simply saying that you're eating it for them – perhaps they wanted you to try it, or are buying you lunch.

182

Doing and Asking Favors

Chapter 13

그럼 갈게요.
"Well then, I'll go."

You can say this phrase when leaving, as if to say "I'll be off then." Although it's not doing the other person a favor (unless they really didn't want to hang out with you), you can use this form here because you're leaving in order to allow the other person to continue on with their day – you're leaving for them, even though it's not a favor.

Doing Real Favors
Verb Stem + 아/어/etc. + 주다

You can use this form to ask someone to do a real *favor* for you – it is equivalent to saying "please" at the beginning of a sentence.

"But we already learned that we can use 세요 to say 'please', right?" Well, it's true that the 세요 form is a polite way to ask someone to do something, and could also translate as "please." However, asking someone to do something for you with 세요 does not make it a favor; it's simply a polite way to make a *command* – 하세요 literally means "Do it (please)."

Using this form instead gives the meaning of asking for a real favor – asking someone to do something *for you* – instead of just telling someone nicely to do something using the 세요 form. Both can translate to "please," but this form will be useful for asking or doing real favors to others.

This form is also not appropriate for times when you need to be formal, but it's fine for all other situations. We'll learn a more formal version later in this chapter.

To make this form, take a verb and conjugate it to the 요 form. Then remove the 요, add a *space*, and then conjugate the verb 주다 ("to give") any way that you'd like in the sentence.

하다 → 해
해 + 주다 → 해 주다

팔다 → 팔아
팔아 + 주다 → 팔아 주다

같이 가 줄 수 있어요?
"Can you please go together with me (as a favor)?"

Doing and Asking Favors

그냥 해 주세요.
"Please just do it for me (as a favor)."

사진을 찍어 주세요.
"Please take a photo for me (as a favor)."

귀여운 멍멍이를 사 줬어요.
"He bought me a cute doggy (as a favor)."

제 친구가 같이 가 줬어요.
"My friend went together with me (as a favor)."

포장해 주세요.
"Please wrap it up for me (as a favor)."

Note that 포장(을) 하다 is the verb you'll use when ordering food "to go" from a restaurant. Another way to translate the above sentence would be "I'll get it to go."

> **Adv** Literally, using this form means "to give the act of (verb)" – 해 주다 would therefore mean "to give the act of doing."

Both of these forms (게요 and 주다) are also often combined together. As you might expect, when combined together they give the meaning that *you* (the speaker) are doing a real *favor* for someone else.

제가 해 줄게요.
"I'll do it for you."

파스타를 만들어 줄게요.
"I'll make pasta for you."

한국어를 가르쳐 줄게요.
"I'll teach you Korean."

내년에 새로운 핸드폰을 사 줄게요.
"I'll buy you a new cell phone next year."

Doing and Asking Favors

Chapter 13

Advanced

제발...

Another way to say "please" is by using the adverb 제발, which means "please." Using 제발 is a strong way to say "please" and should only be used when you are *begging* someone for something.

제발 가르쳐 주세요.
"Please, teach it to me."

Politely Doing Real Favors – 드리다

We learned that we can use verbs with the 주다 form to do real *favors* for others. When being more polite (such as to anyone older than yourself, or to a stranger), you can change 주다 to the *humble verb* 드리다 to show more respect to the person who you are doing the favor for.

This form should only be used when *you* are the one who is doing the favor, and not when talking about someone else doing a favor (for that, you can use the 주다 form instead).

제가 해 드릴게요.
"I'll do it for you."

물을 사 드릴게요.
"I'll buy you water."

제가 편지를 써 드릴게요.
"I'll write you a letter."

포장해 드릴게요.
"I'll wrap it up for you."

Doing and Asking Favors

Asking and Giving Permission
Verb Stem + 아/어/etc. + 도 되다

You can use this form to ask for *permission* – "Is it okay if (I)...?" Previously, we've only learned one way to ask permission:

저도 같이 갈 수 있어요?
"Can I go together?"

Using this new form will allow us to ask for permission in a different way, instead of only asking if you "can" do something.

To make this form, take a verb stem and conjugate it to the 요 form. Then remove the 요, and add 도 ("also," "even," "too"). Finally, use the verb 되다 and conjugate it any way that you'd like in the sentence.

하다 → 해
해 + 도 되다 → 해도 되다

먹다 → 먹어
먹어 + 도 되다 → 먹어도 되다

저도 가도 돼요?
"Is it okay if I go too?"

제가 먼저 먹어도 돼요?
"Is it okay if I eat first?"

There is an exception for the verb 이다 ("to be"). 이다 conjugates as 이어도 when used after a *consonant*, or 여도 when used after a *vowel*. The same applies to the verb 아니다, which becomes 아니어도.

이다 → 이어도 / 여도
아니다 → 아니어도

제가 학생이어도 되죠?
"It's okay if I'm a student, right?"

어제 선생님이 주신 숙제를 그냥 안 해도 되나요?
"Is it okay if I just don't do the homework that the teacher gave me yesterday?"

Doing and Asking Favors

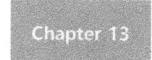

Chapter 13

사진을 같이 찍어도 될까요?
"Would it be okay if we took a photo together?"

Just as you can use this form to ask for permission, you can also use it to give permission.

이제 집에 가도 돼요.
"You can go home now."

숙제를 끝냈으니까 티비를 봐도 돼요.
"You can watch TV because you finished the homework."

> **Adv**: You might also commonly see 이다 as 이라도 after a *consonant*, or 라도 after a *vowel*. 아니다 can also similarly become 아니라도.

Now that we've learned the basics of doing and asking for favors, let's go over the conversation and get some additional practice.

백찬일: 지민 씨, 저 좀 도와줄 수 있어요?
"Ji-min, can you help me a bit?"

도와주다 and 도와 드리다

We previously learned that 도와주다 means "to help," but this verb originally comes from the *irregular verb* 돕다 ("to help") combined with 주다 ("to give"), and works just like the 주다 form we learned in this chapter. 도와주다 is much more commonly used than 돕다 (so common that it's written as one word), but you will still see 돕다 from time to time.

Because 도와주다 comes from this same form, we can also change 주다 to 드리다 and get the *humble verb* 도와 드리다.

도와 드리고 싶지만 시간이 없어서 못 합니다.
"I want to help you but I can't because I don't have time."

제가 도와 드릴까요?
"Shall I help you?"

숙제를 도와 드릴게요.
"I'll help you with your homework."

In the same way, we can also change the 주다 (from 도와주다) to 주시다 and get the *honorific verb* 도와주시다.

Chapter 13

Doing and Asking Favors

선생님이 저를 많이 도와주셨어요.
"The teacher helped me a lot."

전지민: 뭐?
"What?"

Judging by this casual reply, we can tell that 전지민 must be older than 백찬일, and also likely close (friends, etc.).

백찬일: 이 문제를 풀어 주세요. 전 못 하겠어요.
"Solve this problem for me. I can't do it."

풀다 can mean both "to solve" (such as in the conversation) or "to untie" (the opposite of 묶다 – "to tie").

전지민: 난 수학은 잘 몰라. 그 문제 하나는 그냥 안 해도 되지 않아?
"I don't know math well. Can't you just not do that one problem?"

You'll notice that this sentence uses two Topic Markers – in 난 and 수학은. While most sentences will only use one Topic Marker (or none), this sentence is an example of when using two is acceptable. You can think of this sentence as translating as the following: "As for me, when it comes to math, I don't know it well."

Even
Verb Stem + 아/어/etc. + 도

Literally, using this form (Verb Stem + 아/어/etc. + 도 되다) means "it's okay even if one does the act of (verb)." Saying 해도 돼요 would therefore mean "It's okay even if (someone) does it."

We can actually take this form apart and only use the first piece (아/어/etc. + 도) by itself to mean "even if (someone) does (verb)." This might sound a bit complicated, but we've actually already learned how to use it; you can use it in the exact same way as we've just learned when asking for and giving permission, but also in many more situations and with more verbs besides only 되다. Let's take a look at a few examples.

저도 가도 돼요?
"Is it okay (even) if I go too?"

저도 가도 괜찮아요?
"Is it alright (even) if I go too?"

Doing and Asking Favors

제가 먼저 시작해도 철수 씨가 안 도와줄 거예요.
"Even if I start it first Chul-soo won't help me."

제가 한국 사람이 아니라도 한국어를 할 수 있어요.
"I can speak Korean even though I'm not a Korean."

난 네가 안 먹어도 신경 안 써.
"I don't care even if you don't eat it."

신경(을) 쓰다 literally means "to use one's nerves," but it's used as an *idiom* to mean "to care" or "to mind." We'll learn more about idioms in the appendix of this book.

백찬일: 안 돼요. 도와주세요. 108 나누기 30 이 뭐예요?
"No. Help me. What's 108 divided by 30?"

Mathematics

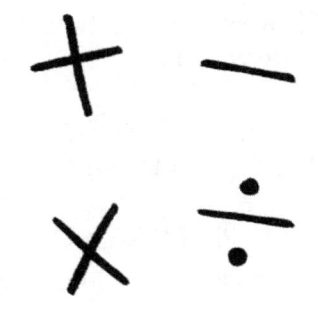

So I bet you've been wondering this whole time, "How can I calculate complex mathematic equations in Korean?" No? Anyone? Well, we won't cover that here, but we will cover a few of the most basic math-related concepts that you should know. Note that Sino Korean numbers (일, 이, 삼, ...) are used for mathematics.

Addition: To add numbers together, or to say "plus," use 더하기.

1 + 1 = 2
1 **더하기** 1 은 2 예요.
"1 plus 1 is 2."

Subtraction: To subtract numbers together, or to say "minus," use 빼기.

3 − 2 = 1
3 **빼기** 2 는 1 이에요.
"Three minus two is one."

Chapter 13: Doing and Asking Favors

Multiplication: To multiple numbers together, or to say "times," use 곱하기.

5 * 5 = 25
5 **곱하기** 5 는 25 예요.
"5 times 5 is 25."

Division: To divide numbers, or to say "divided by," use 나누기.

10 / 5 = 2
10 **나누기** 5 는 2 예요.
"10 divided by 5 is 2."

전지민: 계산기를 써도 되지?
"I can use a calculator, right?"

"To Calculate" – 계산(을) 하다

계산기 comes from 계산(을) 하다, which means "to calculate." But 계산(을) 하다 has an additional usage – "to take care of payment."

계산은 누가 할 거죠?
"Who's going to pay for it?"

제가 계산할게요.
"I'll take care of (paying for) it."

저기요! 여기 계산해 주세요.
"Excuse me! Please take care of payment here."
"Please bring us the bill."

백찬일: 네, 써도 괜찮아요.
"Yes, it's okay to use it."

This sentence is another example of using 도 with a verb besides 되다 – here, 괜찮다 ("to be okay," "to be alright").

전지민: 그래. 그럼 도와줄게.
"Okay. Then I'll help you."

Doing and Asking Favors

백찬일: 다음에 제가 맛있는 요리를 해 줄게요.
"Next time I'll make you some delicious food."

다음 means "next," and can be used with 에 as an *adverb* to mean "next time." On its own, 다음 can be used as an *adjective*.

다음에 같이 가요.
"Let's go together next time."

다음 게임을 보자.
"Let's watch the next game."

전지민: 아싸! 저번에 만들어 준 게 정말 맛있었어.
"Alright! The thing you made for me last time was really delicious."

You can shout 아싸 when you're excited about something – similarly to saying "Alright!" or "Yes!" in English. Note that because this is an *exclamation* (something that you shout out), it shouldn't be used in *formal* situations.

저번 means "last time." You can also use 지난번 to mean the same thing.

지난번에 우리가 여기 왔을 때 같이 먹은 게 뭐였지?
"What was it that we ate together the last time when we came here?"

We previously learned that the 에 particle is *optional* when used after 어디; it's also *optional* after 여기, 거기, and 저기.

이번 means "this time." In addition, it can be used as an *adjective* when talking about an event, or a time.

이번에 더 빨리 가르쳐 줄게요.
"I'll teach you faster this time."

이번 학기가 더 어려울까요?
"Would this semester be more difficult?"

이번 토요일에 만날 거예요.
"We'll meet this Saturday"

다음번 means "next time." It can be used in the same way as 다음, but can only refer to the actual *time* ("next time") and *cannot* be used as an adjective.

Chapter 13: Doing and Asking Favors

다음번에는 그냥 사이다를 마시자.
"Next time, let's just drink soda."

백찬일: 이번에 더 맛있게 해 줄게요.
"This time I'll make it even more delicious."

하다 and 만들다

While 해 줄게요 means "I'll *do* it for you," often the verb 하다 can replace the verb 만들다 ("to make"). The verb 하다 can be used with a variety of adverbs in this way. Let's just take a look at a few examples.

맛있게 하다 – "to make it (taste) delicious"

맛있게 해 주세요.
"Please make it taste delicious."

멋있게 하다 – "to make it (look) cool"

이발사가 제 머리를 멋있게 해 줬어요.
"The barber made my hair look cool."

재미있게 하다 – "to make it entertaining," "to make it fun"

동영상을 재미있게 해 줄게요.
"I'll make the video entertaining."

Practice

Translate to Korean:

1. "Please go to the store (for me)."

   _____.

2. "I'll write the essay for you."

   _____.

Doing and Asking Favors

3. "Can I take a little rest?"

   _____.

4. "What's 2 times 3?"

   _____.

5. "I don't care even if you go."

   _____.

6. "Please do the dishes and the laundry."

   _____.

7. "I can learn Korean even if I'm an American."

   _____.

8. "Can I go home now?"

   _____.

9. "Even if I leave now I'll be late."

   _____.

10. "Even if I eat I'm always hungry."

    _____.

Translate to English:

11. 내일까지 할게요.

    _____.

Chapter 13 — **Doing and Asking Favors**

12. 800 나누기 50 은 16 이 맞아요?

_____.

13. 지금 안 해도 괜찮아요.

_____.

14. 날 항상 도와주셨어.

_____.

15. 제가 계산해도 될까요?

_____.

16. 도와 드리고 싶지만 지금 바빠서 못 합니다.

_____.

17. 다음에 도와주시겠어요?

_____.

18. 날씨가 덥지 않아도 난 안 갈래.

_____.

19. 자기소개를 해 주세요.

_____.

20. 아빠가 자동차로 여기까지 데리고 와 주셨어요.

_____.

Doing and Asking Favors

Chapter 13

New Phrases

내일 뵐게요.	"I'll see you tomorrow." (hum.)
아싸!	"Alright!," "Yes!"

New Vocabulary

멍멍이	"doggy"
야옹이	"kitty"
포장(을) 하다	"to wrap up (to go)"
도와 드리다	"to help" (hum.)
돕다	"to help"
풀다	"to untie," "to solve"
문제(를) 풀다	"to solve a problem"
묶다	"to tie"
스트레스	"stress"
스트레스(를) 풀다	"to relieve stress"
신경	"nerve"
신경(을) 쓰다	"to care," "to mind"
더하기	"plus" [addition]
빼기	"minus" [subtraction]
곱하기	"times" [multiplication]
나누기	"divided by" [division]
계산기	"calculator"
계산(을) 하다	"to calculate," "to take care of payment"
영수증	"receipt"
잔돈	"(money) change"
청구서	"a bill (for payment)"
신용 카드	"credit card"
체크 카드	"debit card" (literally, "check card")
지폐	"paper money," "bills"
현금	"cash"
동전	"coins"
수표	"(bank) check"

Chapter 13: Doing and Asking Favors

여권	"passport" (pronounced 여꿘)
신분증	"identification (card)"
다음	"next" (adjective)
지난	"last" (adjective)
다음에	"next time"
저번	"last time"
지난번	"last time"
이번	"this time," "this"
다음번	"next time"
이발사	"barber"
이발소	"barbershop"
동영상	"video"
바닥	"the floor," "the ground"
금	"gold"
은	"silver"
금색	"gold (color)"
은색	"silver (color)"
올빼미	"owl"
늑대	"wolf"
토끼	"rabbit"
파리	"fly"
벌	"bee"
모기	"mosquito"
풀	"grass"
흙	"dirt," "soil"
직접	"directly" (adverb)
간접	"indirectly" (adverb)
세다	"to count"
무게	"weight"
몸무게	"bodyweight"
에세이	"essay"
자기소개	"self introduction"
자기소개(를) 하다	"to introduce oneself"

Don't

Chapter 14

Conversation

택시 기사:	자동차 안에서 먹지 마세요.
동수:	아, 죄송합니다. 그러면 조금 잘게요.
택시 기사:	곧 도착할 거니까 지금 자면 안 돼요.
동수:	네, 알겠습니다.
택시 기사:	거의 다 왔어요. 앞에 차가 많으니까 여기서 내리면 좋겠어요.
동수:	감사합니다. 여기서 내릴게요.
택시 기사:	아, 잠시만 기다려 주세요! 돈을 안 내면 안 되죠?

Don't: Verb Stem + 지 말다

Up until now we've been unable to say "don't" (and we've just accepted everything that's happened). While saying "don't" can be rude in any language depending on how it's used, there are still times when you will need to use it.

197

Chapter 14

Don't

To say "don't," we'll use the verb 말다. This verb is not used by itself, but means "to stop" or "to not do."

To make this form, take a verb stem (an *action verb*) and attach 지. Then, conjugate the verb 말다; for example, you could change it to 마세요, or 말아 주세요, among others.

하다 → 하
하 + 지 → 하지 + 말다

먹다 → 먹
먹 + 지 말다 → 먹지 말다

놀다 → 놀
놀 + 지 말다 → 놀지 말다

> 그렇게 빨리 먹지 마세요. 배가 아플 거예요.
> "Don't eat so quickly. Your stomach will hurt."

> 하지 마!
> "Don't (do it)!"

Note that conjugating 말다 to 마 is for *casual speech* only.

> 저를 쳐다보지 말아 주세요.
> "Please don't stare at me."

> 그러지 마요.
> "Don't be that way."

Although 마요 uses a 요, it's not entirely polite because you're still telling someone "don't." Be careful when using this to people who aren't close to you, but feel free to use it with older friends (or in situations when you'd normally use *informal speech*).

> **Advanced**
>
> You can also use 말다 with "let's" to say "let's not."
>
> > 그냥 가지 말자.
> > "Let's just not go."
>
> > 하지 말자.
> > "Let's not (do it)."

Now that we've covered how to say "don't," let's move onto the conversation.

Don't

Chapter 14

택시 기사: 자동차 안에서 먹지 마세요.
"Please don't eat inside of the car."

동수: 아, 죄송합니다. 그러면 조금 잘게요.
"Ah, I'm sorry. Well then I'll just sleep a little."

> **Advanced**
>
> Another use of the 게요 form is for giving a *response* to someone about something that you are going to do. Let's take a look at two examples:
>
> 1. 먹을 거예요.
> 2. 먹을게요.
> "I'll eat it."
>
> The first sentence means that they are going to eat it regardless of what is happening – it's simply a plain sentence ("I'll eat it."). While the second sentence translates the same way in English, it is being said in *response* to something that someone else said. Perhaps someone had just asked them if they will eat something, so the second sentence could be a response to that; it means that you're *responding* to them and are not simply saying a plain sentence. If you were to instead reply with the first sentence, it would sound a bit like saying "I'm going to eat it, *no matter* what you say." The second sentence, however, sounds a bit more like "I'm going to eat it, *because* of what you just said."
>
> This is the reason that the 게요 form can be used when you're doing something for someone else, even if it's not a real favor, because you're using it as a *response* to something or someone.
>
> Using 조금 잘게요 is as a *response* to what the driver said – "Please don't eat inside of the car."

택시 기사: 곧 도착할 거니까 지금 자면 안 돼요.
"You shouldn't sleep because we'll arrive soon."

Sometimes saying "don't" can be rude (such as in a *formal* situation, or when you want to sound polite), so in those cases there can be better to say what you mean – "should not." And while we'll already be learning how to say "should not," let's also learn how to say "should."

Should Not: Verb Stem + (으)면 안 되다

Literally, saying "should not" in Korean is saying "It is not okay if...."

To make this form, take a verb stem and attach 으면 if it ends in a *consonant*, or attach 면 if it ends in a *vowel* (just as we learned in Chapter 2). Then attach 안, followed by 되다 ("to be okay"). Let's take a look at a few examples.

빨간 불에 길을 건너면 안 돼요.
"You shouldn't cross the street at a red light."

Don't

제가 하면 안 되나요?
"Should I not do it?"

술을 마시고 운전하면 안 됩니다.
"You should not drink and drive."

그렇게 빨리 먹으면 안 돼요.
"You shouldn't eat so quickly."

신발 신고 방에 들어가면 안 되죠.
"You should not wear shoes and go in the room."

죄송하지만, 여기서 사진을 찍으시면 안 됩니다.
"I'm sorry, but you should not take photographs here."

The above example could also translate to "I'm sorry, but you *can't* take photographs here." Using "should not" though sounds a bit more polite, and might be something that a security guard could say.

Also note that 여기에서 is often shortened to 여기서, just as 어디에서 is often shortened to 어디서. The same applies to 거기에서 (거기서) and 저기에서 (저기서).

Should: Verb Stem + 는 것이 좋겠다

Saying "should" in Korean is a bit different from "should not."

To make this form, take a verb stem (of an *action verb*) and attach 는. Then attach 것이 (or 게), followed by 좋겠다 (the *future tense* of 좋다).

하다 → 하는 것이 좋겠다
먹다 → 먹는 것이 좋겠다

Verb stems ending in ㄹ will conjugate as if they ended in a *vowel* instead.

팔다 → 파는 것이 좋겠다

Let's take a look at a few examples.

오늘 숙제하는 게 좋겠어요.
"You should do the homework today."

오늘은 집에 있는 게 좋겠어요.
"You should stay home for today."

Don't

제가 병원으로 가는 게 좋겠어요?
"Should I go to the hospital?"

한국어를 더 열심히 공부하면 좋아요.
"You should study Korean harder."

이제 공부를 시작하는 게 좋겠어요.
"You should start studying now."

Should: Verb Stem + (으)면 좋겠다

Another similar way to say "should" is by using (으)면 좋겠다 – literally, "It will be good if...." Although this form is less commonly used, you should still be aware of it. This works in the same grammatical way as the form we learned for "should not."

지금 하면 좋겠어요.
"It'll be good if you do it now."
"You should do it now."

잘되면 좋겠어요.
"It'll be good if it goes well."

잘되다 means "to go well" – its opposite is 잘 안 되다 ("to not go well").

This form also has one more usage – "(I/you) hope (that)."

잘되면 좋겠어요.
"I hope (that) it goes well."

진짜가 아니면 좋겠어요.
"I hope (that) it's not real."

내일 쉴 수 있으면 좋겠어요.
"I hope (that) I can rest tomorrow."

Don't

Should: Verb Stem + 는 것이 낫다

Although it's common and fine to use either of the 좋겠다 forms to say "should," there is an even better, and more common way – using 낫다 ("to be preferable," "to be better").

낫다 is an *irregular verb*, and the ㅅ goes away when conjugating it. In the 요 form, it becomes 나아요. However, in other forms, it will conjugate as if its verb stem ended in a *consonant* – for example, when used with (으)면 it will become 나으면, and in past tense it will become 나았다. Here's a quick example of 낫다:

그것보다 이게 나을 거예요.
"This will be more preferable than that."
"This will be *better* than that."

Let's look at a few examples.

가는 게 나아요.
"You should go."

그것보다 이걸 사는 게 나아요.
"You should buy this instead of that."

모르는 길은 천천히 가는 게 나아요.
"When it comes to roads you don't know, you should go slowly."

In addition, this form can also be used to mean "should not," by simply using a *negative verb*.

안 가는 게 나아요.
"You should not go."

그분을 안 믿는 게 나아요.
"You should not trust him."

비가 올 때 운전하지 않는게 나아요.
"You should not drive when it rains."

동수: 네, 알겠습니다.

"Okay, I understand."

택시 기사: 거의 다 왔어요. 앞에 차가 많으니까 여기서 내리면 좋겠어요.

"We've almost arrived. It'll be good if you get off here because there are a lot of cars in front of us."

Almost (On Purpose): 거의

In English, "almost" can be used in two different situations – when you almost did something *on purpose*, and when you almost did something *by mistake*.

On Purpose: "I almost finished all of my homework."
By Mistake: "I almost died!"

Don't

Chapter 14

Both sentences would use the same "almost" in English, but in Korean these would be different.

거의 is an *adverb* that means "almost." You can use it whenever what you almost *do* (or what you almost *are*) is *on purpose*.

숙제를 거의 다 했어요.
"I almost finished all of my homework."

다 is an *adverb* that means "all." We'll talk more about 다 soon. 거의 and 다 are frequently combined (거의 다), and together mean "almost all."

그 사람은 거의 한국 사람이에요.
"That person is almost a Korean."

거의 같아요.
"It's almost the same."

책을 거의 다 읽었어요.
"I read almost all of the book."

Almost (By Mistake): Verb Stem + (을/ㄹ) 뻔하다

In order to say "almost" for something that was *by mistake*, use the verb 뻔하다 instead of the *adverb* 거의.

To make this form, take a verb stem and attach 을 if it ends in a *consonant*, or attach ㄹ if it ends in a *vowel*. Then conjugate the verb 뻔하다 – this will usually be in *past tense*.

하다 → 하
하 + ㄹ 뻔하다 → 할 뻔하다

먹다 → 먹
먹 + 을 뻔하다 → 먹을 뻔하다

The three rules for verbs that we learned in Chapter 2 also apply to this form.

정말 죽을 뻔했어요!
"I really almost died!"

넘어질 뻔했어요.
"I almost fell down."

203

Chapter 14

Don't

개 똥을 밟을 뻔했어요.
"I almost stepped on dog poop."

어제 아침에 못 일어날 뻔했어요.
"I almost couldn't wake up yesterday morning."

버스를 놓칠 뻔했어요.
"I almost missed the bus."

놓치다 means "to miss," and can be used for anything from the bus to an *opportunity*. It can't be used for a person though – remember to use 보고 싶다 for "to miss (a person)."

"All" – 다

다 is an *adverb* that means "all."

이미 다 먹었어요.
"I already ate it all."

숙제를 다 했어요.
"I did all of the homework."

다 좋아해요.
"I like it all."

아이들은 다 그래요.
"Kids are all that way."

다 봤어요.
"I saw it all."

다 can also have the meaning of "finish" when used with *action verbs*.

이미 다 먹었어요.
"I already finished eating it."

숙제를 다 했어요.
"I finished the homework."

다 오다 ("to all come") means "to arrive," and can be used in the same way as 도착(을) 하다.

Don't

다 왔어요!
"We've arrived!"

"Every" – 모든

모든 is an *adjective*, and means "every." While we already learned many words with "every" in them – 매주 ("every week"), 매일 ("every day"), etc. – you can use 모든 in all other situations to mean "every" where there is not already a separate word.

모든 사람들이 그렇게 생각해요.
"Every person thinks so."

그 남자는 모든 여자들의 이상형이에요.
"That man is every girl's type."

모든 걸 다 잘할 수는 없지?
"You can't do everything (all) well, right?"

"Most" – 대부분

While 대부분 means "most" or "for the most part," it's most often used to mean "most *people*." It can be used as both a *noun* (when placed *before* what it's describing – using the particle 의), or as an *adverb* (when placed *after* what it's describing). Here are a few examples:

대부분 그래요.
"Most (people) are like that."

대부분의 사람들은 8시간 정도 잠을 자요.
"Most people sleep about 8 hours."

한국 사람들은 대부분 빵보다 밥을 더 좋아해요.
"Most Koreans like rice more than bread."

대부분의 학생들은 시험을 위해 공부를 해요.
"Most students study for tests."

동수: 감사합니다. 여기서 내릴게요.
"Thank you. I'll get off here."

Chapter 14

Don't

택시 기사: 아, 잠시만 기다려 주세요! 돈을 안 내면 안 되죠?

"Ah, wait just one moment! You shouldn't not pay, right?"

잠시 and 잠깐

잠시 is a *adverb* that means "a short while" or "a moment." It is *polite*, and can be used in any *formal* situation.

잠시 시간이 있으세요?
"Do you have a moment of time?"

잠시만 기다려 주세요.
"Please wait only a moment."

Optionally, you can also attach 만 to add the meaning of "only."

When speaking *informally* or *casually*, there is a different word that you can use instead – 잠깐.

잠깐만 기다려 줘.
"Please wait a moment."

친구 집에 잠깐 있었어.
"I was at my friend's house for a short while."

잠깐만 can also be used on its own (in *informal* speech).

잠깐만....
"Just a moment...."

Practice

Translate to Korean:

1. "Don't swim here."

_____.

2. "You shouldn't start now."

_____.

Don't

Chapter 14

3. "I almost fell asleep."

_____.

4. "Please don't go in this room."

_____.

5. "I drank all of the milk."

_____.

6. "Every house has a bathroom."

_____.

7. "Most people think so."

_____.

8. "Don't touch the wall. I just painted it."

_____.

Translate to English:

9. 오늘은 밖에 나가지 마세요.

_____.

10. 병원에서 뛰지 말아 주세요.

_____.

11. 그렇게 말하지 마요.

_____.

Chapter 14 — Don't

12. 오늘은 우산을 가져가는 게 좋겠어요.

_____.

13. 야채가 더 많으면 좋겠어요.

_____.

14. 아직 먹으면 안 돼.

_____.

15. 제 노트북을 떨어뜨릴 뻔했어요.

_____.

16. 거의 다 왔어요.

_____.

New Vocabulary

쳐다보다	"to stare"
건너다	"to cross"
낫다	"to be preferable," "to be better"
택시 기사	"taxi driver"
기사	"driver"
곧	"soon" (adverb)
거의	"almost" (adverb)
거의 다	"almost all" (adverb)
놓치다	"to miss"
기회	"opportunity"
넘어지다	"to fall down," "to trip"
밟다	"to step on"
다	"all" (adverb)
다 오다	"to arrive"

Don't

모든	"every" (adjective)
이상형	"(ideal) type"
내리다	"to get off (a vehicle)"
올리다	"to get on (a vehicle)"
잠시	"a short while," "a moment"
잠시만	"only a short while," "just a moment"
잠깐	"a short while," "a moment" (informal)
잠깐만	"only a short while," "just a moment" (informal)
서두르다	"to rush," "hurry"
주차(를) 하다	"to park"
주차장	"parking lot"
중고	"used," "secondhand" (adjective)
중고차	"used car," "secondhand car"
총	"gun"
총(을) 쏘다	"to shoot a gun"
사냥	"hunting"
사냥(을) 하다	"to hunt"
감옥	"jail"
법(률)	"law," "legislation"
법학	"(study of) law"
삭제(를) 하다	"to delete"
저장(을) 하다	"to save"
복사(를) 하다	"to copy," "to duplicate"
프린트(를) 하다	"to print"
온라인	"online"
오프라인	"offline"
치다	"to type"
검색(을) 하다	"to search"
연결(을) 하다	"to connect"
공기	"air"
교환(을) 하다	"to exchange"
교환학생	"exchange student"
대부분	"most"

Chapter 14: Don't

잘되다	"to go well"
잘 안 되다	"to not go well"
페인트(를) 칠하다	"to paint"
잠(이) 들다	"to fall asleep"

More Negative Sentences

Chapter 15

Conversation

양태용: 저는 한국인 친구가 1 명밖에 없어요.

김영희: 저도 1 명 정도 있어요.

양태용: 영희 씨는 한국 사람인데 한국인 친구가 1 명밖에 없어요?

김영희: 네, 불쌍하죠? 제가 나쁜 사람도 아닌데요.

양태용: 그러네요! 정말 착한 사람이에요. 근데 왜 아무도 안 놀아 줘요?

김영희: 하하. 저는 친구를 쉽게 못 만드는 사람이에요.

양태용: 친구 없이 재미없죠? 아니면 혼자가 좋아요?

김영희: 저는 어릴 때부터 친구가 많이 없었어요. 그래도 괜찮아요. 태용 씨가 있으니까요.

양태용: 그렇죠!

Negative Verbs and 도

In the previous book we learned about how to use *negative verbs* (such as 없다 and 모르다). There are more things that we can do with these negative verbs to add flavor to our sentences. We'll learn several of the most common uses in this chapter, but first let's start with the basics. So far we've only learned how to use these negative verbs on their own. For example:

저는 그분을 몰라요.
"I don't know him."

211

Chapter 15: More Negative Sentences

If we add the particle 도 ("also," "even," "too"), we can get a slightly different meaning.

저는 그분도 몰라요.
"I don't know him either."

Note that the above sentence literally means "I don't know him too." Let's look at another example with 도.

저는 커피를 살 돈도 없어요.
"I don't even have the money to buy coffee."

But 도 isn't the only thing that we can use to add flavor to our negative sentences. There are also *adverbs* which can *only* be used in negative sentences, such as 절대로 ("never"), 전혀 ("not at all"), 별로 ("not really"), and 그다지 ("not that," "not so"). Let's take a look at each of them.

절대로 담배를 피우지 마세요.
"Never smoke."

Note that 절대로 is *not* used to mean "never" when saying "I've *never* done something before." We'll cover how to say that you have or haven't done something before in Chapter 18. 절대로 is most commonly used with the 말다 form, as in the above example.

전혀 좋아하지 않아요.
"I don't like it at all."

별로 재미없는데요.
"It's not really that fun."

그다지 어렵지 않아요.
"It's not so hard."

그다지 is similar to 그렇게, but is only used in negative sentences.

> **Adv** 그다지 is often shortened to 그닥.

We'll learn more about negative sentences in the conversation, so let's go ahead and jump right in.

양태용: 저는 한국인 친구가 1명밖에 없어요.
"I only have one Korean friend."

More Negative Sentences

"Korean friend" is normally 한국인 친구, but 한국 친구 is also fine. "American friend" would be 미국인 친구 or 미국 친구, "Japanese friend" would be 일본인 친구 or 일본 친구, and so on.

밖에 + Negative Verb

We previously learned that 밖에 means "outside."

고양이는 집 밖에 있어요.
"The cat is outside of the house."

밖에 can also be used with *negative verbs* to mean "only" or "nothing but." When used this way, it is attached *directly* to the word it follows, without a space.

저는 바나나밖에 안 먹어요.
"I only eat bananas."
"I eat nothing but bananas."

1,000 원밖에 없어요.
"I only have 1,000 Won."
"I have nothing but 1,000 Won."

한국어밖에 할 수 없어요.
"I can only speak Korean."
"I can speak nothing but Korean."

> **Advanced**
>
> ### 밖에 and 만
>
> Even though we've now learned how to use 밖에 with negative sentences, know that this doesn't mean that you have to use 밖에 in every sentence. You're still free to use 만, just as before.
>
> 3 개밖에 안 먹었어요.
> 3 개만 먹었어요.
> "I ate only 3."
>
> Using 밖에 instead of 만 (in negative sentences) adds more emphasis to the meaning of "only" or "nothing but," but the overall meaning of the sentence will not change.

김영희: 저도 1 명 정도 있어요.

"I also have about 1."

양태용: 영희 씨는 한국 사람인데 한국인 친구가 1 명밖에 없어요?

"You're Korean but you only have 1 Korean friend?"

Chapter 15

More Negative Sentences

김영희: 네, 불쌍하죠? 제가 나쁜 사람도 아닌데요.
"Yeah, it's pitiful, huh? I'm not even a bad person."

Not Even: 도 아니다

This isn't really a new concept, but it's worth reviewing. Using the particle 도 with the negative verb 아니다 ("to not be") gives us the meaning of "not even."

마이크 씨가 한국 사람도 아닌데 한국어를 유창하게 말할 수 있어요.
"Mike isn't even a Korean, but he can speak Korean fluently."

제가 원숭이도 아닌데 요즘은 매일 바나나밖에 안 먹고 있어요.
"I'm not even a monkey, but lately I'm eating nothing but bananas."

양태용: 그러네요! 정말 착한 사람이에요. 근데 왜 아무도 안 놀아 줘요?
"Yeah! You're a really nice person. But why doesn't anyone hang out with you?"

착하다 is a more *informal* (or *casual*) way to say 친절하다 ("to be nice"), and means "to be nice" or "to be friendly."

근데 is a shortened version of 그런데 ("but," "however"), which is the 데 form of the *descriptive verb* 그렇다 ("to be so").

Nobody & Nothing: 아무도 and 아무것도

아무도 means "nobody," and is only used in *negative* sentences.

아무도 안 왔어요.
"Nobody came."

아무도 그 새로운 영화를 좋아하지 않아요.
"Nobody likes that new movie."

여기 아무도 없어요.
"There's nobody here."

아무것도 means "nothing" or "anything," and is also only used in *negative* sentences.

오늘 아무것도 안 먹었어요.
"I didn't eat anything today."

More Negative Sentences

Chapter 15

여기 아무것도 없어요.
"There's nothing here."

아무것도 말하지 마세요.
"Don't say anything."

Any: 아무

On its own, 아무 is an *adjective* that means "any," and can be attached before a *noun* (just like "any" in English). This word can be used in both *positive* or *negative* sentences.

아무 자리에 앉아도 돼요.
"You can sit in any seat."

아무 사람이라도 괜찮아요.
"Even if it's any person, it's okay."
"Any person is okay."

철수 씨는 아무 이유 없이 나갔어요.
"Chul-soo left without any reason."

아무 문제도 없었어요.
"There wasn't (even) any problem."

In the above example, 아무 and 도 are separated from each other with the word 문제 ("problem").

Anybody & Anything: 아무나 and 아무것이나

You can use 아무나 and 아무것이나 (or its more-common shortened version, 아무거나) in *positive* sentences as well. 아무나 ("anybody") is the positive version of 아무도 ("nobody"), and 아무것이나 ("anything") is the positive version of 아무것도 ("nothing").

아무나 와도 돼요.
"Anyone can come."

아무나 좀 도와주세요.
"Anyone please help me a bit."

아무거나 먹어도 상관없어.
"For me, it doesn't matter even if we eat anything."
"It doesn't matter whatever we eat."

Chapter 15

More Negative Sentences

아무거나 해도 돼요.
"You can do anything."

Anytime: 아무때나

You can also use 아무때나 to mean "anytime." The 때 here is the same one that we learned in Chapter 2, and means "time."

아무때나 연락 주세요.
"Contact me anytime."

저는 아무때나 괜찮아요.
"For me, anytime's okay."

김영희: 하하. 저는 친구를 쉽게 못 만드는 사람이에요.
"Haha. I'm not someone who can make friends easily."

Notice how the expression "to make friends" is the same in Korean as it is in English – 친구를 만들다.

양태용: 친구 없이 재미없죠? 아니면 혼자가 좋아요?
"It's not fun without any friends, is it? Or do you like being alone?"

"Alone" & "By Oneself" – 혼자(서) & 스스로

혼자(서) is an adverb that means "alone." The 서 is *optional* when used together with an *action verb*, but when used with a *descriptive verb* (such as 좋다), the 서 is dropped.

혼자서 공부했어요.
"I studied alone (and nobody else was there with me)."

Another word that can seem similar to 혼자(서) is 스스로, which means "by oneself." 스스로 can be used to say that you did something without any help, and not to say that you are alone.

스스로 공부했어요.
"I studied on my own (and nobody helped)."

More Negative Sentences

Chapter 15

Or: 아니면

To say "or," use 아니면. Literally, 아니면 means "if not," and comes from the verb 아니다 ("to not be").

You can use 아니면 when asking someone to *choose* between two options – for example, "Do you like milk *or* juice?"

우유 아니면 주스를 좋아해요?
"Do you like milk or juice?"

김치를 좋아해요? 아니면 싫어해요?
"Do you like kimchi? Or do you dislike it?"

갈 거예요? 아니면 안 갈 거예요?
"Are you going? Or are you not going?"

> **Advanced**
>
> Note that in the above example 아니면 is used after the end of the first question – "Are you going?" In English, this would all be said as one sentence – "Are you going or not?" If you're giving someone a choice between two *things* (such as milk or juice), then 아니면 will appear between them in the *same* sentence, but when giving someone a choice between two *verbs* (such as going or not going), 아니면 will appear at the start of the *second* sentence instead.
>
> 아들이에요? 아니면 딸이에요?
> "Is it a boy? Or is it a girl?"
>
> 나랑 같이 갈래? 아니면 여기 있을 거야?
> "Do you wanna go with me? Or do you wanna stay here?"

Or (something): Noun + (이)나

Another way to say "or" is by using (이)나. Using (이)나 is different from using 아니면.

Chapter 15: More Negative Sentences

To use it, take a noun and attach 이나 if it ends in a *consonant*, or attach 나 if it ends in a *vowel*.

Using (이)나 is different from 아니면 for two reasons. First, it can only be used with nouns (아니면 can be used with both *nouns* and *verbs*). More importantly, it is *not* used when asking someone to choose between two options. Although it can translate as "or," it can also translate as "or *something*." For example, take a look at this sentence:

저는 빵이나 치즈를 먹을 거예요.
"I'll eat bread or cheese."

This sentence is not saying that there is a choice, but is only listing two things – bread or cheese. Because it uses (이)나, it means that the speaker *does not care* whether they eat bread or cheese. If you wanted to say that you will eat bread, or you will eat cheese (and are therefore choosing one of them), you would need to use 아니면.

저는 빵 아니면 치즈를 먹을 거예요.
"I'll eat bread or cheese."

Using 아니면 means that there is a *choice*, so it means that the speaker will eat bread, *or* cheese, but definitely not both. If the speaker eats bread, then they won't eat cheese, and vice versa.

Using (이)나 means that there is *no choice*, so it means that the speaker does not care whether they eat bread or cheese, or both, or even neither. Let's look at another example.

과일이나 야채를 먹고 싶어요.
"I want to eat fruits or vegetables (or something)."

To help make it easier to understand, I added "or something" in parentheses. If the speaker doesn't end up eating fruit or vegetables, they probably wouldn't mind, since they used (이)나 in the sentence.

(이)나 can also mean "or somewhere" when used with *locations*, such as in this example:

집이나 학교로 갈까?
"Should we go home or to school (or somewhere)?"

To summarize, if you're giving someone an *option*, use 아니면. If you're simply listing things and the choice *does not matter*, use (이)나.

More Negative Sentences

Chapter 15

Advanced

Because (이)나 means "or (something)," it can also be used on its own, and does not need to be used with two different nouns – you can use it after *one* single noun too.

김치나 넣을까요?
"Should I put in kimchi or something?"

그냥 옷이나 사.
"Just buy clothes or something."

Although (이)나 can be used by itself, it won't often be used by itself with the verbs 있다 or 없다. Instead of asking "김치나 없어요?" it would be better to ask "김치나 뭐 없어요?" ("Do you have kimchi or something?") using 뭐 (here, meaning "something"). You can read more about using 뭐 to mean "something" in the "Advanced Notes" in Chapter 7.

Or (something): Verb Stem + 거나

While (이)나 can only be used with *nouns*, 거나 can only be used with *verbs*.

To use it, take a verb stem and attach 거나.

오후에 학교에 가거나 도서관에 갈 거예요.
"I'll go to school in the afternoon or go to the library (or something)."

한국어를 공부하거나 음악을 들어요.
"I'll study Korean or listen to music (or something)."

Just like when using (이)나, this form is not used for presenting *options* – for that, use 아니면 instead.

Adv

Another word that you can use is 혹은, which has the same meaning as 아니면, but is *Sino Korean* (originally comes from Chinese).

김영희: 저는 어릴 때부터 친구가 많이 없었어요. 그래도 괜찮아요. 태용 씨가 있으니까요.

"I haven't had a lot of friends since I was young. Anyway I'm okay. Because I have you."

그래도 comes from the verb 그렇다, conjugated to the "even" form we learned previously (Verb Stem + 아/어/etc. + 도). It means "even so," but can also translate to "still" or "anyway."

양태용: 그렇죠!

"Yeah!"

Chapter 15: More Negative Sentences

Practice

Translate to Korean:

1. "Never tell another person."

   _____.

2. "Chul-soo isn't my type at all."

   _____.

3. "That color doesn't really suit you."

   _____.

4. "I don't have anything I can give as a present."

   _____.

5. "Bring anyone."

   _____.

6. "Do you want to eat shrimp, or lobster?"

   _____.

7. "Should we study in the library or a cafe (or somewhere)?"

   _____.

8. "It's not even my birthday today, but I got a lot of presents."

   _____.

9. "Please give me water or soda (or something)."

   _____.

More Negative Sentences

Chapter 15

10. "On the plane I'll watch a movie or sleep (or something)."

_____.

Translate to English:

11. 집도 없고 차도 없어요.

_____.

12. 제가 해 줄 수 있는 것도 없어요.

_____.

13. 전혀 비슷하지 않아요.

_____.

14. 유럽에서는 영국밖에 아는 나라가 없어요.

_____.

15. 요즘은 아무도 저에게 연락하지 않아요.

_____.

16. 미국 사람이세요? 아니면 캐나다 사람이세요?

_____.

17. 아무거나 마실 것 좀 주세요.

_____.

18. 저는 아무 색이나 다 잘 어울려요.

_____.

Chapter 15: More Negative Sentences

19. 너도 그다지 잘한 건 없잖아.

_____.

20. 선물로 꽃이나 인형은 어때요?

_____.

New Vocabulary

절대로	"never" (negative)
전혀	"not at all" (negative)
그다지	"not that," "not so" (negative)
별로	"not really" (negative)
담배	"cigarette," "tobacco"
피(우)다	"to smoke"
끊다	"to quit" (smoking, etc.)
그만두다	"to quit" (job, etc.)
불쌍하다	"to be pitiful," "to be poor"
유창하다	"to be fluent"
착하다	"to be nice," "to be friendly"
근데	"but," "however"
그런데	"but," "however"
그렇지만	"nevertheless," "however"
아무	"any"
아무도	"nobody" (negative)
아무것도	"nothing," "anything" (negative)
혼자(서)	"alone" (adverb)
스스로	"by oneself" (adverb)
주스	"juice"
아니면	"or"
(이)나	"or (something)"
그래도	"even so," "still," "anyway"
키위	"kiwi"
이유	"reason," "cause"

More Negative Sentences

상관없다	"to not matter"
상관있다	"to matter"
둘다	"both (of them)" (noun)
어울리다	"to match well," "to suit," "to go with"
연락(을) 하다	"to contact"
캐나다	"Canada"
마늘	"garlic"
뿌리	"root"
특히	"especially," "particularly" (adverb)

Chapter 15: More Negative Sentences

Have to Do

Chapter 16

Conversation

상현:	저는 지금 나가야 돼요. 밤까지 여기 있을 거예요?
수빈:	네... 하지만 8시 전에 친구를 만나러 나갈 거예요.
상현:	그럼 설거지 좀 해 주세요.
수빈:	꼭 오늘 해야 하나요?
상현:	네, 내일 어머니가 오셔서요.
수빈:	알았어요. 나가기 전에 할게요.

Have to Do: Verb Stem + 아/어/etc. + 야 되다

You can use this form to say that you "have to" *do* something. It can also translate as "need to," so feel free to translate it either way.

To make it, take a verb stem and conjugate it to the 요 form, but remove the 요. Then attach 야, followed by the verb 되다 – conjugated in any way that you'd like.

하다 → 해
해 + 야 되다 → 해야 되다

먹다 → 먹어
먹어 + 야 되다 → 먹어야 되다

Have to Do

Chapter 16

차갑다 → 차가워
차가워 + 야 되다 → 차가워야 되다

밥을 먹어야 돼요.
"I have to eat."

그 책을 내일까지 다 읽어야 되죠?
"You have to read all of that book by tomorrow, right?"

난 빨리 가야 돼!
"I have to go right away!"

도서관에서 조용히 해야 돼요.
"You have to be quiet in the library."

> **Adv** Note how "to be quiet," the *descriptive verb*, is 조용하다, but 조용히 하다 (also, "to be quiet") can be used as an *action verb*. 조용히 하다 literally means "to do (something) quietly."
>
> 조용한 방에서 조용히 하세요.
> "Please be quiet in a quiet room."

친구한테 편지를 써야 돼요.
"I need to write a letter to a friend."

수영장에 가기 위해서 일단 운동을 많이 해야 돼요.
"In order to go the pool, first of all I need to exercise a lot."

Now that we've seen how to use this form, let's start the chapter conversation.

상현: 저는 지금 나가야 돼요. 밤까지 여기 있을 거예요?
"I have to leave now. Will you be here until nighttime?"

밤 means "night," but when used on its own can translate more naturally to "nighttime."

수빈: 네... 하지만 8시 전에 친구를 만나러 나갈 거예요.
"Yeah... but I'll leave before 8 o'clock to meet a friend."

Before: Noun + 전에

To say "before," use 전에.

다음 달 15일 전에 뵐게요.
"I'll see you before the 15th of next month."

Have to Do

Chapter 16

제가 이미 2 시간 전에 다 했어요.
"I already finished it 2 hours ago."

전에 한 번 봤어요.
"I saw it once before."

하루 전에 하지 말고 미리 하는 게 좋겠어요.
"You should do it in advance, and not do it one day before."

After: Noun + 후에

To say "after," use 후에.

1 시간 후에 만나도 될까요?
"Would it be okay if we meet after an hour?"

그 영화는 12 월 후에 나와요.
"That movie is coming out after December."

우리는 2 시 후에 공연을 시작할 거예요.
"We will start the performance after 2 o'clock."

저는 이번 달 15 일 후에 시간이 더 많을 거예요.
"I will have more time after the 15th of this month."

> **Adv** You can also use 뒤에 ("behind," "after") in place of 후에, and the meaning will be the same.

상현: 그럼 설거지 좀 해 주세요.
"In that case do the dishes."

While 그럼 (or 그러면) translates as "well then," it can also be used to mean "in that case." Since 그렇다 means "to be so," 그러면 literally means "if it is so."

수빈: 꼭 오늘 해야 하나요?
"Do I have to do it today?"

We learned in the previous book that 꼭 means "surely" or "certainly." It's also used frequently with "have to," such as in the conversation. When used together with "have to," 꼭 makes the meaning *stronger* – instead of just "have to," think of it as meaning "*have* to."

227

Chapter 16

Have to Do

꼭 해야 돼요.
"I have to do it (or else)."

내일 꼭 와요.
"Make sure to come tomorrow."

Must Do: Verb Stem + 아/어/etc. + 야 하다

In the same way as "have to," you can use this form to mean "must." Its meaning is exactly the same as "have to," but is a bit more direct and slightly *stronger*.

To make it, take a verb stem and conjugate it to the 요 form, but remove the 요. Then attach 야 like before, but this time followed by the verb 하다 – conjugated in any way that you'd like.

하다 → 해
해 + 야 하다 → 해야 하다

In the example sentences below, I've translated this form as "must" to show that it has a stronger meaning, but know that it has the same meaning as "have to" (or "need to") and could also be translated in the same way.

빨리 나가야 하죠!
"You must leave right away!"

친구를 위해서 생일 선물을 만들어야 해요.
"I must make a birthday present for my friend."

그리고 그 선물을 포장해야 해요.
"And I must wrap that present."

한국어를 더 배워야 해요.
"I must learn more Korean."

매일 꼭 일을 해야 하나요?
"Must you work everyday?"

뭐해야 할까요?
"What would we need to do?"

어떻게 해야 돼요?
"How do I have to do it?"

Have to Do

Chapter 16

지금 해야 할 일이 있어요.
"There's something I must do now."

In Chapter 2 we learned that in addition to meaning "work" or "job," 일 is also used to mean "a matter" or "a concern" – although a more natural English translation could simply be "thing." The above sentence could therefore also be translated to "There's a matter I must do today."

상현: 네, 내일 어머니가 오셔서요.
"Yeah, because tomorrow mother's coming."

수빈: 알았어요. 나가기 전에 할게요.
"Okay. I'll do it before I leave."

알았다 (here, 알았어요) can be used in the same way as 알겠다, which we previously learned in the phrase 알겠습니다.

Before: Action Verb Stem + 기 전에

You can use this form to say "before" when using an *action verb*.

To use it, take a verb stem and attach 기, then 전에.

하다 → 하
하 + 기 전에 → 하기 전에

먹다 → 먹
먹 + 기 전에 → 먹기 전에

놀다 → 놀
놀 + 기 전에 → 놀기 전에

여행가기 전에 한 번 만나자.
"Let's meet once before you go on a trip."

밥을 먹기 전에 손을 씻으세요.
"Please wash your hands before eating."

외출하기 전에 날씨를 확인하세요.
"Please check the weather before you go outside."

Chapter 16

Have to Do

앞머리를 자르기 전에 한 번 더 생각할게요.
"I'll think about it one more time before cutting my bangs."

After: Action Verb Stem + (은/ㄴ) + 후에

You can use this form to say "after" when using an *action verb*.

To use it, take an *action verb* that's been conjugated to an *adjective* in the *past tense*. We learned how to do this in Chapter 4.

하다 → 한
먹다 → 먹은
팔다 → 판

그 책에 대해서 알아본 후에 사세요.
"Buy that book after finding out about it."

지하철에서 내린 후에 전화하세요.
"Call me after you get off from the subway."

밥을 먹은 후에 설거지를 하세요.
"Do the dishes after you've eaten."

날 도와준 후에 가도 되잖아.
"Look, you can leave after you've helped me."

> **Advanced**
>
> Here as well, you can use 뒤에 in place of 후에, and the meaning will be the same.
>
> 첫 사랑을 찾았지만 이미 결혼한 **뒤**였어요.
> "I found my first love, but it was after already getting married."
>
> There is also one more option that you have when using this form – 다음에. Feel free to use 후에, 뒤에, or 다음에.
>
> 그 책에 대해서 알아본 **후에** 사세요.
> 그 책에 대해서 알아본 **뒤에** 사세요.
> 그 책에 대해서 알아본 **다음에** 사세요.
> "Buy that book after finding out about it."

Have to Do

Chapter 16

Advanced

It's been a while since we first learned about the 서 form (for showing *cause* and *effect*), so I wanted to talk about another important way that this form is used – in a similar way as 고 ("and").

Strong Relation: Verb Stem + 아/어/etc. + 서

We previously learned that we can connect verbs using the 고 ("and") form.

제가 집에 가고 자고 싶어요.
"I want to go home and sleep."

When using the 고 form, the two sentences do not *need* to have any relationship to each other (but they can if you want). The 고 form is flexible, and can be used anywhere.

We also previously learned (in Chapter 5) that we can use the 서 form to connect verbs which show a *cause* and an *effect*.

너무 많이 먹어서 배가 아파요.
"My stomach hurts because I ate too much."

The 서 form also has one additional use for connecting verbs together – for showing that two verbs are *related* to each other. You can use the 서 form to show that one action happens *right after* the other, and therefore the two actions are related. Let's look at a few examples:

제가 집에 가서 자고 싶어요.
"I want to go home and sleep."

Although the meaning of the above sentence is the same as the first sentence using the 고 form, the meaning shown here is that you will sleep *right after* returning home (and not hours later, or the next day, etc.).

밖에 나가서 놀 거예요.
"I'm going to go outside and play."

In this above sentence as well, the speaker is saying that they will play *right after* going outside.

요리해서 가족과 같이 먹을 거예요.
"I'm going to cook and eat with my family."

도시락을 만들어서 소풍을 다녀왔어요.
"I made a box lunch and went on a picnic (and came back)."

Using 다녀오다 instead of 가다 simply *emphasizes* that you've returned, and that you're not still on a picnic; this information can be important in a conversation, such as if you're talking on the phone with a friend, who might still think that you're on the picnic. *Grammatically* though, both verbs (다녀오다 or 가다) would be fine in the above sentence.

지난 주말에 친구들을 초대해서 파티를 했어요.
"Last weekend I invited friends and had a party."

Note that using the 서 form in this way (to show an action happening after the other) is only for *action verbs*.

231

Chapter 16: Have to Do

Practice

Translate to Korean:

1. "I really have to do it right away."

   _____

2. "Why do you have to leave before 5 o'clock?"

   _____

3. "After 2 o'clock, I'll be too busy."

   _____

4. "Before you clean the house please throw away the trash."

   _____

5. "I must do the dishes after I make lunch."

   _____

6. "I must buy new shoes in order to exercise."

   _____

Translate to English:

7. 샤워를 해야 돼요.

   _____

8. 일단 집에 가야 돼요.

   _____

Have to Do

9. 그것을 알기 위해서 내일까지 기다려야 돼요.

   _____.

10. 식사 후에 약을 먹을 거예요? 아니면 식사 전에 먹을 거예요?

    _____.

11. 문을 닫기 전에 열쇠를 챙기세요.

    _____.

12. 선생님이 되기 위해서 어떻게 해야 할까요?

    _____.

New Phrases

예(를) 들어서...	"For example..."

New Vocabulary

일단	"first (of all)"
조용하다	"to be quiet" (descriptive verb)
조용히 하다	"to be quiet" (action verb)
전에	"before"
후에	"after"
미리	"in advance," "ahead of time" (adverb)
외출(을) 하다	"to go out(side)"
확인(을) 하다	"to check," "to confirm"
앞머리	"bangs"
머리(를) 자르다	"to get a haircut," "to cut one's hair"
알아보다	"to find out," "to look into"
별	"star"
매력	"charm," "attractiveness"
매력적이다	"to be charming," "to be attractive"

Chapter 16: Have to Do

잠시 후	"after a short while," "after just a moment"
주변	"surroundings," "vicinity"
근처	"neighborhood," "vicinity"
파티(를) 하다	"to have a party"
다녀오다	"to go and come back"
도시락	"packed lunch," "box lunch"
공연	"performance," "show"
챙기다	"to pack," "to take along (something)"
여행(을) 하다	"to travel," "to take a trip"
여행(을) 가다	"to go on a trip"
확실하다	"to be certain," "to be sure"
확실히	"certainly," "surely"
태도	"attitude"
사과(를) 하다	"to apologize"
후회(를) 하다	"to regret"
존경(을) 하다	"to respect," "to look up to"

Try to Do

Chapter 17

Conversation

현진:	선영 씨, 여기로 와 보세요.
선영:	네?
현진:	이거 좀 드셔 보세요.
선영:	아! 맛있네요! 이게 뭐죠?
현진:	무궁화 향을 넣은 쿠키예요.
선영:	일반 동그란 모양의 쿠키보다 맛있어요.
현진:	제가 만든 거예요.
선영:	정말 대단해요.
현진:	하지만 더 맛있게 만들려고 노력하고 있어요.

In this chapter we'll learn about two different ways to say "try," as well as when to use each one. To begin, let's learn the most standard way to say "to try doing something."

Try & Intending: Verb Stem + (으)려고 (하다)

You can use this form when you want to show that you *intend* to do something. Depending on the sentence, this might translate as either "intend" or "try."

Chapter 17: Try to Do

To make this form, take a verb stem and attach 으려고 if it ends in a *consonant*, or attach 려고 if it ends in a *vowel*. Then *optionally* you can attach the verb 하다, and conjugate it any way you'd like. If you choose to not use 하다, instead add 요 to the end when using *informal speech*.

하다 ➔ 하
하 + 려고 하다 ➔ 하려고 하다

먹다 ➔ 먹
먹 + 으려고 하다 ➔ 먹으려고 하다

Verbs ending in ㄹ will conjugate as if they ended in a vowel instead.

팔다 ➔ 팔
팔 + 려고 하다 ➔ 팔려고 하다

요즘 다이어트하려고 하고 있어요.
"I'm trying to diet these days."

내일은 친구를 만나려고 해요.
"I'm intending to meet a friend tomorrow."

30 분 후에 은행에 가려고요.
"I'm intending to go to the bank after 30 minutes."

내가 지금 자려고 하고 있으니까 좀 조용히 해 줘.
"Please be quiet because I'm trying to sleep now."

저를 설득하려고 하지 마세요.
"Don't try to persuade me."

벌써 가려고?
"You're already intending to go?"
"You're already going to go?"

Sometimes a more natural translation of this form in English will be "going to," as in the above sentence. Note though that using 려고 is still different from using a regular *future tense* form, because 려고 shows that the speaker *intends* to do something and is not saying that they *will* do something.

> **Adv**: The 래(요) form that we learned in Chapter 10 is similar to the form (으)려고 하다. In addition to meaning "want to," the 래(요) form can also be used to show *intention* – you can think of it as a combination of "want" and "intention."

Try to Do

Chapter 17

현진: 선영씨, 여기로 와 보세요.
"Come here, Sun-yung."

You might've realized it by now, but names in Korean will more often come *first* in a sentence.

여러분, 안녕하세요!
"Hello, everyone."

철수 씨도 그렇게 생각하세요?
"Do you think so too, Chul-soo?"

Try and See: Verb Stem + 아/어/etc. 보다

Although this form can also translate as "try," it's quite different from 려고. You can use this form to mean that you are going to *do* something and then see how it goes; you can think of it meaning "to try (and see)."

To make this form, take a verb stem and conjugate it to the 요 form, but remove the 요. Then conjugate the verb 보다 ("to see") any way that you'd like in the sentence.

한 번 드셔 보세요.
"Eat it once (and see how it tastes)."
"Try (eating) it once."

여기에 앉아 보세요.
"Sit here (and see how it goes)."
"Try sitting here."

선생님을 만나 보고 결정하세요.
"Try meeting the teacher and then deciding."

그럼 생각해 볼게요.
"Well then I'll think about it."

너도 써 보면 알 거야.
"If you try (using) it you'll know too."

웨딩드레스를 입어 보고 싶어요.
"I want to try on a wedding dress."

Chapter 17

Try to Do

선영: 네?

"What?"

네 can also be used as a polite way to ask someone to *repeat* what they've just said, like "Pardon?" in English.

When speaking casually, you can use 응 (or 어) in the same way.

응?
"Huh?"

> **Adv** A common alternative to 네 is 예, which means the same thing. 예 is used often in *dialects* of Korean (people in each area of Korea will speak slightly differently from others, just like people from New York speak differently from people from California). However, it's common enough that you can learn it without knowing about dialects yet.

현진: 이거 좀 드셔 보세요.

"Try this."

선영: 아! 맛있네요! 이게 뭐죠?

"Ah! That's good! What is this?"

현진: 무궁화 향을 넣은 쿠키예요.

"It's a cookie with hibiscus fragrance put in it."

While 향 means "fragrance" or "scent," 냄새 means "smell." 냄새 can be used for both pleasant and unpleasant smells.

쓰레기 냄새예요.
"It's the smell of trash."

고기 냄새가 나요.
"It smells like meat."

Try to Do

Chapter 17

Culture Notes

무궁화 is the national flower of South Korea. The name comes from 무궁 (meaning "eternity" or "immortality") and 화, which is a Sino Korean word meaning "flower." However, 화 is not used by itself – instead, use the Pure Korean word 꽃 (which means "flower").

Advanced

The word 꽃, while pronounced 꼳 by itself, is often pronounced as 꼿 when combined with other words. Let's take a look at an example.

꽃을 샀어요?
"Did you buy flowers?"

According to the rules of sound changes, this sentence would be pronounced 꼬츨 사써요. However, because 꽃 is often pronounced as 꼿, this sentence would instead sound like 꼬슬 사써요. This is also easier to pronounce.

선영: 일반 동그란 모양의 쿠키보다 맛있어요.
"It's more delicious than regular round-shaped cookies."

일반 means "regular" or "normal," and can be used as an *adjective*.

일반 사람들은 밤에 자고 아침에 일어나요.
"Normal people sleep at night and wake up in the morning."

모양 ("shape") can be used *before* what you want to describe (with the particle 의), such as in the conversation.

예쁜 모양의 비누를 선물로 샀어요.
"I bought some pretty-shaped soap as a present."

Culture Notes

It's considered polite in Korea to accept gifts using both hands.

Chapter 17

Try to Do

현진: 제가 만든 거예요.
"I made it."

Note that 제가 만든 거예요 literally means "It is something that I made."

선영: 정말 대단해요.
"That's really great."

현진: 하지만 더 맛있게 만들려고 노력하고 있어요.
"But I'm trying to make it taste better."

We learned that 맛있게 means "deliciously," so 맛있게 만들다 can literally translate as "to make it deliciously." However, it's used here in the same way as 맛있게 하다 – "to make it (taste) delicious" – which we learned in Chapter 13.

맛있게 해 주세요.
맛있게 만들어 주세요.
"Please make it taste delicious."

More on 려고

While we learned that 하다 is *optional* in the 려고 form, it can also be replaced by other verbs. This is because the form 려고 shows *intention* by itself. You can see an example in the conversation with 노력(을) 하다, but there are also many other verbs which you can use with 려고.

요즘 다이어트하려고 등산을 하고 있어요.
"I'm hiking (intending) to diet these days."
"I'm trying to diet these days by hiking."

여행을 가려고 돈을 모으고 있어요.
"I'm saving up money (intending) to go on a trip."

게임을 덜 하려고 노력하고 있어요.
"I'm trying to play games less."

Try to Do

Advanced

"Too Bad" – 아깝다, 아쉽다, and 안타깝다

These three words are defined in the vocabulary list, but they can be a bit tricky to get the hang of even though they're used frequently. This is especially because all three of them can translate as "to be too bad" in a natural English sentence. However, each is used a bit differently. Let's go over an example of each one.

아깝다 "to be sad about losing a thing/opportunity"

이번 시험에서 한 문제를 틀려서 아깝게 1등을 못 했어요.
"Sadly, I couldn't get first place because I missed one problem on this test."
"It's too bad I couldn't get first place because I missed one problem on this test."

아쉽다 "to be unsatisfying"

함께 캠핑을 갈 수 없어서 아쉬워요.
"It's unsatisfying that we couldn't go camping together."
"It's too bad that we couldn't go camping together."

안타깝다 "to be sad and frustrated"

이번 경기에 제가 좋아하는 선수가 안 나와서 안타까워요.
"I'm sad that the athlete I like didn't come out in this game."
"It's too bad that the athlete I like didn't come out in this game."

In addition, here is one more for review – 안됐다 – which we already saw used once in Chapter 9. 안됐다 originally comes from the *past tense* of 안 되다, but is written without a *space*.

안됐다 "to be sorry (to hear)"

그 말을 들으니까 안됐네요.
"I'm sorry to hear that."
"It's too bad to hear that."

Practice

Translate to Korean:

1. "Can I try this shirt on?"

_____.

2. "I want to try swimming in the ocean."

_____.

3. "I want to try the pizza that Chul-soo made."

_____.

241

Chapter 17 — Try to Do

4. "I'm intending to go to Korea next spring."

_____.

5. "I'm intending to go to the movie theater."

_____.

6. "I'm different from regular people."

_____.

7. "I bought a star-shaped cake."

_____.

8. "Lately I'm trying to drink a lot of water."

_____.

Translate to English:

9. 그림을 그리려고 하고 있어요.

_____.

10. 독일 소시지를 먹어 보고 싶어요.

_____.

11. 새로운 친구를 만들려고 노력하고 있나요?

_____.

12. 혼자서 운전해도 될까요?

_____.

Try to Do

13. 예전 남자 친구를 잊으려고 노력하고 있어요.

_____.

14. 화장실에 가려고 기다리고 있어요.

_____.

15. 새로운 방법으로 화장을 해 봤어요.

_____.

16. 장미 모양의 아이스크림은 일반 아이스크림보다 더 맛있을까요?

_____.

New Vocabulary

여러분	"everyone"
다들	"everyone" (informal)
노력(을) 하다	"to make an effort," "to try"
다이어트(를) 하다	"to diet"
설득(을) 하다	"to persuade," "to convince"
돈(을) 모으다	"to save (up) money"
웨딩드레스	"wedding dress"
입어 보다	"to try (something) on"
무궁화	"hibiscus (flower)"
향	"fragrance," "scent"
냄새	"smell"
냄새(가) 나다	"to smell (like)"
쿠키	"cookie"
일반	"general," "normal" (adjective)
보통	"regular(ly)," "normal(ly)"
모양	"shape"
비누	"soap"
대단하다	"to be great," "to be incredible"

Chapter 17
Try to Do

신기하다	"to be awesome," "to be amazing"
책임	"responsibility"
틀리다	"to miss (a problem)"
캠핑(을) 가다	"to go camping"
아깝다	"to be sad about losing a thing/opportunity"
아쉽다	"to be unsatisfying"
안타깝다	"to be sad and frustrated"
답답하다	"to be frustrating"
예전	"the past," "the old days," "before"
예전에	"in the past," "in the old days," "before" (adverb)

Have Ever

Chapter 18

Conversation

알렉스:	미국에 가 본 적이 있습니까?
정미:	아니요. 없어요.
알렉스:	기회가 되면 한 번 와 보세요. 제가 안내해 드릴게요.
정미:	그래요? 미국 어디서 사세요?
알렉스:	캘리포니아주 로스엔젤레스시에 삽니다.
정미:	제 동생도 거기에 살아요.

Have Ever
Verb Stem + 아/어/etc. 본 적(이) 있다

To make this form, take a verb and conjugate it to the 요 form, but remove the 요. Add 본 적(이), and then the verb 있다; conjugate 있다 in any way that you'd like.

하다 → 해
해 + 본 적(이) 있다 → 해 본 적이 있다

먹다 → 먹어
먹어 + 본 적(이) 있다 → 먹어 본 적이 있다

해 본 적이 있어요?
"Have you ever done it before?"

Have Ever

한국에 가 본 적이 있어요?
"Have you ever been to Korea before?"

그럼 옷을 만들어 본 적은 있어요?
"Well then, have you ever made clothes before?"

Notice how the above example sentence uses the *Topic Marker* (은/는) instead of the *Subject Marker* (이/가). Using the *Subject Marker* is acceptable as well, but know that the meaning will be a bit different – "Well then, how about making clothes? Have you ever done *that* before?"

길에서 넘어져 본 적도 있어요?
"Have you ever fallen down in the street before as well?"

Also note how the above sentence uses the particle 도 to add the meaning of "too" or "as well."

> **Adv** This form actually comes directly from the 보다 form that we learned last chapter (Verb Stem + 아/어/etc. 보다). 해 본 is the past tense *adjective* form. 적 is a *Sino Korean word* that means "experience" (although 적 cannot be used by itself in a sentence – use 경험 instead to say "experience"). Literally this form means "to have the *experience* of having tried something."

However, when we use the verb 보다 ("to see") with this form, we get a slightly shorter result.

이 영화를 본 적이 있어요?
"Have you ever seen this movie before?"

Note how the sentence only has 본 적이 있다, and *not* 봐 본 적이 있다. This is because 본 originally comes from the verb 보다 anyway, so it's not necessary to repeat it.

You can also use this same form with 없다 (instead of 있다) to mean "have not ever" or "have never."

제 친구를 만나 본 적이 없어요?
"Have you never met my friend before?"

병원에 입원해 본 적이 없죠?
"You've never been in the hospital before, right?"

김치를 먹어 본 적 없어요.
"I've never tried kimchi before."

Have Ever

알렉스: 미국에 가 본 적이 있습니까?

"Have you ever been to America before?"

Adv | While you might be tempted to use the "have ever" form whenever you want to say that you've done something, this form is only commonly used when you want to say that you have the *experience* of doing something. To simply say that you've *tried* doing something before, or that you've simply done something before, such as in the sentence "I've been to America," use the 보다 form that we learned last chapter. To say "I've been to America before" as an *experience*, (note that this sentence emphasizes that it is a past *experience*), use the 본 적 form in this chapter.

정미: 아니요. 없어요.

"No. I haven't."

You can use 있다 or 없다 to reply that you *have* or *haven't* done something before, when asked using this form.

알렉스: 기회가 되면 한 번 와 보세요. 제가 안내해 드릴게요.

"If you have the opportunity come sometime. I'll show you around."

기회(가) 되면 literally means "if it becomes an opportunity." You'll notice many expressions in Korean that use the *Subject Marker* (이/가) along with 되다 in this way, so keep an eye out for them as they come up.

정미: 그래요? 미국 어디서 사세요?

"Yeah? Where do you live in America?"

Notice how "in America" in this sentence is arranged as "America where" in Korean.

한국 어디 있어요?
"Where in Korea are you?"

태국 어디를 여행했어요?
"Where did you travel in Thailand?"

알렉스: 캘리포니아주 로스엔젤레스시에 삽니다.

"I live in Los Angeles, California."

Have Ever

State & City: 주 & 시

~주

~시

When saying a *state*, add 주 to the end. 주 is a *Sino Korean word* that means "state."

뉴욕**주**
"New York (state)"

When saying a *city*, add 시 to the end; 시 is a *Sino Korean word* that means "city."

뉴욕**시**
"New York (city)"

When saying a state and a city together, the state will come first, followed by the city – in order from largest to smallest.

미국 텍사스주 휴스턴시를 여행했어요.
"I traveled in Houston, Texas, in America."

정미: 제 동생도 거기에 살아요.
"My younger sibling lives there too."

Have Ever

Chapter 18

Advanced

First, Second, Third...

Previously we've learned how to say "first place" (using 위 and 등), as well as "first" as an *adjective* (using 첫). Now let's learn how to say "second," "third," and more.

번째

We can say "second," "third," and any other higher amount by using a *Pure Korean number* with 번째. These can be used as both *nouns* and *adjectives*.

두 번째 "second"
세 번째 "third"
네 번째 "fourth"
열 번째 "tenth"

If you happen to like math, these kinds of numbers are also known as "ordinal numbers."

지금 세 번째 책을 쓰고 있어요.
"I'm now writing the third book."

어제는 이모의 두 번째 결혼식이었어요.
"Yesterday was my aunt's second wedding (ceremony)."

If you want to say "first" using this method (instead of just using the *adjective* 첫), it becomes 첫 번째 – using 한 번째 would be *incorrect*.

드디어 제 친구의 첫 번째 앨범이 나왔어요.
"Finally my friend's first album came out."

Both 첫 and 첫 번째 mean "first," so you can use either one.

드디어 제 친구의 첫 앨범이 나왔어요.
"Finally my friend's first album came out."

We can also use these ordinal numbers as *adverbs* – first(ly), second(ly), third(ly), etc. – by adding 로 to the end.

제가 마라톤에서 첫 번째로 들어왔어요.
"I came in first in the marathon."

두 번째로 노래를 부른 사람이 누구예요?
"Who's the person who sang a song second?"
"Who sang second?"

Practice

Translate to Korean:

1. "Have you ever come to America before?"

_____.

Have Ever

Chapter 18

2. "Have you ever been to karaoke before?"
   _____

3. "I've never seen a Korean drama before."
   _____

4. "Have you ever played an online game before?"
   _____

5. "Have you ever read this book before?"
   _____

6. "Have you ever tried mountain climbing before?"
   _____

Translate to English:

7. 비행기를 타 본 적이 있어요?
   _____

8. 가족과 소풍을 가 본 적이 있어요?
   _____

9. 고양이를 키워 본 적이 있어요?
   _____

10. 저는 아직 레몬을 먹어 본 적이 없어요.
    _____

Have Ever

11. 정말 혼자서 운전을 해 본 적이 없어요?

_____.

12. 최근 3 년 동안 머리를 잘라 본 적이 없어요.

_____.

New Vocabulary

입원(을) 하다	"to be hospitalized"
기회(가) 되다	"to have an opportunity"
안내(를) 하다	"to guide," "to show around"
캘리포니아	"California"
태국	"Thailand"
텍사스	"Texas"
뉴욕	"New York"
세다	"to be strong," "to be powerful"
힘(이) 세다	"to be physically strong"
테이블	"table"
천	"cloth"
비닐	"plastic" (literally, "vinyl")
비닐봉지	"plastic bag"
비닐봉투	"plastic bag"
잊다	"to forget"
까먹다	"to forget" (informal)
양력	"Western calendar," "Gregorian calendar"
음력	"Lunar calendar"
달력	"a calendar"
숯	"charcoal"
검은	"black" (adjective)
검은색	"black" (noun)
주황	"orange" (adjective)
주황색	"orange" (noun)
핑크색	"pink" (noun)

Chapter 18: Have Ever

회색	"grey" (noun)
쥐색	"grey" (literally, "mouse color") (noun)
갈색	"brown (color)"
번째	ordinal counter
결혼식	"wedding (ceremony)"
드디어	"finally," "at last"
앨범	"album"
마라톤	"marathon"
경험	"experience"
최근	"recent," "the last" (adjective)
최근에	"recently," "these days"
약혼(을) 하다	"to get engaged"
다이아몬드	"diamond"

Verbs to Nouns

Chapter 19

Conversation

소현:	와아! 그림이 정말 예뻐요! 누가 그렸어요?
희진:	고마워요. 제가 그렸어요.
소현:	저는 그렇게 못 그려요. 그림을 그리기가 너무 어려워요.
희진:	연습을 많이 하면 할 수 있어요.
소현:	이렇게 그리는 것은 시간이 많이 걸리죠?
희진:	그렇게 많이 안 걸려요. 한 하루, 이틀이면 돼요.
소현:	하하. 저는 됐어요.
희진:	그림 그리기 싫으면 조각을 해 보세요. 저는 그림을 좋아해서 계속 하고 있는 거예요.

Earlier in Chapter 4 we learned how to turn an action verb into an *adjective*. In this chapter we'll learn how to turn an action verb into a *noun* – an example would be changing the verb "to swim" into "swimming," which is a noun. Knowing how to do this will let us make a much larger variety of sentences (such as "I like swimming.").

> **Adv** Changing an action verb into a noun is known as "nominalization," from the Latin root *nom*, meaning "name" or "noun."

There are three ways to turn an action verb into a noun, and each one is different.

Verbs to Nouns

1. Action Verb Stem + 기

This is the most common way to change an action verb into a noun.

To make this form, take an action verb stem and attach 기.

하다 → 하
하 + 기 → 하기

먹다 → 먹
먹 + 기 → 먹기

살다 → 살
살 + 기 → 살기

저는 영화 보기를 좋아해요.
"I like watching movies."

요리하기가 어려워요.
"Cooking is difficult."

책 읽기를 좋아하세요?
"Do you like reading books?"

오늘은 수영하기에 좋은 날씨예요.
"Today is good weather for swimming."

You can use the above form 에 좋다 to mean "to be good for."

남들 앞에서 노래하기를 싫어해요.
"I dislike singing in front of other people."

다른 도시에서 운전하기가 쉽지 않아요.
"Driving in another city is not easy."
"Driving in a different city is not easy."

다른 is an *adjective* that comes from 다르다 ("to be different"), and also means "other" or "another."

This form is also the preferred way when you are creating a *list* of items (such as a to-do list).

Verbs to Nouns

Chapter 19

8:00 – 일어나기 ("waking up")
8:10 – 양치하기 ("brushing teeth")
8:15 – 샤워하기 ("showering")

You might have realized it (or not), but we've also already used this form (adding 기) in several previous grammar lessons. For example:

가기 전에 설거지를 해 주세요.
"Please do the dishes before going."

제가 한국어를 **좋아하기** 때문에 공부하고 있어요.
"I'm studying because I like Korean."

저는 돈을 **벌기** 위해서 열심히 일하고 있어요.
"I am working hard in order to earn money."

When used in grammatical forms such as these ones above, 기 *must* be used; you don't need to relearn anything already covered in this book or the previous book. In other cases, when these verbs are not part of a specific grammatical form, you can use either 기, or 는 것 (which we will learn next).

---

2. Action Verb Stem + 는 것

Changing an action verb into a noun with this form is a tiny bit more *formal* than using the 기 form, but besides that they are similar in meaning.

To make this form, take an action verb stem and attach 는 것.

하다 → 하
하 + 는 것 → 하는 것

먹다 → 먹
먹 + 는 것 → 먹는 것

For verb stems ending in ㄹ, remove the ㄹ first.

살다 → 살
살 – ㄹ → 사
사 + 는 것 → 사는 것

저는 영화 보는 것을 정말 좋아해요.
"I really like watching movies."

255

Chapter 19

Verbs to Nouns

책을 읽는 것이 재미있어요.
"Reading books is fun."

운동을 하는 것이 건강에 좋아요.
"Exercising is good for your health."

그룹 과제를 하는 것을 좋아하는 사람은 없어요.
"There is no person who likes doing group assignments."

저는 영화관에서 파는 캐러멜 팝콘을 먹는 것을 좋아해요.
"I like eating the caramel popcorn they sell in movie theaters."

자기 전에 일기를 쓰는 것이 저의 습관이에요.
"Writing in my journal before sleeping is my habit."

We've also previously used this form in Chapter 14 for saying "should" (by adding 는 것이 좋겠다).

3. Action Verb Stem + (음/ㅁ)

Using this form is different from the previous two. Because of this, it cannot be exchanged with either of the other two forms.

To make this form, take an action verb stem and attach 음 if it ends in a *consonant*, or attach ㅁ if it ends in a *vowel*.

하다 → 하
하 + ㅁ → 함

먹다 → 먹
먹 + 음 → 먹음

For verb stems ending in ㄹ, do not remove the ㄹ.

팔다 → 팔
팔 + ㅁ → 팖

만들다 → 만들
만들 + ㅁ → 만듦

When changing an action verb into a noun with this form, the new noun will act like it's a completely new, *unique* noun; often, nouns that are created this way will have their own entry in the dictionary. Here are a few examples:

Verbs to Nouns

배우다 ("to learn") → 배움 ("learning," "study")
가르치다 ("to teach") → 가르침 ("teachings")
추다 ("to dance") → 춤 ("a dance")
자다 ("to sleep") → 잠 ("sleep")
죽다 ("to die") → 죽음 ("death")

The above two examples are often used together with their original verbs – 춤(을) 추다 ("to dance") and (잠[을]) 자다 ("to sleep"). This should help to give you an idea of how action verbs turned into nouns using this form will act as separate, unique new words. Here are a few more examples:

살다 ("to live") → 삶 ("life")
돕다 ("to help") → 도움 ("help")*
걷다 ("to walk") → 걸음 ("a step," "a pace")*

*도움 and 걸음 are two common exceptions.

잠이 더 필요해요.
"I need more sleep."

그분의 가르침이 아주 훌륭했어요.
"His teachings were very wonderful."

아무도 삶과 죽음을 피할 수 없어요.
"Nobody can avoid life and death."

제가 어렸을 때 책을 많이 읽은 것이 도움이 되었어요.
"Having read a lot of books when I was young was helpful."

도움이 되다 (literally "to become help") is a common way to say "to be helpful."

As a tip, if you're not sure whether to use this form (음/ㅁ), or to use one of the other two (기 or 는 것), I'd recommend to *not* conjugate verbs using this form on your own as it's the least commonly used. Instead, 는 것 and 기 will be fine in most situations.

257

Chapter 19

Verbs to Nouns

This form (음/ㅁ) has one additional usage, for *writing comments* (such as on the "comments" section for a list of names).

김철수 (28) – 숙제 안함.
"Kim Chul-soo (28) – Doesn't do homework."

김영희 (25) – 아주 좋은 학생임.
"Kim Yung-hee (25) – Is a very good student."

Let's move onto the conversation.

소현: 와아! 그림이 정말 예뻐요! 누가 그렸어요?
"Wow! The drawing's really pretty! Who drew it?"

와아! (also written 와~!) is a common way to show that you're surprised. You can think of it as meaning "Wow!"

희진: 고마워요. 제가 그렸어요.
"Thanks. I drew it."

Remember that 고마워요 comes from the verb 고맙다, which is slightly *less formal* than the verb 감사하다.

소현: 저는 그렇게 못 그려요. 그림을 그리기가 너무 어려워요.
"I can't draw like that. It's too hard to draw."

While the general translation for 그렇게 is "so" or "in that way," another acceptable translation is "like that."

그림(을) 그리다 ("to draw") is another example of a noun created from an action verb using the third form we learned (음/ㅁ). Literally it means "to draw a drawing." There are several expressions in Korean that use this sort of repetition.

Verbs to Nouns

Chapter 19

잠(을) 자다 "to sleep (a sleep)"
춤(을) 추다 "to dance (a dance)"
꿈(을) 꾸다 "to dream (a dream)"
걸음(을) 걷다 "to walk (a step)"

희진: 연습을 많이 하면 할 수 있어요.
"You can if you practice a lot."

소현: 이렇게 그리는 것은 시간이 많이 걸리죠?
"Does it take a lot of time to draw like this?"

"To Take Time" – 시간(이) 걸리다

시간(이) 걸리다 means "to take time," and can be used in many ways.

시간이 얼마나 걸려요?
"How much time does it take?"

30 분밖에 안 걸릴 거예요.
"It'll only take 30 minutes."

Note that although the above sentence uses a *negative verb* – 안 걸리다 – the English translation uses "only" and does not have a negative verb. Also notice how the verb 걸리다 can also be used on its own to mean "to take (time)," without adding the word 시간.

이틀 넘게 걸렸어요.
"It took over two days."

넘게 is an *adverb* that means "over" or "more than." Its opposite is 도 안 되게 ("under," "less than").

이틀도 안 되게 걸렸어요.
"It took under two days."

Chapter 19

Verbs to Nouns

> A common way to say "it takes (time) to" do something is with the 데 form and the verb 걸리다. When used in this way, add a space before 데.
>
> 자동차로 거기까지 가는 데 3 시간 걸려요.
> "It takes 3 hours to go there by car."
>
> 다 하는 데 2 달 정도 걸렸어요.
> "It took about 2 months to do it."
>
> 옷을 고르는 데 시간이 오래 걸렸어요.
> "It took a long time to choose clothes."
>
> The verb used with the 데 form will remain in the *present tense*, as in the above examples.

희진: 그렇게 많이 안 걸려요. 한 하루, 이틀이면 돼요.
"It doesn't take that long. About 1 or 2 days is enough."

Approximately: 한

We previously learned how to use 정도 for making guesses in Chapter 7. While 정도 is used *after* what you are guessing, 한 is used *before*.

이틀 정도 걸려요.
"It takes about 2 days."

한 이틀 걸려요.
"It takes approximately 2 days."

Both 한 and 정도 can translate as "about" or "approximately," but often they're used together. Although this seems repetitive in English, it sounds natural in Korean.

한 이틀 정도 걸려요.
"It takes about 2 days, approximately."

한 3 명 정도 올 거예요.
"About 3 people will come, approximately."

> Another word that you can use is 약, which works in the same way as 한 and has a similar meaning.
>
> 약 이틀 정도 걸려요.
> "It takes approximately 2 days."

Verbs to Nouns

Chapter 19

Noun + (이)면 되다

We've seen a few examples of how 되다 can be used in expressions to have different meanings – such as 기회(가) 되다 ("to have an opportunity") and 시간(이) 되다 ("to have time"). Here we have another meaning – using (이)면 ("if," from the verb 이다) after a *noun* with 되다 can mean, "It is okay if it is (noun)."

키큰 여자면 돼요.
"It's fine if it's a tall girl."

Also, this form can mean, "It is enough if it is (noun)," as it does in the conversation.

하루면 돼요.
"One day is enough."

3 시간이면 될 거예요.
"3 hours will be enough."

소현: 하하. 저는 됐어요.
"Haha. No thanks."

In the past tense, 되다 takes on another meaning – "No thanks," or "I'm not interested."

아, 됐어요.
"Ah, no thanks."

This phrase can be useful when trying to avoid conversations (such as with sales workers).

희진: 그림 그리기 싫으면 조각을 해 보세요. 저는 그림을 좋아해서 계속 하고 있는 거예요.
"If you don't like drawing try sculpting. I keep doing it because I like drawings."

To Dislike: Noun + (이/가) 싫다

We previously learned that we can use 싫어하다 ("to dislike") to say that we dislike something.

숙제하기를 싫어해요.
"I dislike doing homework."

Verbs to Nouns

Chapter 19

In addition to using 싫어하다 ("to dislike"), you can also use the verb 싫다 ("to be disliked"), to mean "to dislike," when used with the *Subject Marker* (이/가). The meaning is the same.

숙제하기**가** 싫어요.
"I dislike doing homework."

바람 부는 날**이** 싫어요.
"I dislike windy days."

월요일 아침에 일어나기**가** 싫어요.
"I dislike waking up on Sunday mornings."

Remember that 싫어하다 is used with the *Object Marker* (을/를), while 싫다 is used with the *Subject Marker* (이/가)

> **Adv** While the meaning of (이/가) 싫다 and (을/를) 싫어하다 is the same, their nuance is slightly different. Using 싫다 emphasizes the *thing* that you dislike, while using 싫어하다 emphasizes that you *dislike* it. However, this difference is small, and not significant (I just thought that some of you might be curious).

To Like: Noun + (이/가) 좋다

Just as 싫다 can be used similarly to 싫어하다, the verb 좋다 ("to be good") can also be used similarly to 좋아하다 ("to like").

고양이보다 강아지**가** 좋아요.
"I like dogs more than cats."

강아지 means "puppy," but is used often in place of 개 ("dog").

내가 좋아? 아니면 철수**가** 좋아?
"Do you like me? Or do you like Chul-soo?"

휴가지로는 바다**가** 좋아요.
"As a vacation spot, I like the beach."

Again, remember that 좋아하다 is used with the *Object Marker* (을/를), while 좋다 is used with the *Subject Marker* (이/가)

Continually: 계속

계속 is an *adverb* that means "continually." It can be translated in regular conversation as "keep" (such as "to keep doing"). Here are just a few examples:

Verbs to Nouns

Chapter 19

계속 하다 "to keep doing," "to continually do"
계속 보다 "to keep looking," "to continually look"
계속 가다 "to keep going," "to continually go"

머리가 계속 아파요.
"My head keeps hurting."

Adv

Repeatedly: 자꾸

Another similar word to 계속 is the *adverb* 자꾸. This means "repeatedly," so instead of something just continuing (as with 계속), it shows that the action happens over and over again.

자꾸 보고 싶어요.
"I keep wanting to see you."

Person – 것

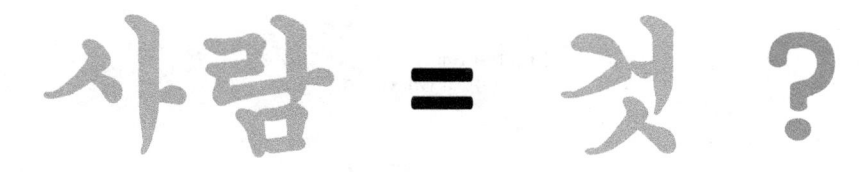

사람 = 것 ?

Let's go back to the conversation sentence and look at the ending – 계속 하고 있는 거예요. In the sentence, 희진 uses 것 at the end (here, 거) to talk about *herself*. Literally, this means "I am a thing that keeps doing it."

While we'd never think of a person as a "thing" in English, in Korean it's fine to use 것 when describing someone (such as yourself, for example).

To make this form, attach 는 것 after an *action verb*, or conjugate a descriptive verb like normal to the *present tense*.

저도 같이 가는 거예요.
("I am a thing that is going together too.")
"I'm going together too."

나도 먹는 거야.
"I'm eating too."

혼자서 운동하는 거예요.
"I'm exercising alone."

지금 미국에서 살고 있는 거예요.
"Now I'm living in America."

Chapter 19 — Verbs to Nouns

> **Adv:** Using this form (는 것이다) is similar to using the standard 요 form, but puts more emphasis on the *person*. Using the standard 요 form instead, or any other form, puts more emphasis on the *action*. However, the difference is small, so feel free to use either one.

Also remember that you can still use 것 for describing *things* (as usual), and not only for people.

한국은 겨울에 추운 거죠?
"Korea is cold in winter, right?"

운전을 하려고 하면 면허증이 필요한 거예요.
"If you intend to drive, you need a license."

> **Adv:** Although I didn't mention this earlier, we've already used this kind of form (것) before with the *future tense* – ㄹ 것이다. When using the ㄹ 것이다 future tense, what you're actually saying is that you are a "thing" which *will* (future ㄹ – which we learned in Chapter 4) do something.
>
> 저도 갈 거예요.
> ("I am a thing which will go too.")
> "I will go too."

Practice

Change the following action verbs into nouns using 기:

1. 김치를 먹다
2. 수학을 공부하다
3. 비행기를 타다

Change the following action verbs into nouns using 는 것:

4. 한국어를 가르치다
5. 책을 읽다
6. 미국에서 살다

Change the following action verbs into nouns using (음/ㅁ):

7. 배우다
8. 가르치다
9. 그리다

Verbs to Nouns

Chapter 19

Translate to Korean:

10. "I like reading books."

_____.

11. "Swimming is fun."

_____.

12. "It will take about 2 hours."

_____.

13. "I kept losing."

_____.

14. "Keep doing it."

_____.

15. "It's important to brush your teeth in the evening."

_____.

Translate to English:

16. 숙제하기가 싫어요.

_____.

17. 비 오는 날에는 밖에 나가기가 싫어요.

_____.

18. 난 네가 좋아.

_____.

Chapter 19 — Verbs to Nouns

19. 이 정도면 돼요.

_____.

20. 한 5 킬로그램 정도 차이 나요.

_____.

21. 캘리포니아주에서 한국까지 가려고 하면 10 시간 넘게 걸려요.

_____.

New Phrases

와아!	"Wow!"
됐어요.	"No thanks.," "I'm not interested."

New Vocabulary

양치(를) 하다	"to brush one's teeth"
다른	"other," "another" (adjective)
그룹	"group"
과제	"assignment," "project"
캐러멜	"caramel"
팝콘	"popcorn"
일기	"journal," "diary"
일기(를) 쓰다	"to write in a journal/diary"
습관	"habit," "custom"
도움	"help"
배움	"learning," "study"
가르침	"teachings"
죽음	"death"
피하다	"to avoid"
도움이 되다	"to be helpful"
걸음	"a step," "a pace"

Verbs to Nouns

Chapter 19

시간(이) 걸리다	"to take time"
넘게	"over," "more than" (adverb)
도 안 되게	"under," "less than" (adverb)
한	"about," "approximately"
조각	"sculpture"
조각(을) 하다	"to sculpt," "to carve a sculpture"
싫다	"to be disliked"
바람(이) 불다	"to be windy"
강아지	"puppy," "dog"
휴가	"a break," "a leave"
휴일	"a day off"
휴가지	"vacation spot"
방학	"school vacation"
축제	"festival"
계속	"continually" (adverb)
면허증	"(driver's) license"
충분하다	"to be enough"
충분히	"enough" (adverb)
부족하다	"to be lacking"
모자르다	"to not be enough"
그만하다	"to stop (doing)"
빗	"comb"
체육	"physical education"
체육관	"gym," "gymnasium"
박하	"peppermint"
계피	"cinnamon"
떠나다	"to go off," "to depart"
떠나가다	"to go off (to somewhere)," "to depart (to somewhere)"
열(이) 나다	"to catch/get a fever"
감기(에) 걸리다	"to catch a cold"
독감에 걸리다	"to catch the flu"
차이(가) 나다	"to be different," "to have a difference"

Chapter 19
Verbs to Nouns

차이(가) 안 나다	"to not be different," "to not have a difference"
면도(를) 하다	"to shave"
오래	"a long time" (adverb)

While

Conversation

Chapter 20

현우:	공부하는 동안에 음악을 조금 틀어도 될까요?
성현:	네, 제가 할게요.
현우:	아, 그런 음악 말고요! 전 랩을 싫어해요.
성현:	미안해요. 저는 랩을 들으면서 춤 추는 걸 좋아해요.
현우:	지금 춤을 추지 마세요. 저는 공부하는 중이에요.
성현:	네, 그럼 다른 걸 찾아 볼게요.
현우:	아, 트로트 말고요! 랩이 더 나아요.
성현:	알았어요. 그럼 랩을 다시 들어요.

As you'll learn in this chapter, there's more than one way to say "while" in Korean – by now you should be used to hearing that there is more than one way to do things in Korean. But don't worry. We'll cover each of them in this chapter in detail.

While

While: Verb Stem + (으)면서

You can use this form to say "while" when the *same* person does each action. For example, "I studied while eating." In this example, one person ("I") is doing both actions.

To make this form, take a verb stem and attach 으면서 if it ends in a *consonant*, or attach 면서 if it ends in a *vowel*. Except for the addition of the 서 at the end, this form is conjugated in the same way as (으)면, which we learned in Chapter 2. Here are just a few quick conjugated examples:

하다 → 하면서
먹다 → 먹으면서
알다 → 알면서

티비를 보면서 숙제를 했어요.
"I did homework while watching the TV."

저는 달리면서 밥을 먹었어요.
"I ate while running."

팝콘을 먹으면서 영화를 보고 싶어요.
"I want to watch a movie while eating popcorn."

지금까지 살면서 오늘처럼 행복한 날은 없었어요.
"Until now while living, I didn't have a happy day like today."
"I haven't had a happy day like today in my whole life."

살면서 (literally, "while living"), is commonly used to mean "in one's life." The above example could therefore also more-naturally translate as "Until now in my life, I haven't had as happy of a day as today."

눕다 ("to lie down") is an *irregular verb*, and conjugates as though it were a *descriptive verb* – as 누우면서, and not 눕으면서.

While

답을 이미 알면서 왜 물어봐요?
"Why do you ask while knowing the answer already?"

아빠가 고기를 구우면서 노래를 불렀어요.
"Dad sang a song while cooking the meat."

Another common *irregular verb* is 굽다 – "to cook (with fire)" – which conjugates here as 구우면서, and not 굽으면서.

혼자서도 잘하면서 왜 이렇게 자신이 없어요?
"While you do well even on your own, why do you not have confidence (like this)?"

Note that these irregular conjugations also apply for the (으)면 form that we learned in Chapter 2 as well, and not only when using (으)면서, because both forms are conjugated in the same way.

On the other hand, if you wanted to say "while" when *different* people do each action, you cannot use this form. For example, "I studied while you ate." We'll learn how to make that form next.

While: Verb Stem + 는 동안(에)

You can use this form to say "while" when *different* people do each action.

To make this form, take a verb stem and attach 는 (exactly as you would when changing an *action verb* into an *adjective*, which we learned in Chapter 4). Then attach 동안 ("a period of time"), followed by 에. The particle 에 at the end is *optional*.

하다 → 하는 동안(에)
먹다 → 먹는 동안(에)
알다 → 아는 동안(에)

Chapter 20

While

내가 먹는 동안에 철수가 이야기했어.
"Chul-soo talked while I ate."

내가 먹고 있는 동안에 철수가 이야기했어.
"Chul-soo talked while I was eating."

제가 말하고 있는 동안에 방해하지 마세요.
"Don't interrupt while I'm talking."

제가 청소를 하는 동안에 동생은 빨래를 했어요.
"While I vacuumed, my younger sibling did the laundry."

In addition, you can also use this form to say "while" when the *same* person does each action.

화장실에 있는 동안에 전화가 왔어요.
"I got a phone call while in the bathroom."

시험을 보는 동안에 핸드폰을 쓰면 안 돼요.
"You shouldn't use your cellphone while taking the test."

학교 생활을 하는 동안에 인턴십을 해 보세요.
"Try doing an internship while you're a student."

The above sentence would directly translate as "Try doing an internship while living student life."

Since 동안(에) can be used in both situations – when one person, or when different people are doing the actions – it might be tempting to only use this form; this is fine. At first, I would recommend using 동안(에), and then using (으)면서 as you become more comfortable with how the grammar works.

Now that we've learned two common ways to say "while" in Korean, let's go over the conversation.

현우: 공부하는 동안에 음악을 조금 틀어도 될까요?
"Can I turn on some music while we're studying?"

틀다 means "to turn on," but can only be used for turning on *audio electronics* (such as a radio, CD, music, etc.).

제가 자고 있는 동안에 갑자기 라디오를 틀지 마세요.
"Don't suddenly turn on the radio while I'm sleeping."

While

For all other items, use 켜다 ("to turn on").

티비를 켰어요.
"I turned on the TV."

불을 켰어요.
"I turned on the light."

성현: 네, 제가 할게요.
"Yeah, I'll do it."

현우: 아, 그런 음악 말고요! 전 랩을 싫어해요.
"Ah, not that kind of music! I don't like rap."

Not: Noun + 말고(요)

You can use 말고(요) to tell someone "not" in a sentence. The 요 is removed when you're speaking *casually*.

저 말고요.
"Not me."

커피 말고 차를 주세요.
"Please give me tea, not coffee."

이것들 말고 다른 건 없나요?
"Not these ones, but is there another one?"

Note that using 말고(요) is different from using 아니고(요), which simply means "it is not," or "I am not," among other translations.

제가 미국 사람이 아니고, 캐나다 사람이에요.
"I'm not an American, I'm Canadian."

미국 사람 말고요. 한국 사람이에요.
"Not American. He's Korean."

> Adv 말고(요) comes from the verb 말다, which is the same verb that we previously learned how to use in Chapter 14 – for example, using 마세요.

While 싫어하다 means "to dislike," keep in mind that sometimes simply "to not like" will be a more natural translation – in this way it can be used similarly to 좋아하지 않다.

273

While

Chapter 20

성현: 미안해요. 저는 랩을 들으면서 춤 추는 걸 좋아해요.
"Sorry. I like dancing while listening to music."

현우: 지금 춤을 추지 마세요. 저는 공부하는 중이에요.
"Don't dance now. I'm in the middle of studying."

In the Middle of: Verb Stem + 는 중(이다)

You can use this form to say that you are in the *middle* of doing something – meaning that you're *currently* doing something. While its literal meaning is similar to using the *Progressive Tense* (고 있다), it more strongly *emphasizes* that you are currently doing something (and therefore might not be finished for a while).

To make this form, take a verb stem and attach 는 (exactly as we just did for 동안). Then attach 중, followed by the verb 이다 conjugated any way you'd like.

지금 숙제하고 있는 중이에요.
"I'm in the middle of doing homework now."

아직 고민하는 중이에요.
"I'm still worrying."

지금 가는 중이에요.
"I'm in the middle of going."
"I'm on my way."

Or, you can also use 중(이다) directly after certain *nouns* instead. While it can't be used after every noun, here are some common cases where you will find it:

아직 고민 중이에요.
"I'm still in the middle of concern."
"I'm still worrying."

다이어트 중이에요.
"I'm in the middle of a diet."
"I'm on a diet."

생각 중이에요.
"I'm in the middle of thinking."
"I'm thinking about it."

While

사장님은 회의 중이십니다.
"The boss is in the middle of a meeting."
"The boss is in a meeting."

성현: 네, 그럼 다른 걸 찾아 볼게요.

"Okay, well then I'll try to find something else."

현우: 아, 트로트 말고요! 랩이 더 나아요.

"Ah, not trot! Rap is better."

Note that the sentence 랩이 더 나아요 literally translates as "Rap is more preferable." You could also translate it more naturally to match the conversation as, "Rap would be much better."

Culture Notes

트로트 ("trot") is Korea's oldest form of pop music, and is mainly influenced by Japanese and American songs. If you were a "K-pop" fan in the early 1900s, you would've listened to a lot of trot. While trot remained popular into the 1970s, more popular music slowly began to take its place. Nowadays there are only a few singers who still create trot music, and it is a slowly disappearing form of pop music. If you want to make a special impression on older Koreans, consider singing a trot song for them the next time you're in a 노래방.

성현: 알았어요. 그럼 랩을 다시 들어요.

"Alright. Well then we'll listen to rap again."

Chapter 20

While

While: Verb + 가

There's one more common way to say "while" – using 가. This form is a bit different from (으)면서 and 동안(에), in that this form is used when the second action happens immediately *after* the first action. For example, "I ran *then* stopped and took a photo." While the actual meaning of this form is one action happening right after another action, it is often used to mean "while," which is why I've included it here. For example, "I stopped to take a photo *while* running."

This form is extremely simple to make. To make it, take a verb (including the stem) and attach 가.

뛰어가다가 사진을 찍으려고 멈췄어요.
"I ran then stopped (intending) to take a photo."
"I stopped to take a photo while running."

잠을 자다가 침대에서 떨어졌어요.
"I slept then fell down from the bed."
"I fell down from the bed while sleeping."

영화를 보다가 잠들었어요.
"I watched a movie then fell asleep."
"I fell asleep while watching a movie."

학교로 걸어가다가 돈을 주웠어요.
"I walked to school then picked up some money."
"I picked up some money while walking to school."

줍다 ("to pick up") is another *irregular verb* which conjugates as 주웠어요 – and not as 줍었어요.

Practice

Translate to Korean:

1. "I sang a song while dancing."

_____.

2. "I put on makeup while drying my hair."

_____.

3. "While I did homework my younger sibling studied next to me."

_____.

4. "I showered while my friend ate."

_____.

While

5. "Today I'll wear pants, not a skirt."

   _____.

6. "Who turned on this music?"

   _____.

7. "I'm in the middle of watching a movie with mom."

   _____.

8. "I made a new friend while traveling."

   _____.

Translate to English:

9. 음악을 들으면서 요리를 했어요.

   _____.

10. 친구와 전화 통화를 하면서 버스를 기다렸어요.

    _____.

11. 운전을 하는 동안에 전화가 와서 받지 못했어요.

    _____.

12. 제가 옷을 입어 보는 동안에 아빠가 계산을 했어요.

    _____.

13. 저는 그것 말고 이게 더 좋아요.

    _____.

While

14. 제가 에어컨을 켰으니까 창문을 닫아 주세요.

_____.

15. 아직 여행하고 있는 중이에요.

_____.

16. 오늘 학교를 가는 동안에 연예인을 봤어요.

_____.

New Phrases

힘내세요.	"Cheer up."

New Vocabulary

방해(를) 하다	"to interrupt"
전화(가) 오다	"to get a phone call"
전화(를) 걸다	"to make a phone call"
통화	"telephone conversation"
전화 통화(를) 하다	"to talk on the phone"
대화	"conversation"
대화(를) 하다	"to have a conversation," "to converse"
문자	"text message"
생활	"(daily) life"
생활(을) 하다	"to live"
학교 생활	"school life"
인턴십	"internship"
자신	"confidence"
굽다	"to cook (with fire)"
틀다	"to turn on (sound)"
라디오	"radio"
랩	"rap"
회의	"conference," "meeting"

While

고민	"concern," "worry"
고민(을) 하다	"to be concerned," "to (slightly) worry"
트로트	"trot (music)"
멈추다	"to stop (moving)"
뛰어가다	"to go running"
뛰어오다	"to come running"
줍다	"to pick up"
여전히	"as usual," "as always," "as ever" (adverb)
진정(을) 하다	"to calm down"
힘(을) 내다	"to cheer (oneself) up"
눈물	"tear(s)"
눈물(이) 나다	"to cry," "to bawl"
음성	"voice"
간식	"snack," "refreshment"
안주	"snack (served with alcohol)"
반찬	"side dish"
옛날	"in the (really) old days," "in the past"
베이컨	"bacon"
무지개	"rainbow"
하품(을) 하다	"to yawn"
기침(을) 하다	"to cough"
재채기(를) 하다	"to sneeze"
트림(을) 하다	"to burp"
딸꾹질(을) 하다	"to hiccup"
참다	"to endure," "to repress"
때리다	"to hit," "to slap"
무릎	"knee"
근육	"muscle"
피	"blood"
수건	"towel"
손수건	"hand towel"
엉덩이	"buttocks," "butt"
답장	"(written) reply"
답장(을) 하다	"to reply (in writing)"

Chapter 20: While

엽서	"postcard"
치마	"skirt"
에어컨	"air conditioner"
살면서...	"in one's life..."

Answer Keys

Chapter 1

1) 저는 지금 바빠요. 맛있는 스테이크를 먹고 있어요.
2) 저는 책 3 권을 가지고 있어요.
3) 내일 과학 시험이 있어요.
4) 저는 심심하지만, 그 지루한 숙제를 하고 싶지 않아요.
5) 저는 80%만 이해했어요.
6) "I'm looking at the cell phone."
7) "Are you already going?"
8) "Please ask the English teacher tomorrow."
9) "Do you have money?"
10) "I'm doing it now but I can't finish it by tomorrow."

Chapter 2

1) 추우면
2) 길면
3) 더우면
4) 팔면
5) 가르치면
6) 영화를 정말 좋아하면 이 영화도 보세요.
7) 오늘 공원에 가면 물을 가지고 가세요. // 오늘 공원에 갈 때 물을 가지고 가세요.
8) 제가 졸업하면 같이 초밥을 먹으러 가고 싶어요.
9) 제가 졸업했을 때 초밥을 먹었어요.
10) 제가 어렸을 때 고양이를 좋아했어요.
11) "If I have time today, I can help."
12) "I can help when I have time today."
13) "What's wrong? Why do you want to move to a different city?"
14) "Please do it by 2 o'clock tomorrow."
15) "When I was 8 years old, I went to school everyday."

Chapter 3

1) 저는 안 갈 거예요.
2) 이번 달 23 일에 일할 거예요?

Answer Keys

3) 내일까지 25 불이 있을 거예요.
4) 오늘은 빨래를 했고 내일은 설거지를 할 거예요.
5) 5 시에 시간이 되면 알려주세요.
6) 자동차로 일하러 나갔어요.
7) "When will you do it?"
8) "I will start now."
9) "Let's eat!"
10) "You already ate?"
11) "Please sign on the contract in pencil."
12) "I didn't start, but I will do it tomorrow."

Chapter 4

1) 이것은 제가 산 컴퓨터예요.
2) 책은 읽을 수 있는 거예요.
3) 저는 읽을 책이 필요해요.
4) 저는 같이 놀 수 있는 친구가 없어요.
5) 시간이 조금 더 필요해요.
6) 제가 만든 김치가 철수 씨가 만든 김치보다 더 맛있었어요.
7) "You said that's a novel? Not a dictionary?"
8) "Did you hear what he said?"
9) "Is there something that we can play together?"
10) "Is there someone who will help?"
11) "Who's the person who made this movie?"
12) "Now I need something to eat."

Chapter 5

1) 저는 영어 선생님을 위한 선물을 샀어요.
2) 저는 제 친구를 위해서 노래를 불렀어요.
3) 저는 어머니를 위한 자동차를 샀어요.
4) 그 카메라가 아이를 위한 것이 아니에요.
5) 영희 씨는 한국어를 공부하기 위해서 그 책을 샀어요.
6) 저는 건강하기 위해 매일 운동해요.
7) "Who ate the food that's for Chul-soo?"

Answer Keys

8) "I need that."
9) "I don't need that."
10) "Did you prepare for going to Europe?"
11) "You need a lot of practice in order to speak Korean well."
12) "There are many things that I need in order to help."

Chapter 6

1) 제 책을 재미있게 읽었어요?
2) 저는 실수로 피자를 너무 뜨겁게 만들었어요.
3) 저는 비싼 운동화 없이 높이 뛸 수 없어요.
4) 조금 더 크게 말하세요.
5) 제 어머니가 만든 스테이크를 맛있게 먹었어요.
6) 철수 씨가 일부러 천천히 뛰었어요.
7) "Please speak quietly in the library."
8) "I had fun playing with my friend and enjoyed eating lunch."
9) "My friend moved far away."
10) "I took out my camera in vain."
11) "I couldn't enjoy watching the game because it tied at 5 to 5."
12) "I ate it without ketchup by mistake."

Chapter 7

1) 제일 좋아하는 책이 뭐예요?
2) 저는 그 책을 제일 좋아해요.
3) 이 셔츠를 아직 좋아해요.
4) 영어를 얼마나 공부했어요?
5) 그분은 저 같은 친구가 없어요.
6) 그분은 저같이 친절한 친구가 없어요.
7) 어느 게 제 샌드위치예요?
8) 그래서 제가 한국어를 공부해요.
9) "What's your favorite movie?"
10) "I don't even like that kind of movie."
11) "They still didn't come yet."
12) "I can't do it as well as Chul-soo."

Answer Keys

13) "I can't speak as well as Chul-soo can."
14) "Did you do something today?"
15) "Sometime I'll go to Korea."
16) "There is no food as delicious as the sandwiches they sell at that store."

Chapter 8

1) 하시다
2) 드시다
3) 주무시다
4) 계시다
5) 안 계시다
6) 가시다
7) 돌아가시다
8) 아시다
9) 혹시 미국 사람이세요?
10) 어제 왜 같이 안 가셨어요?
11) 뭘 드시고 싶으세요?
12) 성함이 어떻게 되세요?
13) 이 쪽으로 오세요.
14) 언제 주실 수 있어요?
15) "Where is your house?"
16) "How old are you?"
17) "Who's that person?"
18) "I couldn't give it to them yet."
19) "Please bring it to me tomorrow."
20) "I'll see you next time."

Chapter 9

1) 김치를 정말 좋아하네요!
2) 철수 씨는 햄버거를 못 먹네요.
3) 한국어를 많이 공부하고 있죠!
4) 한국어가 쉽죠?
5) 미국 사람이 아니군요.

Answer Keys

6) 철수 씨는 스테이크도 못 먹는군요.
7) 맞나요?
8) 한국 음악을 좋아하시나요?
9) "Now they're a little busy."
10) "It's your first time here, right?"
11) "Oh, they'll go home now."
12) "By chance do you know the teacher at this school who teaches math?"

Chapter 10

1) 안녕.
2) 언제 가셔?
3) 맛있네!
4) 잘 지냈어?
5) 나는 이제 밥 먹고 싶어.
6) 좀 더워.
7) 누구한테서 받았어?
8) 친구랑 놀았어?
9) 찌개가 너무 뜨겁잖아!
10) 나랑 영화 보러 같이 갈래?
11) 너 진짜 괜찮아?
12) 그게 뭐야?
13) 김영희 씨는 아주 예뻐.
14) "Don't you wanna go?"
15) "You're my good friend."
16) "I won't eat it so you eat it."
17) "You're really not a Korean? Your Korean is so good."

Chapter 11

1) 오는데
2) 맛있는데
3) 사는데
4) 하고 싶은데
5) 먼데

Answer Keys

6) 뜨거운데
7) 그런데
8) 좋은데
9) 심심한데
10) 인데
11) 가게에 갈까요?
12) 누구일까요?
13) 거기 많은 사람들이 있을까요?
14) 새로운 컴퓨터를 샀는데, 아직 게임할 수 없어요.
15) "If you have time to study shall we study together?"
16) "How would this be? Would Chul-soo like it?"
17) "Shall I help you a little?"
18) "It's not time to eat yet, right?"

Chapter 12

1) 숙제를 먼저 하자.
2) 한국에 같이 가자.
3) 오늘 밤에 영화 보러 가자.
4) 시작해요.
5) 같이 점심 먹어요.
6) 밤까지 같이 놀아요.
7) "Let's go home."
8) "Let's practice Korean together."
9) "Let's go to my house together."
10) "Let's go bowling."
11) "We don't have time now so let's hurry up and leave."
12) "Let's do the dishes and clean the house."

Chapter 13

1) 가게에 가 주세요.
2) 제가 에세이를 써 줄게요.
3) 제가 조금 쉬어도 돼요?
4) 2 곱하기 3 은 뭐예요?

Answer Keys

5) 난 네가 안 가도 신경 안 써.
6) 설거지하고 빨래를 해 주세요.
7) 제가 미국 사람이라도 한국어를 배울 수 있어요.
8) 이제 제가 집에 가도 돼요?
9) 지금 나가도 늦을 거예요.
10) 밥을 먹어도 항상 배가 고파요.
11) "I'll do it by tomorrow."
12) "Is 800 divided by 50 really 16?"
13) "It's alright if you don't do it now."
14) "They always helped me."
15) "Would it be okay if I pay for it?"
16) "I want to help you, but I can't because I'm busy now."
17) "Will you please help me next time?"
18) "Even if the weather's not hot, I don't wanna go."
19) "Please introduce yourself."
20) "Dad brought me here by car."

Chapter 14

1) 여기서 수영하지 마세요.
2) 지금 시작하면 안 돼요.
3) 잠이 들 뻔했어요.
4) 이 방에 들어가지 말아 주세요.
5) 제가 우유를 다 마셨어요.
6) 모든 집에는 화장실이 있어요.
7) 대부분의 사람들은 그렇게 생각해요.
8) 벽을 만지지 마세요. 제가 방금 페인트를 칠했어요.
9) "Don't go outside today."
10) "Please don't run in the hospital."
11) "Don't talk like that."
12) "You should bring an umbrella today."
13) "There should be more vegetables."
14) "You shouldn't eat yet."
15) "I almost dropped my laptop."
16) "We've almost arrived."

Answer Keys

Chapter 15

1) 절대로 다른 사람에게 말하지 마세요.
2) 철수 씨는 제 이상형이 전혀 아니에요.
3) 그 색은 별로 안 어울려요.
4) 선물로 줄 수 있는 것이 아무것도 없어요.
5) 아무나 데리고 오세요.
6) 새우 아니면 랍스타를 먹고 싶어요?
7) 도서관이나 카페에서 공부할까요?
8) 오늘 제 생일도 아닌데 선물을 많이 받았어요.
9) 사이다나 콜라를 주세요.
10) 비행기에서 영화를 보거나 잠을 잘 거예요.
11) "I don't have a house and a car."
12) "There's not even something I can do for you."
13) "It's not similar at all."
14) "There's no country that I know in Europe but England."
15) "Nobody contacts me lately."
16) "Are you American or Canadian?"
17) "Please give me anything to drink."
18) "For me, any color would all suit you well."
19) "Look, you didn't do anything that well either."
20) "How about flowers or a plush toy as a present?"

Chapter 16

1) 저는 정말 빨리 해야 돼요.
2) 왜 5시 전에 나가야 돼요?
3) 2시 후에는 너무 바쁠 거예요.
4) 집을 청소하기 전에 쓰레기를 버려 주세요.
5) 점심을 만든 후에 설거지를 해야 해요.
6) 운동을 하기 위해서 새로운 신발을 사야 해요.
7) "I have to take a shower."
8) "First of all I need to go home."
9) "I need to wait until tomorrow in order to know that."
10) "Are you going to take your medicine after your meal or before your meal?"

Answer Keys

11) "Take your keys before closing the door."
12) "How can I become a teacher?"

Chapter 17

1) 이 셔츠를 입어 봐도 돼요?
2) 바다에서 수영을 해 보고 싶어요.
3) 철수 씨가 만든 피자를 먹어 보고 싶어요.
4) 내년 봄에 한국에 가려고 하고 있어요.
5) 영화관에 가려고 해요.
6) 저는 일반 사람들과 달라요.
7) 저는 별 모양의 케이크를 샀어요.
8) 요즘 물을 많이 마시려고 하고 있어요.
9) "I'm trying to draw."
10) "I want to try a German sausage."
11) "Are you trying to make a new friend?"
12) "Could I drive by myself?"
13) "I'm trying to forget my past boyfriend."
14) "I'm waiting to go to the bathroom."
15) "I tried putting on my makeup in a new way."
16) "Could rose-shaped ice cream be more delicious than regular ice cream?"

Chapter 18

1) 미국에 와 본 적이 있어요?
2) 노래방에 가 본 적이 있어요?
3) 저는 한국 드라마를 본 적이 없어요.
4) 온라인 게임을 해 본 적이 있어요?
5) 이 책을 읽어 본 적이 있어요?
6) 등산을 해 본 적이 있어요?
7) "Have you ever ridden in an airplane before?"
8) "Have you ever gone on a picnic with your family before?"
9) "Have you ever had a cat before?"
10) "I've never eaten a lemon before yet."
11) "You've really never driven alone before?"

Answer Keys

12) "I haven't ever cut my hair for the last 3 years."

Chapter 19

1) 김치를 먹기
2) 수학을 공부하기
3) 비행기를 타기
4) 한국어를 가르치는 것
5) 책을 읽는 것
6) 미국에서 사는 것
7) 배움
8) 가르침
9) 그림
10) 저는 책을 읽는 것을 좋아해요.
11) 수영하기가 재미있어요.
12) 한 2 시간 정도 걸릴 거예요.
13) 제가 계속 졌어요.
14) 계속 하세요.
15) 저녁에 양치하는 것이 중요해요.
16) "I dislike doing homework."
17) "I dislike going outside on rainy days."
18) "I like you."
19) "This is about enough."
20) "It's about a 5 kilogram difference."
21) "If you're intending to go from California to Korea, it takes over 10 hours."

Chapter 20

1) 춤을 추면서 노래를 불렀어요.
2) 머리를 말리면서 화장을 했어요.
3) 제가 숙제를 하는 동안에 동생은 옆에서 공부했어요.
4) 친구가 밥을 먹는 동안에 샤워를 했어요.
5) 오늘은 치마 말고 바지를 입을 거예요.
6) 누가 이 음악을 틀었어요?
7) 엄마와 영화를 보고 있는 중이에요.

Answer Keys

8) 여행을 하면서 새로운 친구를 만들었어요
9) "I cooked while listening to music."
10) "I waited for the bus while talking to my friend on the phone."
11) "A phone call came while I was driving so I couldn't get it."
12) "While I was trying on clothes my dad paid for them."
13) "I like this better, not that."
14) "Please close the window because I turned on the air conditioner."
15) "I'm still in the middle of traveling."
16) "I saw a celebrity while going to school today."

Answer Keys

Appendix A. Introduction to Idioms

Of course, there's more to the Korean language than just vocabulary words and grammar forms. Just like in English, being able to speak using appropriate cultural references and idioms will help your Korean sound much more natural. And the best part is, you don't even need to be fluent in Korean before adding a bit of flavor to your speech – you can add this flavor by using *idioms*.

An *idiom* is a saying (or phrase) that is said so commonly that almost everyone knows its meaning. Idioms can also have unique meanings of their own that might not match the meaning of the words they are made of. For example, a common idiom in English is "a piece of cake." While we know that this idiom is talking about something being *incredibly* easy, the words are describing cake. The Korean language has many similar useful expressions that you can learn to improve your speaking abilities.

We've actually already learned a few idioms in this book, but you might not have realized it. An example is 신경(을) 쓰다, which we learned in Chapter 13. 신경 means "nerves" and 쓰다 means "to use," but "to use one's nerves" in Korean is an *idiom* that means "to care" in English.

Before beginning this section, I recommend first reading through this book completely at least once, including all of the "Advanced Notes." While knowing and using idioms (when appropriate) can be helpful, they will be much more useful once you are able to back up your newfound skills with actually being able to speak and understand basic Korean sentences.

Over time, new idioms will appear, and old ones will become less popular. This happens in both Korean and English – when was the last time you heard someone say "fit as a fiddle" in a regular conversation? However, while it's important to keep up with the times, the idioms taught in this appendix will be only the most common, relevant, and long-enduring ones that you should be able to safely use for years to come. I've avoided including any brand new idioms, as there is no way of telling how long they will stay around ("YOLO" anyone?). I've also avoided including any old-fashioned idioms in this appendix, as they will be much less common – imagine what your friends would think if you started saying "lickety-split" instead of "A.S.A.P." in your conversations? On the other hand, if you say "lickety-split" and they like you even more then they sound like pretty cool friends.

This appendix is not made to be a complete guide to idioms, nor is it a list of all of the most common expressions. However, you will be able to use all of these in regular conversation, and they are all commonly used. Before exploring additional idioms on your own, I recommend learning these ones first. As usual, I'll guide you through the meaning of each one as we go.

Appendix A. Introduction to Idioms

"to like" – 마음에 들다

Literal Meaning: "to enter the mind/heart"

Vocabulary: 마음 is a metaphorical word for "mind," "heart," or a person's "feelings." 들다 is a verb that means "to go in," or "to enter."

Explanation: If something enters your heart, then it must be something that you like.

이 옷이 정말 마음에 들어요.
"I really like these clothes."

"to (over-)compliment" 비행기(를) 태우다

Literal Meaning: "to give someone a ride in an airplane"

Vocabulary: 비행기 means "airplane." 태우다 means "to give (someone) a ride."

Explanation: If you're offering someone a ride in an airplane, then perhaps you're doing a bit too much for them.

비행기를 태우지 마세요.
"Don't overcompliment me."

"to be extremely easy" – 누워서 떡 먹기

Literal Meaning: "lying down and eating rice cake"

Vocabulary: 누워서 comes from the verb 눕다 ("to lie down"). 떡 is rice cake, and 먹기 means "eating."

Explanation: Lying down and eating rice cake is easy to do. You can think of this idiom as Korea's version of the expression "a piece of cake."

그건 나한테 누워서 떡 먹기야.
"That's a piece of cake for me."

"to be snooty" – 코(가) 높다

Literal Meaning: "one's nose is high"

Appendix A. Introduction to Idioms

Vocabulary: 코 means "nose," and 높다 means "to be high."

Explanation: If someone holds their head up, and looks down on other people, then their nose may appear high.

그 여자는 코가 너무 높아서 남자 친구가 없어요.
"That girl doesn't have a boyfriend because she's too snooty."

"to be (overly-)picky" – 눈(이) 높다

Literal Meaning: "one's eyes are high"

Vocabulary: 눈 means "eye(s)," and 높다 means "to be high."

Explanation: Just like with 코가 높다, if someone holds their head up and looks down on other people, they will also be overly picky using their eyes.

영희 씨는 눈이 높아요.
"Yung-hee is too picky."

"to be blinded" – 눈(이) 부시다

Literal Meaning: "one's eyes are dazzling"

Vocabulary: 눈 means "eye(s)," and 부시다 means "to be dazzling."

Explanation: If your eyes are dazzling (from a bright light), it will be difficult to see. You can use this phrase when the sun is in your eyes ("It's too bright!") or when you see someone who dazzles you ("She's so beautiful!").

아! 눈부셔!
"Ah, it's too bright!"

눈이 부시게 아름다워요.
"She's dazzlingly beautiful."

"to make sense" – 말(이) 되다

Literal Meaning: "the words are okay"

Vocabulary: 말 means "word(s)," and 되다 here means "to be okay."

Appendix A. Introduction to Idioms

Explanation: If the words are okay, then it will make sense.

당연히 말이 되죠.
"Of course it makes sense."

"to not make sense" – 말도 안 되다

Literal Meaning: "even the words are not okay"

Vocabulary: 말 means "word(s)." After 말 is the particle 도 ("also," "even," "too"), followed by 안 되다 ("to not be okay").

Explanation: If the words aren't even okay, then it will not make sense.

그게 말도 안 돼요.
"That doesn't (even) make sense."

"to look familiar" – 눈에 익다

Literal Meaning: "to be familiar to the eyes"

Vocabulary: 눈 means "eye(s)," and 익다 means "to be familiar."

Explanation: Something that is familiar to your eyes is something that *looks* familiar to you.

그 그림이 눈에 익어요.
"That picture looks familiar."

"to be generous/resourceful" – 손(이) 크다

Literal Meaning: "to have big hands"

Vocabulary: 손 means "hand(s)," and 크다 means "to be big."

Explanation: You can think of someone with large hands helping many other people; this can either be due to *generosity*, or due to *resourcefulness*.

우리 엄마는 손이 크셔서 항상 음식을 너무 많이 만드세요.
"My mom is generous so she always makes too much food."

Appendix A. Introduction to Idioms

"to do as one wishes" – 마음대로 하다

Literal Meaning: "to do as the mind/heart"

Vocabulary: 마음 means "mind" or "heart." 대로 means "as" or "like" (대로 is not covered in this book).

Explanation: If you're doing as your mind or heart tells you, then you're doing whatever you want.

마음대로 하세요.
"Do as you wish."

"to relax" – 마음(을) 놓다

Literal Meaning: "to put down the mind/heart"

Vocabulary: 마음 means "mind" or "heart," and 놓다 means "to put down" or "to let go."

Explanation: If you can put down your mind (and your worries) then you will be able to relax.

마음을 놓을 수가 없었어요.
"I couldn't relax."

"a small size" – 쥐꼬리만큼

Literal Meaning: "as much as a mouse tail"

Vocabulary: 쥐꼬리 means "mouse tail," and 만큼 means "as much as."

Explanation: A mouse tail is small and short.

쥐꼬리만큼밖에 안 먹었어요.
"I only ate a tiny piece."

"a small amount" – 눈곱만큼

Literal Meaning: "as much as eye gunk"

Vocabulary: 눈곱 (pronounced 눈꼽) means "eye gunk," and 만큼 means "as much as."

Appendix A. Introduction to Idioms

Explanation: Even though it's gross, eye gunk is only a small amount.

한국어를 눈곱만큼밖에 못 해요.
"I can only speak Korean a little bit."

"to be overcharged" – 바가지(를) 쓰다

Literal Meaning: "to wear a large bowl on your head"

Vocabulary: 바가지 means "a large bowl," and 쓰다 means "to wear (on your head)."

Explanation: You would feel embarrassed and upset to wear a large bowl on your head. In the same way, if you were overcharged (ripped off) at a store you would feel embarrassed and upset.

오늘 시장에서 바가지를 썼어요.
"I got ripped off in the market today."

"to overcharge" – 바가지(를) 씌우다

Literal Meaning: "to put a large bowl on someone's head"

Vocabulary: 바가지 means "a large bowl" and 씌우다 means "to make someone wear something on their head" (forcing someone to 쓰다 something).

Explanation: Making someone else wear a large bowl on their head would cause them to feel embarrassed and upset. In this idiom, overcharging (ripping-off) someone is the same as putting a large bowl over their head.

바가지(를) 씌우지 마세요.
"Don't rip me off."

"to be old" – 나이(를) (많이) 먹다

Literal Meaning: "to eat (many) years"

Vocabulary: 나이 means "age (in years)," and 먹다 means "to eat."

Explanation: In Korean, you *consume* (eat) one year every year that you are alive. People who are older are simply people who have eaten more years.

Appendix A. Introduction to Idioms

이제 나이를 많이 먹어서 몸이 예전과 같지 않아요.
"Now I'm older so my body isn't like it was before."

Another common way to use this idiom is by using 나이(가) 많다 (literally, "to have many years"). This is much more polite than using 늙다 ("to be old").

"to put forth effort" – 애(를) 쓰다

Literal Meaning: "to use effort"

Vocabulary: 애 means "effort," and 쓰다 means "to use."

Explanation: Trying hard to do something takes effort – you are using effort to get something done. 애(를) 쓰다 is similar to 노력(을) 하다, which we learned in Chapter 17.

그런 일에 애를 쓰고 싶지 않아요.
"I don't want to put my effort in that kind of work."

Appendix A. Introduction to Idioms

Appendix B. Major Korean Holidays

Just as it's important to know when April Fools' Day is (it's for your own good), or what the 4th of July is in the United States, it's important to know when and what 추석 is in Korea. If you've never heard of 추석 before, then you're in the right place. Let's cover all of the major, serious holidays in Korea... as well as a few fun ones.

Note that this list does not include every single holiday celebrated in Korea, but this is okay. After all, did you know that Leif Erikson Day (leader of the first Europeans to set foot in America) is celebrated in the United States on October 9th? You can learn additional holidays later on as you continue learning more Korean.

In addition, you'll notice that many religious holidays will be absent from this list; this is simply because these holidays are not well-known or celebrated among the majority of Koreans.

January 1st – 신정

신정 is Korea's "New Year's Day." Most people will take the day off to relax. However, many jobs will require their employees to work anyway.

February 14th – 발렌타인 데이

You should be able to guess which day this is by reading it out loud. However, don't be fooled by the name. Valentine's Day in Korea is unique, in that women give chocolates to men, and not vice versa. Specifically, women will give chocolates to men who they like, to their male friends, and to their male coworkers. Men do not give women chocolates or gifts on this day. I think I just heard a bunch of men sigh in relief, but keep reading.

March 14th – 화이트 데이

화이트 데이 (White Day) is the opposite of Valentine's Day. On White Day, Men give chocolates to women, including women who they like, their female friends, and their female coworkers.

Appendix B. Major Korean Holidays

While not listed separately here, there is one more day that you can be aware of which is similar to Valentine's Day and White Day – 블랙 데이 (Black Day). On Black Day, both men and women who did not receive any chocolates on Valentine's Day or White Day will meet together to eat 짜장면 (Chinese-style noodles with black bean sauce).

April 1st – 만우절

만우절 is Korea's version of April Fool's Day. Just like April Fool's Day in other countries (such as America), some Koreans will try to trick others on this day. Although most people will not participate (usually only students will pay attention to this date), keep an eye out for suspicious activity, as well as anyone trying to trick you. Or perhaps, you'll be the one doing the tricking.

May 5th – 어린이날

어린이날 is Children's Day, and every year kids are given money on this day. Families will also plan trips for this day. Hearing about free money and a vacation *almost* makes me want to be a kid again.

May 8th – 어버이날

어버이날 is Parent's Day (어버이 is another word for "parents"). Unlike Children's Day, parents don't usually receive money and a vacation on this day (although some children may give money to their parents). Instead, children will give pink carnations to their parents.

Appendix B. Major Korean Holidays

May 15th – 스승의 날

스승의 날 is Teacher's Day (스승 is another word for "teacher"). On Teacher's Day, students will give pink carnations to their teachers. These can be current students, or previous students who want to show respect to their previous teachers. Also, many schools will close on Teacher's Day, giving teachers an actual vacation from their work.

October 9th – 한글날

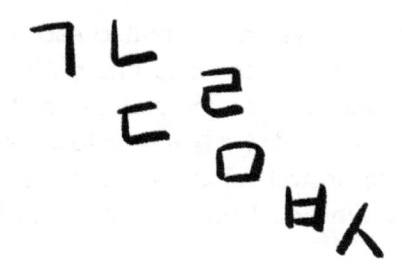

한글날 (literally, "Hangul Day") is the day for celebrating the creation of the Korean alphabet. Typically on this day, Koreans will remember 한글 and feel appreciation for 세종대왕 (King Sejong) who was largely responsible for developing the alphabet.

November 11th – 빼빼로 데이

빼빼로 ("Pepero") is the name of a popular snack in Korea. 빼빼로 are thin cookie tubes coated with chocolate, though there are a variety of other flavors and coatings. This holiday was started by the company that made 빼빼로 in an effort to increase product sales, believe it or not (sarcasm). Although Pepero Day is technically a corporate-created holiday, the day has become so well-known that I've included it on this list. November 11th was selected by the company because the date 11/11 resembles four 빼빼로 sticks. People also use this day as an opportunity to give 빼빼로 to friends and significant others, as two 빼빼로 sticks resemble two people standing together.

Appendix B. Major Korean Holidays

Changing Holidays

There are also a few Korean holidays that do not have a set date, and which will change every year. In America, we have holidays like this as well, such as Mother's Day (which is the second Sunday in May) and Thanksgiving (which is the fourth Thursday in November). American holidays are celebrated according to the *Western calendar* (also called the Gregorian calendar). In Korea, however, holidays with changing dates are celebrated according to the *Lunar calendar*.

In order to know when these holidays are celebrated each year, you will need to know how to convert a date on the Lunar calendar to one on the Western calendar – this is not a simple process, and I wouldn't recommend trying it. More preferably, you can simply do a search online – type in "음력 #월 #일" into your favorite search engine and you should be able to find the answer for the current year easily (I'd recommend this method). Or, you can also try simply asking a Korean what day a certain holiday is for the current year.

Here are the major Korean holidays that have changing dates. Each of these is listed by its date on the Lunar calendar, so you will need to convert it first to the Western calendar in order to know when it is celebrated each year.

1월 1일 – 설날

설날 is Korea's New Year's Day on the Lunar Calendar. On 설날, family members meet and spend time together. Children are also given money. Traditionally Koreans will also eat 떡국 ("rice cake soup") on this day.

4월 8일 – 부처님 오신 날

부처님 오신 날, literally "the day Buddha came," is the celebration of Buddha's Birthday. This day is also called 석가탄신일 (also meaning "Buddha's Birthday"). This holiday is mostly celebrated by Buddhists, who will use this day to visit a Buddhist temple.

Appendix B. Major Korean Holidays

8월 15일 – 추석

추석 is Korea's Thanksgiving. Korean families will meet together on this day to eat. In addition, many families will visit the graves of past relatives to pay respects.

Appendix B. Major Korean Holidays

Appendix C. Reading Practice

Practicing Korean is just as important as studying, but it can be difficult to jump right into reading novels and newspapers when you're still learning the basics of the Korean language. That's why I've created this reading practice appendix for you – to give you a few examples of real-life Korean in use.

This section is intended to be used after you've completed reading through this book, including the "Advanced Notes." You should be able to work your way through this appendix using only what you've learned in this book (as well as the first book). If you're stuck on a vocabulary word, I'd recommend checking the glossaries in both books (or a dictionary). If you're stuck on a grammar concept, I'd recommend that you re-read the chapter that covers it.

Included in this section is an example recipe, a play script, and a few jokes in Korean (each with English translations directly below them). Also included are additional vocabulary sections for new words in this appendix. Enjoy!

레시피 – 소불고기

불고기용 [1] 소고기 (eye of round/sirloin/T-bone/flank) [400 그램]
진간장 [2] [3T][3]
물엿 [1T]
설탕 [1/2T]
키위 [1/2 개]
참기름 [1/2T]
양파 [1 개]
당근 [1/2 개]
다진 마늘 [1T]
파 [1 대][4]
굴소스 [1/2T]
소금과 후추 [약간]

1. 고기는 키친타월로 핏물을 조금 닦아서 준비합니다.
2. 양파 1/2 개, 키위는 믹서기에 갈고,

Appendix C. Reading Practice

3. 2 에 진간장, 물엿, 설탕, 참기름, 다진 마늘, 굴소스, 후추를 조금 넣어서 한 번 더 갑니다.
4. 남은 양파 1/2 개와 당근을 채 썹니다.
5. 파 1 대는 굵게 어슷 썹니다.
6. 큰 보울에 고기와 간 양념을 넣어 비닐 장갑을 낀 손으로 주물러 줍니다.
7. 6 에 채 썬 양파와 당근, 파를 넣어 섞습니다.
8. 냉장고에 7 의 양념된 고기를 넣고 4 시간 정도 기다립니다.
9. 팬에 기름을 넣지 않고 양념된 고기를 넣고 센 불에 볶습니다.
10. 고기가 어느 정도 익으면 중간 불로 줄여서 계속 익힙니다.
11. 간을 보고 싱거우면 소금을 조금 넣어 줍니다.[5]

Recipe – "Barbequed Beef"

Beef for making "barbequed beef" (eye of round/sirloin/T-bone/flank) [400 grams]
Strong soy sauce [3 tbsp.]
Starch syrup [1 tbsp.]
Sugar [1/2 tbsp.]
Kiwi [1/2]
Sesame oil [1/2 tbsp.]
Onion [1]
Carrot [1/2]
Minced garlic [1 tbsp.]
Green onion [1]
Oyster sauce [1/2 tbsp.]
Salt and pepper [a little]

1. For the meat, prepare it by cleaning a bit of the blood with a paper towel.
2. For half of the onion and the kiwi, grind it in a blender....
3. And to (step) 2 add the strong soy sauce, starch syrup, sugar, sesame oil, minced garlic, oyster sauce, and a little pepper, then grind it once more.
4. Finely chop the remaining half of the onion and carrot.
5. For the green onion, slice it thick diagonally.
6. In a large bowl, put in the meat and the ground seasonings, then massage it with a hand wearing a plastic glove.
7. Add the finely chopped onion, carrots, and green onions to (step) 6, then mix.
8. Put the seasoned meat from (step) 7 in the refrigerator, and wait for about 4 hours.
9. Don't add oil to the pan, add the seasoned meat, and (pan) fry it on a high (strong) flame.
10. When the meat is somewhat done, lower it to a medium flame and continue cooking it.
11. Taste it, and if it's bland add a little salt.

Appendix C. Reading Practice

Recipe Notes

[1] 불고기용 means "for the purpose of 불고기." 용 is a Sino Korean word that is added at the end of certain words to mean "for (the purpose of)."

[2] 진간장 means "strong soy sauce," and comes from the descriptive verb 진하다 ("to be strong," "to be thick," "to be dark") and the word 간장 ("soy sauce").

[3] 'T' is used to mean "tablespoon," and 't' is used to mean "teaspoon."

[4] Green onions can also be counted using 대 (appliance or car counter).

[5] While both 간(을) 보다 and 맛(을) 보다 mean "to taste (something)," 간(을) 보다 is specifically used when tasting to see whether something is seasoned well or not.

New Vocabulary

진간장	"strong soy sauce"
물엿	"(starch) syrup"
다지다	"to be minced," "to be finely chopped"
참기름	"sesame oil"
키친타월	"kitchen towel"
핏물	"blood (liquid)"
믹서기	"blender"
갈다	"to grind"
남다	"to be remaining," "to be left over"
채 썰다	"to slice/chop thin," "to slice/chop fine"
굵다	"to be chunky," "to be thick"
어슷	"diagonally," "slanted" (adverb)
보울	"bowl"
양념	"seasoning"
주무르다	"to massage"
양념(이) 되다	"to be seasoned"
팬	"pan"
어느 정도	"somewhat," "to a certain degree" (adverb)
익다	"to be done (cooked)"

Appendix C. Reading Practice

중간	"medium," "the middle," "the center"
익히다	"to cook (something)"
간(을) 보다	"to taste (something)"

연극 – 해와 달이 된 오누이

등장인물:

엄마, 호랑이, 오빠, 여동생, 해설

1 막 [1]

해설: 옛날 옛날에, 어느 [2] 한 오누이와 엄마가 함께 살고 있었습니다.

엄마: 벌써 밤이네. 아이들이 기다리고 있을 건데.... 얼른 가야겠어.[3]

호랑이: 어흥!

엄마: 어머, 누구세요?

호랑이: 떡 하나 주면 안 잡아먹지!

엄마: 여기 있어요. 제발 목숨만은....[4]

해설: 그렇게 여섯 고개를 하나하나 넘어갈 때마다 [5] 호랑이는 계속 나타났습니다. 마지막 고개를 넘어갈 때였습니다....

호랑이: 어흥! 떡 하나 더 주면 안 잡아먹지!

엄마: 이제 떡이 없는데.... 어떡하지?[6]

호랑이: 뭐, 떡이 없어? 그럼 너라도 [7] 잡아먹어야겠는데! 앙!

Appendix C. Reading Practice

2 막

호랑이: 이제 옷도 갈아 입었으니까 아이들이 엄마로 생각할 거야.

해설: 잠시 후....

호랑이: 얘들아! 엄마가 왔어. 어서 문 열어.

오빠: 어? 우리 엄마 목소리가 아니예요!

호랑이: 에취! 에~취![8] 감기에 걸려서 그래.

여동생: 그럼 손을 보여주세요. 우리 엄마 손은 뽀얗고 하얀데.

해설: 호랑이가 손을 보여줍니다.

오빠: 어, 주황 바탕에 검은 줄무늬.... 호랑이 손 같은데?

여동생: 오빠, 그럼 어떡해?

3 막

여동생: 우리 어디로 도망가지?

오빠: 저기 나무가 있네. 저기로 올라가면 되겠어. 근데 어떻게 올라가지?

여동생: 저기 도끼가 있잖아. 도끼로 찍고 올라가면 되지.

오빠 & 동생: 영~차! 영~차!

호랑이: 아니,[9] 이 녀석들이 어디 갔지?

여동생: 우리 여기 있지!

호랑이: 어떻게 저기까지....

오빠: 손에 참기름을 바르고 올라왔지. 아마 넌 못 할 거야!

호랑이: 옳지. 참기름을 발라야겠네.

해설: 잠시 후....

호랑이: 아! 아파!

Appendix C. Reading Practice

해설: 호랑이가 나무 밑으로 [10] 미끄러져 내렸습니다.

여동생: 하하하! 이 바보. 도끼로 찍고 올라와야 되는데.

오빠: 야! 그걸 말해 주면 안 되지!

호랑이: 아! 도끼가 있었네! 녀석들, 너흰 독 안에 든 쥐야![11]

오빠: 호랑이가 올라오잖아! 이제 어떡하지?

여동생: 하느님, 저희들을 살려 주세요! 튼튼한 줄을 내려 주세요!

해설: 하늘에서 줄이 내려왔습니다. 오누이는 그 줄을 잡고 하늘로 올라가서 해와 달이 되었습니다. 하지만 호랑이는....

호랑이: 저도 줄을 주세요!

해설: 하늘에서 썩을 줄이 내려왔습니다. 호랑이는 그 줄을 잡고 올라가다가 밑으로 떨어져서 죽었습니다.

Play – "The Brother and the Sister Who Became the Sun and the Moon"

Characters:

Mom, Tiger, Older Brother, Younger Sister, Narrator

Act 1

Narrator: Once upon a time, a brother and sister lived together with their mother.

Mom: It's already night. The kids will be waiting.... I must leave right away.

Tiger: Roar!

Mom: Oh dear, who are you?

Tiger: If you give me a rice cake I won't eat you!

Mom: Here it is. Please spare my life....

Appendix C. Reading Practice

Narrator: In that way, every time that the mother passed over six hills one by one, the tiger kept appearing. It was when she was passing over the last hill....

Tiger: Roar! If you give me one more rice cake I won't eat you!

Mom: I don't have any rice cakes now.... What do I do?

Tiger: What, you don't have any rice cakes? Well then I have to eat you at least! (Munch!)

Act 2

Tiger: I've changed my clothes, so the kids should think of me as their mother.

Narrator: After a while....

Tiger: Kids! Mom's home. Quick, open the door.

Older Brother: Huh? That's not mom's voice!

Tiger: Atchoo! Aa-choo! It's because I've got a cold.

Younger Sister: Well then show us your hands. Mom's hands are milky and white.

Narrator: The tiger shows its hands.

Older Brother: Uh, black stripes on a yellow background.... It's like tiger hands?

Younger Sister: Brother, well then what do we do?

Act 3

Younger Sister: Where can we run away to?

Older Brother: There's a tree over there. We should climb up there. But how do we climb up?

Younger Sister: Look, there's an axe over there. We should chop with the axe to climb up.

Older Brother & Younger Sister: One, two! One, two!

Tiger: Wait, where did these brats go?

Appendix C. Reading Practice

Younger Sister: We're up here!

Tiger: How did you get up....

Older Brother: We spread sesame oil on our hands and climbed up here. You probably won't be able to do that!

Tiger: Right. I need to spread on some sesame oil.

Narrator: After a while....

Tiger: Ah! That hurts!

Narrator: The tiger slid down to the bottom of the tree.

Younger Sister: Hahaha! You idiot. You have to chop with the axe to climb up.

Older Brother: Hey! You shouldn't tell him that!

Tiger: Ah! You had an axe! Brats, you're fish in a barrel!

Older Brother: Look, the tiger's coming up! What do we do now?

Younger Sister: God, please save us! Please send down a strong cord!

Narrator: A cord came down from the sky. The brother and sister grabbed the cord and climbed up to the sky, and then became the sun and the moon. But as for the tiger....

Tiger: Please give me a rope too!

Narrator: A rotten cord came down from the sky. The tiger grabbed that cord, and while climbing up, fell down and died.

New Vocabulary

오누이	"brother and sister"
등장인물	"character (in book, movie, etc.)"
해설	"narrator"
막	act counter
옛날 옛날에	"A long, long time ago...," "Once upon a time..."

Appendix C. Reading Practice

얼른	"at once," "right away" (adverb)
어흥	"(tiger) roar"
어머	"Oh dear."
잡아먹다	"to catch and eat"
목숨	"one's life," "one's breath"
살리다	"to save," "to spare"
고개	"hill," "pass"
하나하나	"one by one" (adverb)
넘어가다	"to pass over," "to cross over"
나타나다	"to appear," "to show up"
앙	munching sound
얘들아!	"(You) guys!," "(You) kids!"
에취!	"Atchoo!"
보여주다	"to show"
뽀얗다	"to be milky(-white)"
바탕	"background," "foundation"
줄무늬	"stripes," "striped pattern"
도망(을) 가다	"to run away," "to escape"
올라가다	"to climb up (somewhere)," "to go up (somewhere)"
도끼	"axe"
찍다	"to chop," "to hack," "to take (photo)"
영차!	"One, two!," "Heave-ho!"
녀석	"brat," "fellow"
올라오다	"to climb up (here)," "to go up (here)"
옳다	"to be right," "to be proper," "to be correct"
미끄러져 내리다	"to slide down"
하느님	"God"
튼튼하다	"to be durable," "to be sturdy," "to be strong"
내리다	"to let down," "to lower"
내려오다	"to come down," "to descend (to here)"
썩다	"to rot," "to decay"

Appendix C. Reading Practice

Play Notes

[1] 막 is used as a counter for an "act" (such as in a play). It is used with Sino Korean numbers. Not listed here is the counter for "scene" – which is 장, and is also used with Sino Korean numbers. "Act 1, Scene 1" would be 1막 1장.

[2] In addition to meaning "which," 어느 can also mean "a (certain)" or "one;" it's often used when telling stories. You might also see 어느 날 "a certain day" or "one day," used commonly.

[3] It's common in casual speech (or writing) to remove the verb 하다 or 되다 when saying "have to;" after all, both 하다 and 되다 have a similar meaning (we learned about this form in Chapter 16). When doing this, it's common to also remove the space between the words; both 해야 되겠어 or 해야 하겠어 would become 해야겠어.

[4] This is not a complete sentence, but if she finished it the sentence would probably be 제발 목숨만은 살려 주세요.

[5] You can attach 마다 to the 때 form (that we learned in Chapter 2) to mean "every time that someone does something." 누가 내 이름을 말할 때마다 would mean "every time that someone says my name."

[6] 어떡하다 is a common shortening of 어떻게 하다.

[7] Another use for (이)라도 is meaning "at least." Its literal meaning of "even," however, does not change.

[8] You can use "~" in writing to show that a sound is longer than usual.

[9] In English, we can say "wait" or "no" when we say something incorrectly in casual speech; for example, "I have 3... wait, 4 hamsters at home." In Korean you can do this (in casual speech) using 아니.

[10] In addition to "underneath," 밑 can also mean "the foot" or "the bottom" of something.

[11] The expression 독 안에 든 쥐 literally translates as "a mouse inside a jar." This phrase is an idiom, and an equivalent expression in English would be "fish in a barrel."

농담

Q. 아프지도 않은데 집에서 매일 쓰는 약은?
A. 치약

Appendix C. Reading Practice

Q. 사람들이 가장 좋아하는 물은?
A. 선물

Q. 개 중에 가장 예쁜 개는?
A. 무지개

Q. 중학생들과 고등학생들이 타는 차는?
A. 중고차

Q. 아몬드가 죽으면?
A. 다이아몬드

Q. 개미를 3 부분으로 나누면?
A. 죽어요.

Jokes

Q. What is a medicine that you use everyday even when not sick?
A. Toothpaste.

Q. What water do people like most?
A. Presents.

Q. What's the prettiest dog among (all) dogs?
A. Rainbow.

Q. What car do middle school and high school students ride?
A. A secondhand car.

Q. What happens to an almond when it dies?
A. Diamond.

Q. What happens if you divide an ant in three parts?
A. It dies.

While English jokes of this style will often begin with "what is," in Korean it's more common to simply leave the joke as an incomplete question by using the Topic Marker (은/는) or the 면 form.

Appendix C. Reading Practice

Special Thanks

I could not have made this book without the support of the following individuals. You helped to evolve this book into something special. I'd like to give a special thank you to each person here who contributed to this book's creation.

trevarr
Richard Hamilton
Jan Pech
Joel Tersigni
Eike
Wade
Fe Darr
Jonathan Tillman
Rhel ná DecVandé
Olga Aareskjold
Arnfasta
Dennis Ehrhardt
Rachel "토끼" Bibb
George Trombley
Christopher Langdon
Charles Vought
Jacob G Cohen
Catarina Kwan
Ian Blizzard
Nelson Morris
Edward Voss
Ted Morse
Ambrose Hill
Stephen Santoro
Natalie Tae Martinson
Victoria Lynn Yoak
Henry Colomb
Daryl Bigwood
MunHyun Bang
Merrill Grady
손소현

Glossary

ㄱ

가까이 "closely" (adverb)	Ch. 6
가르침 "teachings"	Ch. 19
가리키다 "to point," "to indicate"	Ch. 12
가위바위보 "rock-paper-scissors"	Ch. 12
가짜 "fake" (adjective)	Ch. 10
간(을) 보다 "to taste (something)"	App. C
간단하다 "to be simple"	Ch. 11
간식 "snack," "refreshment"	Ch. 20
간장 "soy sauce"	Ch. 6
간접 "indirectly" (adverb)	Ch. 13
갈다 "to grind"	App. C
갈색 "brown (color)"	Ch. 18
감기(에) 걸리다 "to catch a cold"	Ch. 19
감옥 "jail"	Ch. 14
강아지 "puppy," "dog"	Ch. 19
갖다 드리다 "to (get and) bring" (hon.)	Ch. 8
갖다 주다 "to (get and) bring"	Ch. 8
같이 "together" (adverb)	Ch. 4
같이 "like," "as" (adverb)	Ch. 7
개미 "ant"	Ch. 1
거대하다 "to be gigantic"	Ch. 11
거의 "almost" (adverb)	Ch. 14
거의 다 "almost all" (adverb)	Ch. 14
거짓말쟁이 "liar"	Ch. 7
건너다 "to cross"	Ch. 14
걸음 "a step," "a pace"	Ch. 19
검색(을) 하다 "to search"	Ch. 14
검은 "black" (adjective)	Ch. 18
검은색 "black" (noun)	Ch. 18
겨자 "(spicy) mustard"	Ch. 6
결국 "in the end," "ultimately" (adverb)	Ch. 6
결혼식 "wedding (ceremony)"	Ch. 18
경기 "match," "game"	Ch. 6
경험 "experience"	Ch. 18
계산(을) 하다 "to calculate," "to take care of payment"	Ch. 13
계산기 "calculator"	Ch. 13
계속 "continually" (adverb)	Ch. 19
계시다 "to exist" (hon.)	Ch. 8
계약 "contract"	Ch. 3
계약서 "contract (paper form)"	Ch. 3
계피 "cinnamon"	Ch. 19
고개 "hill," "pass"	App. C
고르다 "to choose," "to select"	Ch. 7
고민 "concern," "worry"	Ch. 20
고민(을) 하다 "to be concerned," "to (slightly) worry"	Ch. 20
고장(이) 나다 "to break down," "to malfunction"	Ch. 4
고추 "chili pepper"	Ch. 10
고추장 "chili pepper paste"	Ch. 10
고치다 "to repair"	Ch. 4
곧 "soon" (adverb)	Ch. 14
곰 "bear"	Ch. 5
곱하기 "times" [multiplication]	Ch. 13
(곳)에 오신 것을 환영합니다. "Welcome to (place)."	Ch. 8
공 "zero"	Ch. 1
공기 "air"	Ch. 14
공연 "performance," "show"	Ch. 16
공주 "princess"	Ch. 4
공짜 "free" (informal)	Ch. 10
공짜로 "for free" (adverb) (informal)	Ch. 10
공포 영화 "horror movie"	Ch. 11
공휴일 "holiday"	Ch. 6
과제 "assignment," "project"	Ch. 19
관심 "an interest"	Ch. 5
관심(이) 없다 "to not be interested"	Ch. 5
관심(이) 있다 "to be interested"	Ch. 5
괜히 "in vain" (adverb)	Ch. 6
교과서 "textbook"	Ch. 5
교통 "traffic"	Ch. 6
교통 사고 "traffic accident"	Ch. 6
교환(을) 하다 "to exchange"	Ch. 14
교환학생 "exchange student"	Ch. 14
구름 "cloud"	Ch. 3

Glossary

구하다 "to look for," "to seek"		Ch. 5
국 "soup"		Ch. 10
국수 "noodles"		Ch. 10
군대 "the military"		Ch. 5
굴 "oyster"		Ch. 5
굵다 "to be chunky," "to be thick"		App. C
굽다 "to cook (with fire)"		Ch. 20
궁금하다 "to be curious (to know)" (descriptive verb)		Ch. 9
규칙 "rule(s)"		Ch. 11
그냥 "just (as it is)" (adverb)		Ch. 12
그네 "a swing"		Ch. 1
그다지 "not that," "not so" (negative)		Ch. 15
그래도 "even so," "still," "anyway"		Ch. 15
그래서 "So...," "Therefore..."		Ch. 5
그래서... "That's why..."		Ch. 7
그러게요 "That's right.," "Yeah."		Ch. 4
그러나 "However..."		Ch. 5
그런데 "but," "however"		Ch. 15
그럼(요). "Yeah.," "Of course." (casual)		Ch. 10
그렇군요. "Oh, I see."		Ch. 9
그렇지만 "nevertheless," "however"		Ch. 15
그룹 "group"		Ch. 19
그만두다 "to quit" (job, etc.)		Ch. 15
그만하다 "to stop (doing)"		Ch. 19
근데 "but," "however"		Ch. 15
근육 "muscle"		Ch. 20
근처 "neighborhood," "vicinity"		Ch. 16
금 "gold"		Ch. 13
금색 "gold (color)"		Ch. 13
급하다 "to be urgent"		Ch. 6
급히 "urgently"		Ch. 6
기계 "machine"		Ch. 12
기름 "oil," "gas(oline)"		Ch. 4
기린 "giraffe"		Ch. 5
기본 "the basics," "fundamentals"		Ch. 12
기본적이다 "to be basic," "to be fundamental"		Ch. 12
기사 "driver"		Ch. 14
기침(을) 하다 "to cough"		Ch. 20
기타 "guitar"		Ch. 11
기회 "opportunity"		Ch. 14
기회(가) 되다 "to have an opportunity"		Ch. 18
긴장(을) 하다 "to be nervous," "to be tense"		Ch. 9
김치찌개 "kimchi stew"		Ch. 10
까먹다 "to forget" (informal)		Ch. 18
깜짝 놀라다 "to be startled" (descriptive verb)		Ch. 10
깜짝 놀래다 "to startle (someone)" (action verb)		Ch. 10
깨끗이 "cleanly"		Ch. 6
깨다 "to break (something)," "to smash (something)"		Ch. 4
꺼내다 "to take/pull out"		Ch. 6
꼬리 "tail"		Ch. 1
꼴찌 "last place"		Ch. 6
꿀차 "honey tea"		Ch. 8
끈 "string"		Ch. 1
끊다 "to quit" (smoking, etc.)		Ch. 15
끓이다 "to boil (something)"		Ch. 12
끼 meal counter		Ch. 5

ㄴ

나 "I," "me" (casual)		Ch. 10
나누기 "divided by" [division]		Ch. 13
나이(를) (많이) 먹다 "to be old" (idiom)		App. A
나중에 "later" (adverb)		Ch. 11
나타나다 "to appear," "to show up"		App. C
낙지 "(small) octopus"		Ch. 5
날씬하다 "to be slim"		Ch. 11
날짜 "a date," "a day"		Ch. 4
남 "others," "other people"		Ch. 7
남 "south"		Ch. 8
남다 "to be remaining," "to be left over"		App. C
남쪽 "south (side)"		Ch. 8
낫다 "to be preferable," "to be better"		Ch. 14

321

Glossary

낮 "day(time)"		Ch. 1
낮잠 "(daytime) nap"		Ch. 1
낮잠(을) 자다 "to take a (daytime) nap"		Ch. 1
내국 "domestic," "within the country"		Ch. 11
내려오다 "to come down," "to descend (to here)"		App. C
내리다 "to get off (a vehicle)"		Ch. 14
내리다 "to let down," "to lower"		App. C
내일 뵐게요. "I'll see you tomorrow." (hum.)		Ch. 13
냄새 "smell"		Ch. 17
냄새(가) 나다 "to smell (like)"		Ch. 17
너 "you" (casual)		Ch. 10
너무 많이 "too much" (adverb)		Ch. 6
너희 "you" (casual plural)		Ch. 10
넓다 "to be wide," "to be spacious" (pronounced 널따)		Ch. 9
넘게 "over," "more than" (adverb)		Ch. 19
넘어가다 "to pass over," "to cross over"		App. C
넘어지다 "to fall down," "to trip"		Ch. 14
녀석 "brat," "fellow"		App. C
노력(을) 하다 "to make an effort," "to try"		Ch. 17
녹차 "green tea"		Ch. 3
놀라다 "to be surprised" (descriptive verb)		Ch. 10
놀래다 "to surprise (someone)" (action verb)		Ch. 10
높이 "high" (adverb)		Ch. 6
높임말 "honorific speech"		Ch. 10
놓치다 "to miss"		Ch. 14
누군가 "someone"		Ch. 7
누워서 떡 먹기 "to be extremely easy" (idiom)		App. A
눈(이) 높다 "to be (overly-)picky" (idiom)		App. A
눈(이) 부시다 "to be blinded" (idiom)		App. A
눈꼽만큼 "a small amount" (idiom)		App. A
눈물 "tear(s)"		Ch. 20
눈물(이) 나다 "to cry," "to bawl"		Ch. 20
눈에 익다 "to look familiar" (idiom)		App. A
뉴욕 "New York"		Ch. 18
늑대 "wolf"		Ch. 13
늘리다 "to increase (something)"		Ch. 3
늙다 "to be old"		Ch. 2

ㄷ

다 "all" (adverb)		Ch. 14
다 같이 "all together" (adverb)		Ch. 12
다 오다 "to arrive"		Ch. 14
다녀오다 "to go and come back"		Ch. 16
다들 "everyone" (informal)		Ch. 17
다른 "other," "another" (adjective)		Ch. 19
다음 "next" (adjective)		Ch. 13
다음번 "next time"		Ch. 13
다음에 "next time"		Ch. 13
다이아몬드 "diamond"		Ch. 18
다이어트(를) 하다 "to diet"		Ch. 17
다지다 "to be minced," "to be finely chopped"		App. C
다큐멘터리 "documentary"		Ch. 11
닦다 "to wipe," "to dry," "to clean (by wiping)"		Ch. 12
단어 "vocabulary word"		Ch. 9
달력 "a calendar"		Ch. 18
담배 "cigarette," "tobacco"		Ch. 15
답답하다 "to be frustrating"		Ch. 17
답장 "(written) reply"		Ch. 20
답장(을) 하다 "to reply (in writing)"		Ch. 20
당기다 "to pull"		Ch. 2
당연하다 "to be reasonable," "to be natural"		Ch. 9
당연히 "of course," "naturally" (adverb)		Ch. 9
대 "versus," "to"		Ch. 6
대단하다 "to be great," "to be incredible"		Ch. 17
대부분 "most"		Ch. 14
대화 "conversation"		Ch. 20

Glossary

대화(를) 하다	"to have a conversation," "to converse"	Ch. 20
댁	"house" (hon.)	Ch. 8
더빙	"dubbing," "voiceover"	Ch. 11
더하기	"plus" [addition]	Ch. 13
던지다	"to throw"	Ch. 12
도 안 되게	"under," "less than" (adverb)	Ch. 19
도구	"tool"	Ch. 12
도끼	"axe"	App. C
도둑	"thief," "burglar"	Ch. 7
도망(을) 가다	"to run away," "to escape"	App. C
도시락	"packed lunch," "box lunch"	Ch. 16
도와 드리다	"to help" (hum.)	Ch. 13
도움	"help"	Ch. 19
도움이 되다	"to be helpful"	Ch. 19
독감에 걸리다	"to catch the flu"	Ch. 19
독학	"self study"	Ch. 9
돈(을) 모으다	"to save (up) money"	Ch. 17
돌아가다	"to go back"	Ch. 8
돌아가시다	"to die," "to pass away" (hon.)	Ch. 8
돌아오다	"to come back"	Ch. 8
돕다	"to help"	Ch. 13
동	"east"	Ch. 8
동물원	"zoo"	Ch. 5
동사	"verb"	Ch. 9
동아리	"club," "group"	Ch. 3
동영상	"video"	Ch. 13
동전	"coins"	Ch. 13
동쪽	"east (side)"	Ch. 8
돼지불고기	"barbequed pork"	Ch. 10
됐어요.	"No thanks.," "I'm not interested."	Ch. 19
된장찌개	"bean paste stew"	Ch. 10
두껍다	"to be thick"	Ch. 9
뚜껑	"lid"	Ch. 4
둘다	"both (of them)" (noun)	Ch. 15
드디어	"finally," "at last"	Ch. 18
드라마	"drama"	Ch. 11
드리다	"to give" (hum.)	Ch. 8
드시다	"to eat," "to drink" (hon.)	Ch. 8
들다	"to pick up," "to carry"	Ch. 6
들르다	"to stop by," "to drop by"	Ch. 4
등	place counter	Ch. 6
등록(을) 하다	"to register"	Ch. 12
등장인물	"character (in book, movie, etc.)"	App. C
따님	"daughter" (hon.)	Ch. 8
따라가다	"to (go) follow"	Ch. 4
따라오다	"to (come) follow"	Ch. 4
따라하다	"to imitate," "to copy"	Ch. 4
따로	"separately" (adverb)	Ch. 4
딸꾹질(을) 하다	"to hiccup"	Ch. 20
때리다	"to hit," "to slap"	Ch. 20
떠나가다	"to go off (to somewhere)," "to depart (to somewhere)"	Ch. 19
떠나다	"to go off," "to depart"	Ch. 19
떡볶이	"stir-fried rice cakes"	Ch. 10
떼	animal group counter	Ch. 3
뚱뚱하다	"to be fat"	Ch. 11
뛰다	"to run," "to jump"	Ch. 6
뛰어가다	"to go running"	Ch. 20
뛰어오다	"to come running"	Ch. 20
뜨다	"to rise (the sun/moon)"	Ch. 8
뜻	"meaning"	Ch. 1

ㄹ

라디오	"radio"	Ch. 20
라면	"ramen"	Ch. 6
랍스타	"lobster"	Ch. 5
랩	"rap"	Ch. 20
레시피	"recipe"	Ch. 2
로맨스 영화	"romance movie"	Ch. 11
로스앤젤레스	"Los Angeles"	Ch. 2

ㅁ

마늘	"garlic"	Ch. 15
마라톤	"marathon"	Ch. 18
마요네즈	"mayonnaise"	Ch. 6
마음(을) 놓다	"to relax" (idiom)	App. A

Glossary

마음대로 하다 "to do as one wishes" (idiom)	App. A
마음에 들다 "to like" (idiom)	App. A
마지막 "last" (noun)	Ch. 6
마지막에 "at the end"	Ch. 6
막 act counter	App. C
막대기 "stick," "bar," "rod"	Ch. 12
만우절 "April Fool's Day"	App. B
만큼 "as much as"	Ch. 7
만화 "comic," "cartoon"	Ch. 11
많이 드세요. "Eat a lot (and enjoy)."	Ch. 3
말(을) 놓다 "to stop speaking politely," "to put down one's speech"	Ch. 10
말(을) 편하게 하다 "to speak without worrying too much about being polite"	Ch. 10
말(이) 되다 "to make sense" (idiom)	App. A
말도 안 되다 "to not make sense" (idiom)	App. A
말씀 "word" (hon.)	Ch. 8
맛(을) 보다 "to taste (something)"	Ch. 3
맛있게 드세요! "Enjoy (the food)!"	Ch. 8
맛있게 먹다 "to enjoy (eating)"	Ch. 6
매력 "charm," "attractiveness"	Ch. 16
매력적이다 "to be charming," "to be attractive"	Ch. 16
머리(를) 자르다 "to get a haircut," "to cut one's hair"	Ch. 16
머무르다 "to stay," "to remain"	Ch. 4
머스터드 "(yellow) mustard"	Ch. 6
먼지 "dust"	Ch. 5
멀리 "far" (adverb)	Ch. 6
멈추다 "to stop (moving)"	Ch. 20
멍멍이 "doggy"	Ch. 13
메뉴 "menu"	Ch. 8
면도(를) 하다 "to shave"	Ch. 19
면허증 "(driver's) license"	Ch. 19
명사 "noun"	Ch. 9
모기 "mosquito"	Ch. 13
모든 "every" (adjective)	Ch. 14
모양 "shape"	Ch. 17
모욕 "insult"	Ch. 10
모욕(을) 하다 "to insult"	Ch. 10
모자르다 "to not be enough"	Ch. 19
목숨 "one's life," "one's breath"	App. C
몸무게 "bodyweight"	Ch. 13
무게 "weight"	Ch. 13
무궁화 "hibiscus (flower)"	Ch. 17
무대 "(performance) stage"	Ch. 11
무료 "free"	Ch. 10
무료로 "for free" (adverb)	Ch. 10
무릎 "knee"	Ch. 20
무슨 뜻이에요? "What does it mean?"	Ch. 1
무슨 일이 있어요? "What's wrong?"	Ch. 2
무슨일이에요? "What's wrong?"	Ch. 2
무엇인가 "something"	Ch. 7
무지개 "rainbow"	Ch. 20
무협 영화 "martial arts movie"	Ch. 11
묶다 "to tie"	Ch. 13
문법 "grammar"	Ch. 9
문어 "(large) octopus"	Ch. 5
문자 "text message"	Ch. 20
문장 "a sentence"	Ch. 9
문제(를) 풀다 "to solve a problem"	Ch. 13
물론 "of course," "it goes without saying" (adverb)	Ch. 9
물병 "water bottle"	Ch. 1
물엿 "(starch) syrup"	App. C
물통 "water container"	Ch. 1
뭔가 "something"	Ch. 7
미국 나이 "American age"	Ch. 10
미끄러져 내리다 "to slide down"	App. C
미리 "in advance," "ahead of time" (adverb)	Ch. 16
믹서기 "blender"	App. C
밀가루 "flour"	Ch. 12
밀다 "to push"	Ch. 2

Glossary

ㅂ

바가지(를) 쓰다 "to be overcharged" (idiom)		App. A
바가지(를) 씌우다 "to overcharge" (idiom)		App. A
바구니 "basket"		Ch. 11
바닥 "the floor," "the ground"		Ch. 13
바람(이) 불다 "to be windy"		Ch. 19
바로 지금 "right this second" (adverb)		Ch. 6
바보 "idiot," "fool"		Ch. 7
바위 "rock," "boulder"		Ch. 12
바이올린 "violin"		Ch. 11
바퀴 "wheel"		Ch. 1
바퀴벌레 "cockroach"		Ch. 1
바탕 "background," "foundation"		App. C
박하 "peppermint"		Ch. 19
반말 "casual speech"		Ch. 10
반찬 "side dish"		Ch. 20
발렌타인 데이 "Valentine's Day"		App. B
밟다 "to step on"		Ch. 14
밧줄 "rope"		Ch. 1
방금 "just (happened)" (adverb)		Ch. 10
방문 "visit"		Ch. 4
방문(을) 하다 "to visit"		Ch. 4
방학 "school vacation"		Ch. 19
방해(를) 하다 "to interrupt"		Ch. 20
방향 "direction"		Ch. 12
방향으로 "in/toward a direction"		Ch. 12
배(가) 부르다 "to be full"		Ch. 5
배우 "actor"		Ch. 11
배움 "learning," "study"		Ch. 19
배추 "cabbage"		Ch. 12
버스 정류장 "bus station," "bus stop"		Ch. 4
번역 "(written) translation"		Ch. 9
번역(을) 하다 "to translate (writing)"		Ch. 9
번역가 "(written) translator"		Ch. 9
번째 ordinal counter		Ch. 18
벌 "bee"		Ch. 13
벌써 "already" (surprised)		Ch. 3
법(률) "law," "legislation"		Ch. 14
법학 "(study of) law"		Ch. 14
베개 "pillow"		Ch. 4
베다 "to cut (into)"		Ch. 12
베이컨 "bacon"		Ch. 20
변태 "pervert"		Ch. 7
별 "star"		Ch. 16
별로 "not really" (negative)		Ch. 15
병 "disease," "sickness"		Ch. 4
보리 "barley"		Ch. 8
보리차 "barley tea"		Ch. 8
보여주다 "to show"		App. C
보울 "bowl"		App. C
보통 "regular(ly)," "normal(ly)"		Ch. 17
복사(를) 하다 "to copy," "to duplicate"		Ch. 14
복잡하다 "to be complicated"		Ch. 11
볶다 "to pan fry"		Ch. 12
볼링 "bowling"		Ch. 12
볼링(을) 치다 "to bowl"		Ch. 12
뵈다 "to see" (hum.)		Ch. 8
뵙다 "to see" (hum.)		Ch. 8
부끄럽다 "to be/feel embarrassing"		Ch. 10
부사 "adverb"		Ch. 9
부전공 "a minor (study)"		Ch. 1
부족하다 "to be lacking"		Ch. 19
부채 "paper folding fan"		Ch. 12
부처님 오신 날 "Buddha's Birthday"		App. B
북 "north"		Ch. 8
북쪽 "north (side)"		Ch. 8
불량식품 "unhealthy snacks"		Ch. 10
분명하다 "to be clear," "to be plain (to see/understand)"		Ch. 7
불 "a light"		Ch. 12
불(을) 끄다 "to turn off the light"		Ch. 12
불(을) 켜다 "to turn on the light"		Ch. 12
불고기 "barbequed meat"		Ch. 10
불닭 "fire chicken"		Ch. 10
불쌍하다 "to be pitiful," "to be poor"		Ch. 15

Glossary

불투명하다	"to be opaque"	Ch. 7
비기다	"to draw," "to tie"	Ch. 6
비누	"soap"	Ch. 17
비닐	"plastic" (literally, "vinyl")	Ch. 18
비닐봉지	"plastic bag"	Ch. 18
비닐봉투	"plastic bag"	Ch. 18
비다	"to be blank," "to be empty"	Ch. 1
비빔밥	"bibimbap"	Ch. 4
비행기(를) 태우다	"to (over-)compliment" (idiom)	App. A
빈칸	"a blank space"	Ch. 1
빗	"comb"	Ch. 19
빛	"light"	Ch. 12
빼기	"minus" [subtraction]	Ch. 13
빼빼로 데이	"Pepero Day"	App. B
뽀얗다	"to be milky(-white)"	App. C
뿌리	"root"	Ch. 15

ㅅ

사고	"accident"	Ch. 6
사과(를) 하다	"to apologize"	Ch. 16
사극	"historical drama"	Ch. 11
사냥	"hunting"	Ch. 14
사냥(을) 하다	"to hunt"	Ch. 14
사실	"(in) fact," "(in) truth" (noun/adverb)	Ch. 4
(사)실은...	"Actually...," "In fact..."	Ch. 5
사인	"signature"	Ch. 3
사인(을) 하다	"to sign"	Ch. 3
삭제(를) 하다	"to delete"	Ch. 14
산책	"a walk," "a stroll"	Ch. 5
산책(을) 하다	"to take a walk"	Ch. 5
살리다	"to save," "to spare"	App. C
살면서...	"in one's life..."	Ch. 20
상관없다	"to not matter"	Ch. 15
상관있다	"to matter"	Ch. 15
상식	"common knowledge," "common sense"	Ch. 7
상어	"shark"	Ch. 5
상추	"lettuce"	Ch. 12
새우	"shrimp"	Ch. 5

생일	"birthday"	Ch. 2
생일 축하합니다.	"Happy Birthday."	Ch. 2
생활	"(daily) life"	Ch. 20
생활(을) 하다	"to live"	Ch. 20
서	"west"	Ch. 8
서두르다	"to rush," "hurry"	Ch. 14
서점	"bookstore"	Ch. 5
서쪽	"west (side)"	Ch. 8
섞다	"to mix"	Ch. 12
선수	"player," "athlete"	Ch. 6
선풍기	"electric fan"	Ch. 12
설날	"(Lunar) New Year's Day"	App. B
설득(을) 하다	"to persuade," "to convince"	Ch. 17
성	"castle"	Ch. 11
성공	"success"	Ch. 6
성공(을) 하다	"to succeed"	Ch. 6
성인	"adult"	Ch. 7
성함	"name" (hon.)	Ch. 8
세다	"to count"	Ch. 13
세다	"to be strong," "to be powerful"	Ch. 18
세상	"the world"	Ch. 7
세상에서	"in the world"	Ch. 7
세탁기	"washing machine"	Ch. 4
(소리[가]) 작다	"to be quiet"	Ch. 6
(소리[가]) 크다	"to be loud"	Ch. 6
소불고기	"barbequed beef"	Ch. 10
소설	"novel," "fiction story"	Ch. 4
소스	"sauce"	Ch. 6
소풍	"picnic"	Ch. 5
소풍(을) 가다	"to go on a picnic"	Ch. 5
손(을) 닦다	"to wash one's hands"	Ch. 12
손(이) 크다	"to be generous/resourceful" (idiom)	App. A
손수건	"hand towel"	Ch. 20
쇼핑(을) 하다	"to go shopping"	Ch. 1
수건	"towel"	Ch. 20
(수업[을]) 듣다	"to take (a class)"	Ch. 5
수저	"spoon and chopsticks"	Ch. 4
수줍다	"to be shy"	Ch. 10

Glossary

수표 "(bank) check"		Ch. 13
순간 "a moment," "an instant"		Ch. 2
순수하다 "to be pure"		Ch. 11
숟가락 "spoon"		Ch. 4
숯 "charcoal"		Ch. 18
쉬다 "to (take a) rest"		Ch. 11
스스로 "by oneself" (adverb)		Ch. 15
스승의 날 "Teacher's Day"		App. B
스트레스 "stress"		Ch. 13
스트레스(를) 풀다 "to relieve stress"		Ch. 13
스포츠(를) 하다 "to play sports"		Ch. 6
습관 "habit," "custom"		Ch. 19
시간(이) 걸리다 "to take time"		Ch. 19
시간(이) 늦다 "to be late (at night)"		Ch. 12
시간(이) 되다 "to have time"		Ch. 3
(시간[을]) 보내다 "to spend (time)"		Ch. 6
시골 "countryside"		Ch. 12
시끄럽다 "to be noisy," "to be annoying (to hear)"		Ch. 2
시작 "start"		Ch. 3
시장 "(outdoor) marketplace"		Ch. 12
시집(을) 가다 "to get married" (used for females)		Ch. 1
시험(을) 잘 보다 "to do well on a test"		Ch. 10
(시험[을]) 통과하다 "to pass (a test)"		Ch. 5
(시험에) 떨어지다 "to fail (a test)"		Ch. 5
식기 "dishes"		Ch. 4
식기 세척기 "dish washer"		Ch. 4
식사 "a meal"		Ch. 8
식사(를) 하다 "to have a meal"		Ch. 8
식사하셨어요? "Have you eaten anything?"		Ch. 8
신경 "nerve"		Ch. 13
신경(을) 쓰다 "to care," "to mind"		Ch. 13
신기하다 "to be awesome," "to be amazing"		Ch. 17
신뢰(를) 하다 "to trust"		Ch. 7
신발 끈 "shoestring," "shoelaces"		Ch. 1
신분증 "identification (card)"		Ch. 13
신용 카드 "credit card"		Ch. 13
신정 "New Year's Day"		App. B
실수 "mistake," "accident"		Ch. 6
실수로 "by mistake," "accidentally" (adverb)		Ch. 6
실제로(는) "in reality," "actually" (adverb)		Ch. 4
실패 "failure"		Ch. 6
실패(를) 하다 "to fail"		Ch. 6
싫다 "to be disliked"		Ch. 19
심부름 "errand"		Ch. 12
심부름(을) 하다 "to do errands"		Ch. 12
심장 "heart"		Ch. 7
심하다 "to be severe," "to be harsh"		Ch. 5
싱겁다 "to be bland (tasting)"		Ch. 1
썩다 "to rot," "to decay"		App. C
썰다 "to chop," "to slice"		Ch. 12

ㅇ

아가씨 "(unmarried) lady," "(young and single) lady"		Ch. 1
아까 "a while ago," "earlier"		Ch. 2
아깝다 "to be sad about losing a thing/opportunity"		Ch. 17
아니면 "or"		Ch. 15
아드님 "son" (hon.)		Ch. 8
아래 "the bottom," "under"		Ch. 6
아래층 "lower floor," "downstairs"		Ch. 3
아몬드 "almond"		Ch. 5
아무 "any"		Ch. 15
아무것도 "nothing," "anything" (negative)		Ch. 15
아무도 "nobody" (negative)		Ch. 15
아무튼 "Anyway...," "In any case..."		Ch. 4
아쉽다 "to be unsatisfying"		Ch. 17
아싸! "Alright!," "Yes!"		Ch. 13
아저씨 "(unmarried) man," "(middle-aged) man"		Ch. 1
아줌마 "(married) woman," "(middle-aged) woman"		Ch. 1
아직 "still," "(not) yet" (adverb)		Ch. 7

Glossary

아직도 "even still," "(not) yet" (adverb)		Ch. 7
악마 "devil"		Ch. 7
악어 "alligator"		Ch. 5
안경 "glasses"		Ch. 9
안경(을) 쓰다 "to wear glasses"		Ch. 9
안내(를) 하다 "to guide," "to show around"		Ch. 18
안녕. "Hi." (casual)		Ch. 10
안됐다 "to be sorry (to hear)," "to be too bad" (past tense)		Ch. 9
안전하게 "safely"		Ch. 6
안전하다 "to be safe"		Ch. 6
안주 "snack (served with alcohol)"		Ch. 20
안타깝다 "to be sad and frustrated"		Ch. 17
알려주다 "to tell," "to let (someone) know"		Ch. 3
알아보다 "to find out," "to look into"		Ch. 16
앙 munching sound		App. C
앞머리 "bangs"		Ch. 16
애(를) 쓰다 "to put forth effort" (idiom)		App. A
액션 영화 "action movie"		Ch. 11
앨범 "album"		Ch. 18
야! "Hey!" (casual)		Ch. 10
야옹이 "kitty"		Ch. 13
약(을) 먹다 "to take medicine"		Ch. 5
약속 "promise," "appointment"		Ch. 11
약혼(을) 하다 "to get engaged"		Ch. 18
얇다 "to be thin (not thick)" (pronounced 얄따)		Ch. 9
양념 "seasoning"		App. C
양념(이) 되다 "to be seasoned"		App. C
양력 "Western calendar," "Gregorian calendar"		Ch. 18
양쪽 "both sides"		Ch. 8
양치(를) 하다 "to brush one's teeth"		Ch. 19
얘들아! "(You) guys!," "(You) kids!"		App. C
어기다 "to break (a rule, promise, etc.)"		Ch. 11
어느 "which" (adjective)		Ch. 7
어느 정도 "somewhat," "to a certain degree" (adverb)		App. C
어딘가 "somewhere"		Ch. 7
어리다 "to be young (like a child)"		Ch. 2
어린이 "child"		Ch. 7
어린이날 "Children's Day"		App. B
어머 "Oh dear."		App. C
어버이날 "Parent's Day"		App. B
어색하다 "to be awkward"		Ch. 10
어서 "quickly," "promptly" (adverb)		Ch. 8
어서 오세요. "Welcome.," "Come in."		Ch. 8
어슷 "diagonally," "slanted" (adverb)		App. C
어울리다 "to match well," "to suit," "to go with"		Ch. 15
어쨌든 "Anyway...," "In any case..."		Ch. 4
어흥 "(tiger) roar"		App. C
언젠가 "sometime"		Ch. 7
얻다 "to get," "to obtain"		Ch. 4
얼른 "at once," "right away" (adverb)		App. C
얼마(만)큼 "how much," "to what extent" (adverb)		Ch. 7
얼마나 "how much," "to what extent" (adverb)		Ch. 7
얼음 "ice"		Ch. 5
없이 "without" (adverb)		Ch. 6
엉덩이 "buttocks," "butt"		Ch. 20
에세이 "essay"		Ch. 13
S.F. 영화 "sci-fi movie" ("에스 에프")		Ch. 11
에어컨 "air conditioner"		Ch. 20
에취! "Atchoo!"		App. C
여권 "passport" (pronounced 여꿘)		Ch. 13
여러분 "everyone"		Ch. 17
여왕 "queen"		Ch. 4

Glossary

여전히 "as usual," "as always," "as ever" (adverb)		Ch. 20
여행(을) 가다 "to go on a trip"		Ch. 16
여행(을) 하다 "to travel," "to take a trip"		Ch. 16
역 "(train/subway) station"		Ch. 4
역시 "(just) as expected" (adverb)		Ch. 5
연결(을) 하다 "to connect"		Ch. 14
연락(을) 하다 "to contact"		Ch. 15
연세 "age" (hon.)		Ch. 8
연어 "salmon"		Ch. 5
연예인 "celebrity"		Ch. 11
연하다 "to be weak," "to be thin," "to be pale"		Ch. 6
열(이) 나다 "to catch/get a fever"		Ch. 19
열쇠고리 "keychain"		Ch. 7
엽서 "postcard"		Ch. 20
영수증 "recei[t"		Ch. 13
영차! "One, two!," "Heave-ho!"		App. C
예(를) 들어서... "For example..."		Ch. 16
예고편 "movie trailer," "movie advertisement"		Ch. 11
예능 프로그램 "variety show," "variety program"		Ch. 11
예문 "example sentence"		Ch. 9
예전 "the past," "the old days," "before"		Ch. 17
예전에 "in the past," "in the old days," "before" (adverb)		Ch. 17
옛날 "in the (really) old days," "in the past"		Ch. 20
옛날 옛날에 "A long, long time ago...," "Once upon a time..."		App. C
오누이 "brother and sister"		App. C
어묵 "fish cake"		Ch. 10
오락실 "arcade"		Ch. 7
오래 "a long time" (adverb)		Ch. 19
오래간만에 "in a long time" (shortened to 오랜만에)		Ch. 10
오래간만이에요. "Long time, no see."		Ch. 1
오랜만이야. "Long time, no see." (casual)		Ch. 10
오른쪽 "right (side)"		Ch. 8
오리 "duck"		Ch. 5
오징어 "squid"		Ch. 5
오케이. "Okay."		Ch. 12
오프라인 "offline"		Ch. 14
옥수수 "corn"		Ch. 8
온라인 "online"		Ch. 14
올라가다 "to climb up (somewhere)," "to go up (somewhere)"		App. C
올라오다 "to climb up (here)," "to go up (here)"		App. C
올리다 "to get on (a vehicle)"		Ch. 14
올빼미 "owl"		Ch. 13
옳다 "to be right," "to be proper," "to be correct"		App. C
와아! "Wow!"		Ch. 19
와인 "wine"		Ch. 8
완전하게 "completely"		Ch. 6
왕 "king"		Ch. 4
왕자 "prince"		Ch. 4
외국인 "foreigner"		Ch. 11
외출(을) 하다 "to go out(side)"		Ch. 16
왼쪽 "left (side)"		Ch. 8
요리사 "chef"		Ch. 2
욕 "swear (word)"		Ch. 10
욕(을) 받다 "to be sworn at"		Ch. 10
욕(을) 하다 "to swear"		Ch. 10
우체국 "post office"		Ch. 12
우표 "postage stamp"		Ch. 12
옥수수차 "corn tea"		Ch. 8
운동화 "tennis shoes," "exercise shoes"		Ch. 6
원래 "original," "originally"		Ch. 6
원어민 "native speaker"		Ch. 12
웨딩드레스 "wedding dress"		Ch. 17
위 place counter		Ch. 6
위층 "upper floor," "upstairs"		Ch. 3
위험하다 "to be dangerous"		Ch. 6

Glossary

유창하다	"to be fluent"	Ch. 15
은	"silver"	Ch. 13
은색	"silver (color)"	Ch. 13
음력	"Lunar calendar"	Ch. 18
음료	"beverage"	Ch. 8
음성	"voice"	Ch. 20
응	"yes" (casual)	Ch. 10
(이)나	"or (something)"	Ch. 15
이따(가)	"after a while," "later"	Ch. 2
(이)랑	"and," "with" (informal)	Ch. 10
이르다	"to be early"	Ch. 12
이미	"already"	Ch. 3
이발사	"barber"	Ch. 13
이발소	"barbershop"	Ch. 13
이번	"this time," "this"	Ch. 13
이불	"blanket"	Ch. 4
이사(를) 가다	"to move (away)"	Ch. 2
이사(를) 오다	"to move (here)"	Ch. 2
이상형	"(ideal) type"	Ch. 14
이유	"reason," "cause"	Ch. 15
익다	"to be done (cooked)"	App. C
익히다	"to cook (something)"	App. C
인기(가) 많다	"to be very popular"	Ch. 2
인사(를) 하다	"to say hello," "to bow," "to greet"	Ch. 1
인생	"(one's) life"	Ch. 7
인턴십	"internship"	Ch. 20
인형	"doll," "plush toy"	Ch. 6
일	"a matter," "something (to do)"	Ch. 2
일기	"journal," "diary"	Ch. 19
일기(를) 쓰다	"to write in a journal/diary"	Ch. 19
일단	"first (of all)"	Ch. 16
일반	"general," "normal" (adjective)	Ch. 17
일부러	"on purpose," "intentionally" (adverb)	Ch. 6
1 층	"first floor"	Ch. 3
일터	"workplace"	Ch. 9
입어 보다	"to try (something) on"	Ch. 17
입원(을) 하다	"to be hospitalized"	Ch. 18
잊다	"to forget"	Ch. 18

ㅈ

자	"(measuring) ruler"	Ch. 12
자기소개	"self introduction"	Ch. 13
자기소개(를) 하다	"to introduce oneself"	Ch. 13
자랑(을) 하다	"to boast," "to brag"	Ch. 7
자르다	"to cut (off)"	Ch. 12
자막	"subtitles"	Ch. 11
자신	"confidence"	Ch. 20
잔	"glass (counter)"	Ch. 8
잔돈	"(money) change"	Ch. 13
잔소리	"nagging"	Ch. 1
잔소리(를) 하다	"to nag"	Ch. 1
잘 가(요).	"Bye." (casual)	Ch. 10
잘 먹겠습니다.	"Thank you (for the food)."	Ch. 3
잘 안 되다	"to not go well"	Ch. 14
잘 있어(요).	"Bye!" (casual)	Ch. 10
잘 지내다	"to be well"	Ch. 10
잘되다	"to go well"	Ch. 14
잠(이) 들다	"to fall asleep"	Ch. 14
잠깐	"a short while," "a moment" (informal)	Ch. 14
잠깐만	"only a short while," "just a moment" (informal)	Ch. 14
잠시	"a short while," "a moment"	Ch. 14
잠시 후	"after a short while," "after just a moment"	Ch. 16
잠시만	"only a short while, just a moment"	Ch. 14
잡수시다	"to eat" (hon.)	Ch. 8
잡아먹다	"to catch and eat"	App. C
장(을) 보다	"to shop for groceries"	Ch. 5
장가(를) 가다	"to get married" (used for males)	Ch. 1
장난	"prank," "joke"	Ch. 6
장난감	"toy"	Ch. 6
장르	"genre"	Ch. 11
장소	"location," "place"	Ch. 8
재난	"disaster," "calamity"	Ch. 11
재난 영화	"disaster movie"	Ch. 11

Glossary

재다	"to measure"	Ch. 12
재료	"ingredient"	Ch. 5
재미있게 놀다	"to enjoy (playing)," "to have fun"	Ch. 6
재미있게 보다	"to enjoy (watching)"	Ch. 6
재미있게 읽다	"to enjoy (reading)"	Ch. 6
재채기(를) 하다	"to sneeze"	Ch. 20
저번	"last time"	Ch. 13
저울	"scale (for weighing)"	Ch. 12
저장(을) 하다	"to save"	Ch. 14
전공	"a major (study)"	Ch. 1
전에	"before"	Ch. 16
전체	"the whole thing"	Ch. 6
전혀	"not at all" (negative)	Ch. 15
전화 통화(를) 하다	"to talk on the phone"	Ch. 20
전화(가) 오다	"to get a phone call"	Ch. 20
전화(를) 걸다	"to make a phone call"	Ch. 20
절대로	"never" (negative)	Ch. 15
젊다	"to be young (and youthful)"	Ch. 2
점	"dot," "point," "period"	Ch. 1
점수	"score"	Ch. 6
정도	"about," "approximately"	Ch. 7
정류장	"station," "stop"	Ch. 4
정리(를) 하다	"to organize," "to put (something) in order"	Ch. 4
정보	"information"	Ch. 4
제로	"zero"	Ch. 1
제일	"most," "(the) best" (adverb)	Ch. 7
조각	"sculpture"	Ch. 19
조각(을) 하다	"to sculpt," "to carve a sculpture"	Ch. 19
조개	"clam," "shellfish"	Ch. 5
조그마하다	"to be tiny"	Ch. 11
조용하다	"to be quiet" (descriptive verb)	Ch. 16
조용히 하다	"to be quiet" (action verb)	Ch. 16
존경(을) 하다	"to respect," "to look up to"	Ch. 16
존댓말	"polite speech"	Ch. 10
졸업(을) 하다	"to graduate"	Ch. 8
졸업식	"graduation (ceremony)"	Ch. 8
좀	"a little," "kinda" (informal)	Ch. 10
좁다	"to be narrow," "to be cramped"	Ch. 9
좋은 하루 되세요.	"Have a nice day."	Ch. 8
좋은 하루 보내세요.	"have a nice day."	Ch. 8
주로	"mainly" (adverb)	Ch. 6
주말	"weekend"	Ch. 6
주무르다	"to massage"	App. C
주무시다	"to sleep" (hon.)	Ch. 8
주변	"surroundings," "vicinity"	Ch. 16
주스	"juice"	Ch. 15
주유소	"gas station"	Ch. 4
주차(를) 하다	"to park"	Ch. 14
주차장	"parking lot"	Ch. 14
주황	"orange" (adjective)	Ch. 18
주황색	"orange" (noun)	Ch. 18
죽음	"death"	Ch. 19
줄	"cord," "line"	Ch. 1
줄무늬	"stripes," "striped pattern"	App. C
줄이다	"to decrease (something)"	Ch. 3
줍다	"to pick up"	Ch. 20
중간	"medium," "the middle," "the center"	App. C
중고	"used," "secondhand" (adjective)	Ch. 14
중고차	"used car," "secondhand car"	Ch. 14
중에서	"among"	Ch. 7
쥐꼬리만큼	"a small size" (idiom)	App. A
쥐색	"grey" (literally, "mouse color") (noun)	Ch. 18
지각(을) 하다	"to be tardy"	Ch. 12
지금 바로	"right now (immediately)" (adverb)	Ch. 6

Glossary

지나가다 "to pass by," "to go by"	Ch. 3
지난 "last" (adjective)	Ch. 13
지난번 "last time"	Ch. 13
지다 "to set (the sun/moon)"	Ch. 8
지우개 "eraser"	Ch. 12
지키다 "to protect," "to keep (a rule, promise, etc.)"	Ch. 11
지폐 "paper money," "bills"	Ch. 13
지하 "basement"	Ch. 3
직접 "directly" (adverb)	Ch. 13
진간장 "strong soy sauce"	App. C
진실하다 "to be honest"	Ch. 7
진정(을) 하다 "to calm down"	Ch. 20
진지하다 "to be serious"	Ch. 6
진짜 "real," "really" (informal)	Ch. 10
진하다 "to be strong," "to be thick," "to be dark"	Ch. 6
짐 "luggage"	Ch. 2
짐(을) 싸다 "to pack luggage"	Ch. 2
징그럽다 "to be gross," "to be disgusting"	Ch. 11
짱! "Awesome!" (casual)	Ch. 10
쪽 "side"	Ch. 8
찌개 "stew"	Ch. 10
찌다 "to steam"	Ch. 12
찍다 "to chop," "to hack," "to take (photo)"	App. C

ㅊ

차이(가) 나다 "to be different," "to have a difference"	Ch. 19
차이(가) 안 나다 "to not be different," "to not have a difference"	Ch. 19
착하다 "to be nice," "to be friendly"	Ch. 15
참 "really" (adverb)	Ch. 9
참기름 "sesame oil"	App. C
참다 "to endure," "to repress"	Ch. 20
창피하다 "to be/feel ashamed"	Ch. 10
채 썰다 "to slice/chop thin," "to slice/chop fine"	App. C

책임 "responsibility"	Ch. 17
챙기다 "to pack," "to take along (something)"	Ch. 16
처음에 "at first"	Ch. 6
천 "cloth"	Ch. 18
천사 "angel"	Ch. 7
천천히 "slowly"	Ch. 6
청구서 "a bill (for payment)"	Ch. 13
청소(를) 하다 "to clean (the house)," "to vacuum"	Ch. 5
청소기 "vacuum cleaner"	Ch. 5
체육 "physical education"	Ch. 19
체육관 "gym," "gymnasium"	Ch. 19
체크 카드 "debit card" (literally, "check card")	Ch. 13
쳐다보다 "to stare"	Ch. 14
총 "gun"	Ch. 14
총(을) 쏘다 "to shoot a gun"	Ch. 14
총각 "(unmarried) man," "(single) man"	Ch. 1
최근 "recent," "the last" (adjective)	Ch. 18
최근에 "recently," "these days"	Ch. 18
추석 "(Korea's) Thanksgiving"	App. B
추천(을) 하다 "to recommend"	Ch. 11
축제 "festival"	Ch. 19
충분하다 "to be enough"	Ch. 19
충분히 "enough" (adverb)	Ch. 19
층 building floor counter	Ch. 3
치다 "to type"	Ch. 14
치마 "skirt"	Ch. 20
칭찬 "compliment"	Ch. 9
칭찬(을) 받다 "to receive a compliment," "to be praised"	Ch. 9
칭찬(을) 하다 "to compliment," "to praise"	Ch. 9

ㅋ

칸 "(tin) can"	Ch. 1
캐나다 "Canada"	Ch. 15
캐러멜 "caramel"	Ch. 19
캘리포니아 "California"	Ch. 18
캠핑(을) 가다 "to go camping"	Ch. 17

Glossary

케첩 "ketchup"		Ch. 6
코(가) 높다 "to be snooty" (idiom)		App. A
코미디 영화 "comedy movie"		Ch. 11
콘서트 "concert"		Ch. 11
쿠키 "cookie"		Ch. 17
키위 "kiwi"		Ch. 15
키친타월 "kitchen towel"		App. C

ㅌ

태국 "Thailand"		Ch. 18
태도 "attitude"		Ch. 16
태우다 "to give (someone) a ride"		Ch. 4
택배 "(mail) package," "parcel"		Ch. 12
택시 기사 "taxi driver"		Ch. 14
테이블 "table"		Ch. 18
텍사스 "Texas"		Ch. 18
토끼 "rabbit"		Ch. 13
통 "container"		Ch. 1
통역 "(spoken) translation"		Ch. 9
통역(을) 하다 "to translate (speaking)"		Ch. 9
통역사 "interpreter"		Ch. 9
통화 "telephone conversation"		Ch. 20
투명하다 "to be transparent"		Ch. 7
튀기다 "to deep fry"		Ch. 12
트로트 "trot (music)"		Ch. 20
트림(을) 하다 "to burp"		Ch. 20
특별하다 "to be special"		Ch. 4
특이하다 "unusual," "odd"		Ch. 4
특히 "especially," "particularly" (adverb)		Ch. 15
튼튼하다 "to be durable," "to be sturdy," "to be strong"		App. C
틀다 "to turn on (sound)"		Ch. 20
틀리다 "to miss (a problem)"		Ch. 17

ㅍ

파리 "fly"		Ch. 13
파티(를) 하다 "to have a party"		Ch. 16
팝콘 "popcorn"		Ch. 19
팬 "pan"		App. C
퍼센트 "percent"		Ch. 1
페이지 "page (of writing)"		Ch. 9
페인트(를) 칠하다 "to paint"		Ch. 14
편의점 "convenience store"		Ch. 4
평일 "weekday"		Ch. 6
포장(을) 하다 "to wrap up (to go)"		Ch. 13
표범 "panther," "leopard"		Ch. 5
풀 "grass"		Ch. 13
풀다 "to untie," "to solve"		Ch. 13
프로 "percent"		Ch. 1
프린트(를) 하다 "to print"		Ch. 14
플루트 "flute"		Ch. 11
피 "blood"		Ch. 20
피(우)다 "to smoke"		Ch. 15
피리 "(musical) pipe"		Ch. 11
피아노 "piano"		Ch. 11
피에로 "clown"		Ch. 1
피하다 "to avoid"		Ch. 19
필요(가) 없다 "to be unnecessary"		Ch. 5
핏물 "blood (liquid)"		App. C
핑크색 "pink" (noun)		Ch. 18

ㅎ

하고 "and," "with" (informal)		Ch. 10
하나하나 "one by one" (adverb)		App. C
하느님 "God"		App. C
하루 종일 "all day" (adverb)		Ch. 3
하마 "hippopotamus"		Ch. 5
하여튼 "Anyway...," "In any case..."		Ch. 4
하품(을) 하다 "to yawn"		Ch. 20
하프 "harp"		Ch. 11
학교 생활 "school life"		Ch. 20
학원 "academy"		Ch. 3
한 "about," "approximately"		Ch. 19
한 번 "one time," "once," "sometime" (adverb)		Ch. 12
한국 나이 "Korean age"		Ch. 10
한글날 "Hangul Day"		App. B
한쪽 "one side"		Ch. 8
한테 "to (a person)" (informal)		Ch. 10

Glossary

한테(서) "from (a person)" (informal)		Ch. 10
해물 "seafood"		Ch. 5
해설 "narrator"		App. C
해외 "overseas," "abroad"		Ch. 11
햇빛 "sunlight," "sunshine"		Ch. 12
행동(을) 하다 "to act," "to behave"		Ch. 7
향 "fragrance," "scent"		Ch. 17
헤헤. "He, he."		Ch. 7
현금 "cash"		Ch. 13
형용사 "adjective"		Ch. 9
호랑이 "tiger"		Ch. 5
혼자(서) "alone" (adverb)		Ch. 15
홍차 "black tea" (literally, "red tea")		Ch. 3
화이트 데이 "White Day"		App. B
화이팅! "Good luck!," "Break a leg!"		Ch. 6
화장(을) 하다 "to put on makeup"		Ch. 12
화장품 "makeup"		Ch. 12
확실하다 "to be certain," "to be sure"		Ch. 16
확실히 "certainly," "surely"		Ch. 16
확인(을) 하다 "to check," "to confirm"		Ch. 16
환영(을) 하다 "to welcome"		Ch. 8
환영합니다. "Welcome."		Ch. 8
회복 "recovery"		Ch. 5
회복(을) 하다 "to recover," "to get well"		Ch. 5
회색 "grey" (noun)		Ch. 18
회의 "conference," "meeting"		Ch. 20
회장님 "president (of a company)"		Ch. 4
후에 "after"		Ch. 16
후회(를) 하다 "to regret"		Ch. 16
휴가 "a break," "a leave"		Ch. 19
휴가지 "vacation spot"		Ch. 19
휴일 "a day off"		Ch. 19
휴지 "tissue," "toilet paper"		Ch. 5
흙 "dirt," "soil"		Ch. 13
흥미롭다 "to be interesting," "to be amusing"		Ch. 5
힘(을) 내다 "to cheer (oneself) up"		Ch. 20
힘(이) 세다 "to be physically strong"		Ch. 18
힘내세요. "Cheer up."		Ch. 20

CPSIA information can be obtained
at www.ICGtesting.com
Printed in the USA
LVHW012208281018
595072LV00002B/11/P

9 781502 722218